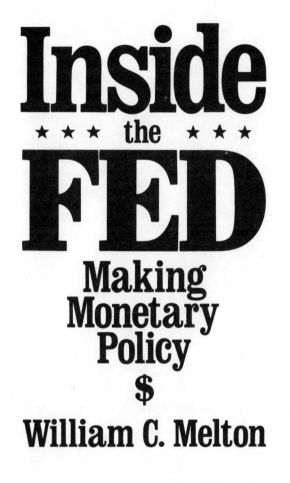

Inside
★ ★ ★ the ★ ★ ★
FED
Making
Monetary
Policy
$
William C. Melton

WITHDRAWN

DOW JONES-IRWIN   Homewood, Illinois   60430

ISBN 0-87094-544-0

Library of Congress Catalog Card No. 84–71297

Printed in the United States of America

2 3 4 5 6 7 8 9 0 K 2 1 0 9 8 7 6 5

In Memoriam
Charlie Sivesind

PREFACE

Nothing so occupies the attention of financial market professionals as the Federal Reserve. And probably no aspect of the U.S. economy is so confusing, to laymen and professionals alike, as monetary policy. In recent years, high and volatile interest rates, together with a series of dramatic policy initiatives, have raised the public's obsession with the Fed to new heights—unfortunately, with little apparent reduction in confusion.

This book was strongly influenced by the author's experiences explaining to corporate treasurers, securities traders, portfolio managers, and interested laymen the nature of monetary policy and the nuances of the Federal Reserve's operations. It assumes only a minimal economics background on the part of the reader, and it traces the development of the mostly simple concepts that lie behind the complex and seemingly impenetrable institutional detail surrounding the monetary policy process.

But the book is much more than an exposition of dry, theoretical concepts. The Federal Reserve's great achievement during the early 1980s—the decisive rupture of an inflation spiral almost two decades in the making—is not only a worthwhile lesson in economics. It is a good story in its own right.

All authors harbor ambitions for their books. This one will fulfill its purpose if it succeeds in fostering a broader understanding of the Fed as an institution and of the monetary policy practice.

Authors typically use a preface to acknowledge their debts while absolving others from responsibility for whatever inadequacies the book may be found to contain. Thus the professional and personal reputations of innocent people are preserved from danger. This practice is well worth emulating.

My own debts are quite extensive. Over the years, teachers, professional colleagues, and fellow financial market participants have given generously of their time and insight. I am most grateful and I regret that they are too numerous to be listed here.

I am proud to count among my good friends individuals who hold almost every side of every current monetary policy issue. I have tried to represent their viewpoints fairly and accurately in this book. Whatever errors may exist are my responsibility alone.

Specific debts to the following persons must be recognized individually. They all took the time to answer my questions during the preparation of this book, and some willingly suffered the tortured prose of early drafts to preserve me from errors. In alphabetical order they are: Donald B. Adams, Irving M. Auerbach, Kenneth H. Bacon, Normand R. V. Bernard, Thomas Brady, E. Gerald Corrigan, Louis V. B. Crandall, Dennis E. Farley, Gary P. Gillum, Cynthia A. Glassman, Frederick H. Jensen, David S. Jones, John P. Judd, Daniel E. Laufenberg, Susan J. Lepper, Rosemary R. Loney, Charles Lieberman, David E. Lindsey, Brian Madigan, George W. McKinney, Jr., Laurence H. Meyer, Anne P. Mills, Carl J. Palash, Richard D. Porter, Larry M. Ricciardelli, Laurence K. Roos, Robert V. Roosa, Thomas D. Simpson, Sharon P. Smith, Wayne J. Smith, Paul A. Spindt, Peter D. Sternlight, Paul A. Volcker, John R. Williams, John F. Wilson, and Burton Zwick. As noted earlier, because of the multiplicity of views these individuals hold regarding monetary policy issues, the reader would do well to check with them directly before associating them with any conclusions expressed in this book.

In addition, Richard H. Hoenig at the Federal Reserve Bank of New York and Joseph R. Coyne at the Board of Governors were most helpful in locating documents, verifying data, and assisting with other vexing tasks.

I owe a special debt to my colleagues at IDS/American Express, Inc., for constant stimulation, and particularly to Bruce R. Smith, Mary J. Metcalf, and Sharon M. Moen, all of whom provided invaluable assistance.

Finally, I thank my family, whose forbearance made this book possible.

William C. Melton

CONTENTS

1

INTRODUCTION

The Federal Reserve and U.S. monetary policy possess all the elements of a good story. Recent years have been punctuated by episodes of high drama. The cast of characters includes individuals whose judgments and actions have been of decisive importance for recent economic history. There are even a few moral lessons to be had.

Among the cast, Paul A. Volcker clearly stands out. Since Volcker became chairman of the Board of Governors in August 1979, monetary policy has been *his* policy, and the Federal Reserve—to a far greater extent than many realize—has been the Volcker Fed.

In the wake of the Fed's dramatic policy departure in October 1979, the economy experienced its sharpest economic downturn since the 1930s, and within a couple of years, there was a striking reversal of more than a decade of accelerating inflation. It's no exaggeration that Fed policy has touched, and continues to touch, the lives of millions.

This book describes why the Fed acted as it did, when it did. It tells the story of monetary policy in recent years, including what went right—and what went wrong.

Monetary policy is always changing, conceptually as well as tactically. This book throws into stark relief some of the intellectual crosscurrents that lie behind the continuing changes in the policy process. And it identifies unresolved issues still on the agenda.

Unfortunately, probably no single part of economic discussion is so arcane and so packed with jargon and buzz words, while being so much the focus of popular interest as is monetary policy. This book

1

aims to explain. Jargon is minimal. It is hoped that what buzz there is in these pages will remain well under the reader's pain threshold.

The financial markets' obsession with the Fed's every nuance has spawned a small industry of "Fedwatchers," people dedicated to the task of anticipating the Fed's next policy move. In part, this book is a product of that industry. One of its objectives is to explicate and clarify the strategy, tactics, and nuances of monetary policy, especially as it has been practiced in recent years. I hope the book will assist the investing public in appraising developments that are often reflected only imperfectly in necessarily terse media accounts. In attempting to provide such assistance, I made some hard choices in relegating most of the arcana of Fedwatching to an appendix. The fact is, the story flows better when unimpeded by such terms as "matched sale-purchase agreements," "customer repurchase agreements," and similar terminology. Aficionados of the policy process—or those who merely want to learn the argot of market professionals—are welcome to indulge themselves in the appendix, which stands on its own as a guide to the Fed's daily open-market operations.

But it would be unfortunate, indeed, if this book were to serve primarily as a Fedwatching manual. Monetary policy is, after all, a branch of what once was commonly termed "political economy." And the Federal Reserve, from the date of its creation in 1914 (under authority of the Federal Reserve Act of 1913), has been part and parcel of the inherently political crafting of the country's economic policy. As a result of changes made over the years in the Fed's powers, its policy role is fully as important as—some might say more important than—that of the White House or the Congress. Moreover, unlike denizens of those two centers of power, the governors of the Federal Reserve are not elected. Their appointments to 14-year terms of office represent one of the longer terms in the entire government. From the outset, the intent was to distance monetary policy from short-term political exigencies. However, as the framers of the original Federal Reserve Act intended, the Fed remains the creation of Congress, accountable only to Congress. How the Federal Reserve's semi-independence and accountability have shaped monetary policy is necessarily a major part of any chronicle of recent economic developments.

The greater part of the task of explaining the Fed is simply telling the story, in coherent fashion, of how policy was shaped during the last several years. In facing up to that task, one naturally seeks role models, and the inspiration for this book is Walter Bagehot (1826–77).

These days, Bagehot is not exactly a household name—but it was one in England during the 19th century. Besides being a leading literary critic, Bagehot made fundamental contributions to political science, including his pathbreaking delineation of the "constitution'" of

Britain. Founder of *The Economist* magazine, he was an astute observer of the economic and political scene. He is credited with inventing the Treasury bill and, as is described in Chapter 10, he wrote the classic statement of principles for the conduct of a central bank during a financial crisis—the widely recognized though often imperfectly understood "lender of last resort" function. That he did in a small volume entitled *Lombard Street*.

In the 19th century, Lombard Street was the principal location of the "bill brokers" of London, functionally equivalent to securities dealers today. Bagehot took the name for his title to emphasize that he was writing about an actual money market, inhabited by actual people. His special gift was to assemble well-known facts and to reveal functions and relationships that had never been perceived before, or if so, only imperfectly. An emphasis on practical relationships, and practical solutions to problems, permeated his work.

This book is also about actual people—chiefly in the Federal Reserve and the financial markets—and how they make monetary policy. As Bagehot would have had it, the emphasis is on the interplay between policymakers and financial market participants—their objectives, uncertainties, mistakes, and achievements.

2

THE SYSTEM

The Federal Reserve System is a huge organization that performs a wide variety of functions, of which monetary policy— though by far the most important—is only one. The System carries out these functions with an organizational structure that has no parallel among central banks abroad or among other domestic governmental agencies. An understanding of the monetary policy process must begin with an understanding of the System itself.

The hydra

Perhaps the best place to start is with an overview, necessarily brief, of the Fed's principal activities. Though it is hardly a matter of common knowledge, the Federal Reserve has almost as many functions as a hydra has heads.

Monetary policy. Paramount in the popular conception, of course, is the Fed's responsibility for monetary policy. Ironically, that function, at least in its modern meaning, was *not* one of the purposes envisioned in the original Federal Reserve Act. The act basically conceived of the Fed as a collection of supercorrespondent banks organized chiefly to improve the country's payments mechanism and to provide for seasonal currency needs, while supporting the soundness of banking through its role as lender of last resort.

The big issues at the time the act was passed were "par banking" and an "elastic currency."[1] Little attention was given to macroeconomic

4

objectives. Those responsibilities were added during the Depression, when the Banking Act of 1935 reconstituted the Federal Open Market Committee and assigned to it various policy responsibilities (discussed later in this chapter).

Payments system.   In addition, as the original act prescribed, the Fed is the operator of a crucial part of the country's payments system. Look at the back of almost any canceled check, and there will be a legend similar to PAY ANY BANK FRB BOSTON, followed by a mass of numbers, all of which indicates that the check was sent through one of the Fed's automated check-processing centers. The payments system is still overwhelmingly paper-based, but it is assuming a more electronic character with each passing year. The paper in question is, of course, the billions of paper checks that the Fed routes from banks where they have been deposited to the banks where the check writers have their accounts.

Processing paper checks is a mammoth job. During 1983, for example, the Fed's check processing facilities cleared almost 17 billion checks having an aggregate value of more than *$11 trillion.* An additional, unknown volume was cleared by banks directly. This is also an expensive job. Allocable expenses of the Fed's share of the operation alone cost about $185 million in 1983. That's why the Fed is trying to replace much of the paper shuffle with various forms of electronic payment devices. One of these is the Fedwire, established shortly after World War I, and greatly expanded and enhanced since that time. The Fedwire carries the bulk of large interbank payments. The total of such transfers during 1983 was nearly $140 trillion—more than double the value of transfers in 1979. But more is on the way. Many social security payments, for example, are handled via computer tapes distributed to banks that post the payments to recipients' accounts with no paper involved at all.

Lender of last resort.   As lender of last resort to the banking system, the Fed in effect backstops the liquidity of all U.S. financial markets, though not necessarily the solvency of an individual *participant* in those markets. This is one of the Fed's most widely recognized responsibilities. In the popular imagination, the lender of the last resort exudes drama and a bit of mystery. However, from the perspective of the Fed personnel who actually make the loans, the activity is more commonplace. They are prepared to process each day applications from banks which, usually for the most humdrum reasons, find themselves temporarily strapped for reserves. These employees monitor loan collateral to ensure its adequacy and post to banks' reserve accounts the funds loaned. Only seldom does anything truly dramatic occur.

From its inception, making advances to banks was regarded as one of the Fed's most essential functions. At one time, in fact, even the architecture of the dozen regional Federal Reserve Banks emphasized the point. As an illustration, consider the entrance foyer at the Cleveland Fed. Resplendent in gleaming, imported yellow marble, it is patterned after the Vatican's Sistine Chapel. Standing in the foyer, admiring the soaring arches and vaults, all of a pure, pale-yellow hue, one experiences a strong sense of the uplifting architectural harmony, until the eyes light upon a plain, black-and-white lettered sign protruding a bit from above one of the lower arches and bearing the stark legend: LOANS.

In recent years, though, the Fed, like everyone else it seems, has been modernizing, and the discount function (as it is called[2]) must make do with a less spectacular architectural form. At the New York Fed, for example, the function area is located on the second floor, behind a set of tellers' windows, the kind a not especially profitable bank in a small town might provide. Apparently, the Fed no longer feels the need to impress its borrowing clientele, at least not by architecture. Behind the tellers' windows are a few offices and several desks, and, during business hours, a huge steamer trunk on casters. There is nothing outwardly impressive about the trunk; except for the casters and its substantial bulk, it looks like one you might find in your Aunt Millie's attic. But on the day not so long ago when the author viewed the trunk, it held approximately $5 billion of collateral, mostly in the form of commercial loan notes deposited with the Fed by the largest New York City banks. Banks that borrow from the Fed must put up suitable collateral to back the loan. Since most banks, if they must borrow, do so only at the end of the day, speed is essential in processing the loan before closing. Hence, collateral is deposited in advance. That's why the function needs a capacious trunk.

Bank supervision.   Almost all banks in the United States are subject to regulation by some governmental authority. State-chartered banks that are not members of the Federal Reserve System are regulated by their states' banking commissions. The Fed itself, however, supervises state-chartered banks that are members of the Fed. (In addition, the Fed regulates bank holding companies.) Nationally chartered banks are regulated by the Comptroller of the Currency. Similarly, thrift institutions with state charters are supervised on the state level, while those with national charters are subject to the Federal Home Loan Bank Board. Money market mutual funds, which provide services similar in some respects to bank deposits, are regulated by the Securities and Exchange Commission. U.S. branches of foreign banks fit into this scheme depending on whether they are state-chartered (and supervised by state banking commissions) or nationally chartered (and supervised by the Comptroller of the Currency). In addition, to ensure uniformity of regulation, the Federal Reserve has residual supervisory authority over all U.S. operations of foreign banks. As a regulatory hodgepodge, this stands comparison to any.

Yet in most respects, the confusion is more apparent than real. From the standpoint of meeting its responsibilities for monetary policy and as lender of last resort, what matters most to the Fed is information. Prior to passage of the Monetary Control Act in 1980, the Fed's access to data from nonmember banks necessary to compile monetary statistics was seriously incomplete. However, the act took care of that problem. Similarly, since virtually all of the larger banks are members of the Federal Reserve System, and since the various regulatory authorities cooperate in sharing information obtained through periodic reports of condition and on-site audits by supervisory personnel, the regulatory network appears much more chaotic than it actually is. (As of this writing, Congress is considering proposals that would considerably modify the Fed's regulatory powers. The ultimate outcome remains to be seen.)

Fiscal agent for the Treasury. The Federal Reserve Banks serve as fiscal agents for the United States Treasury, that is, they process almost all payments to and from the government. This function includes receiving tenders (i.e., offers to buy) for Treasury securities issued in auctions. The Fed also operates the electronic book-entry system that allows government securities to be bought and sold without the necessity of issuing or transferring paper.

In addition, the Fed monitors conditions in the Treasury securities market and informs the Treasury of developments. Though it lacks legal authority to regulate government securities dealers, its role in the market is so important that the Fed can, and does, wield enormous influence. It also assists the Treasury through the Foreign Desk at the Federal Reserve Bank of New York, which intervenes in foreign exchange markets as the Treasury's agent, or for the System's own account with the Treasury's authorization.

Miscellanea. Finally, the Fed prescribes and enforces regulations governing stocks purchased on margin credit and is responsible for enforcing a variety of laws, among them the Truth in Lending Act, which sets standards for disclosure of lending terms on consumer loans.

A bizarre form of organization

The Federal Reserve System is an outstanding example of the fact that form need not follow function. Instead, the Fed's organizational structure is an anachronism utterly unlike that of any other governmental agency or business enterprise. The structure is absolutely perplexing unless it is understood as a historical accretion that functions well enough. In fact, it actually has some peculiar advantages.

The 12 regional Federal Reserve Banks are legally constituted as privately owned banks with special charters. Their shareholders are those commercial banks in the same districts that are members of the Federal Reserve System. This device solved quite a few political problems when the original Federal Reserve Act was being debated by Congress in 1913.

Many felt that the commercial banks that stood to benefit directly from the ability of the Federal Reserve Banks to make advances should reasonably be expected to bear the cost of providing for their establishment through subscribing equity capital. At the same time, there was strong sentiment in banking circles that the Federal Reserve Banks should be largely under the control of the banking community, and not the federal government. Private ownership seemed to meet that objective.

Finally, the various regions of the country wanted assurance that the banks would pay special heed to their own peculiar financial needs and not simply those of, for example, the New York banking community. Regional ownership of regional Federal Reserve Banks provided that assurance. Consequently, a wide variety of seemingly contradictory views appeared to be served through private ownership of the regional banks.[3]

Probably the best two-sentence description of the diverse principles underlying the improbable new System was written by H. Parker Willis, one of the chief draftsmen of the act and the first secretary of the Federal Reserve Board:

> The new act provides for twelve reserve banks, introduces the principle of local control, calls for strict government oversight, shifts reserves from present correspondent banks to new institutions, minimizes the influence of the larger banks in the directorates, and generally diffuses control instead of centralizing it. It leaves banking as such to be practiced by bankers; it rests the control of banking in the hands of government officers.[4]

Formally, the 12 regional banks were subordinate to the Federal Reserve Board in Washington, whose seven members included the Secretary of the Treasury, the Comptroller of the Currency, and five members appointed by the President, subject to confirmation by the Senate. But the regional banks, each with its own governor and board of directors, possessed substantial autonomy. Most important, the boards of directors of the banks had the latitude to determine for themselves the terms on which they would provide reserves to the banking system. This power was often described (incompletely and rather misleadingly) as the power to set their own discount rates, even though the Board could veto changes in the rates.

Under the leadership of Governor Benjamin Strong of the Federal Reserve Bank of New York, the System did achieve some coordination of its provision of reserves through open-market purchases and sales of securities, but following his death in 1928, a lack of leadership and petty mutual antagonisms between the Board and the various banks prevented such operations from being used as an effective policy instrument. In retrospect, extreme fragmentation of control over monetary policy clearly was a macroeconomic disaster waiting to happen.

The disaster arrived with the onset of the Depression. The Federal Reserve Banks, with the partial exception of the Federal Reserve Bank of New York, showed themselves utterly incapable of moving quickly to counter the spreading financial crisis.[5] Consequently, one of the highest priorities of the New Deal was passage of legislation—especially the Banking Act of 1935—that provided for centralized control over the Federal Reserve's monetary policy.

The reforms were thorough. The Federal Reserve Board was rechristened the Board of Governors, and the Secretary of the Treasury and the Comptroller of the Currency were removed from membership. Also, the standing of the Board was enhanced by designating its members as governors (traditionally the title of the head of a central bank), while the banks' governors were demoted to presidents.

One might naively have supposed that all control over policy would simply have been turned over to the Board of Governors, but that did not occur. Regional sentiments were still strong enough that, as so often happens, an apparently inconsistent, but politically sensible, compromise was produced.

Authority over monetary policy was vested in the Federal Open Market Committee (FOMC), composed of the members of the Board of Governors as well as five of the regional bank presidents. Of these five, the New York Fed's president is a permanent member. The other 11 banks annually rotate among themselves the remaining four places. This structure may appear bizarre and patently illogical, but messier political deals have surely been struck in the past, and no doubt many more will be in years to come.

The establishment of the FOMC deprived the regional banks of substantially all of their independent power to make policy. But it did not change their legal structure. They remained privately owned, continued to have boards of directors, and continued to pay dividends to their shareholding member banks (though the amount of the dividend was beyond their purview). All that remained of the authority of their boards of directors was the largely symbolic ritual of meeting every two weeks to "establish" (subject to review by the Board of Governors) their bank's discount rate. They possessed no authority whatever to determine the availability of reserves to the banking system.

From time to time, proposals have been put forth in Congress to tidy up this messy structure by dispensing with the legal formality of regional banks.[6] Invariably such initiatives have gotten nowhere, and it is not hard to see why. In the first place, administrative streamlining would save little money, if any. Almost all of the operational functions performed by the regional banks, such as check clearing, would have to be performed by somebody, no matter what the System's organizational matrix looked like. Second, regional concerns and regional pride are still important, and it will be a snowy day in hell before a city containing a regional bank would willingly see it eliminated or reduced in importance, even symbolically, merely to relieve the clutter on someone's organization chart. Finally, the regional banks have no independent power to make policy, so why should the valuable time of Congress be wasted on a harmless anachronism?

There appear to be only two substantive grounds for the proposals. One is a concern that private bankers, who by law hold three of the nine directorships on the boards of the regional banks, might exert undue influence on policymakers, or might have preferential access to information not available to other members of the public. The other is a concern that the process of selecting bank presidents—who, of course, rotate as voting FOMC members—is not subject to congressional approval in the same fashion as Board appointments are. To some, their selection by the bank boards (subject, of course, to review by the Board) seems profoundly undemocratic.

These are by no means trivial concerns. But as far as influence on policy is concerned, it is frankly difficult to see how participation on an anachronistic board of directors could add measurably to the policy clout which industry lobbyists (not only banking lobbyists) wield. No doubt, members of Congress are particularly well placed to understand the merit of this argument.

As for access to confidential information, that is only attractive if one can make money with it. And it strains belief to imagine that the members of the boards could do so and not be found out, for there are few such secrets in the money markets, and none remain secret for very long. In any event, ever since 1935, bank presidents serving on the FOMC have been prohibited from divulging to their directors (to whom they are only nominally subordinate) any confidential information about decisions of the committee.[7]

In practice, the only exchange of nonpublic information appears to flow in the reverse direction: board members routinely supply information concerning their banks, regional business, and financial developments to the bank's president and senior staff.

The one exception is, of course, the ability of the boards to recommend discount rate changes. Through their presence, directors obviously know whether a vote has been taken to make such a recommendation. But unfortunately for the would-be profiteer, in the vast majority of cases, the Board of Governors takes no action on such recommendations, and it is hard to make money on inside information without confidence that the information will be translated into policy.[8] In fact, the only case in which a true problem might arise is when the Board of Governors desires to change the discount rate and notifies the regional boards of its willingness to "consider" a change, should they be inclined to "recommend" one. Then and only then would board members have advance information of an imminent policy change.

The role of the bank boards in the selection of bank presidents is rather less than meets the eye. As in so many other respects, the power of the boards, once essentially absolute, shriveled as the authority of the Board grew. The regional boards do appoint their presidents, but such appointments are subject to review by the Board, and as part of that process, Board members interview final candidates. Naturally, neither the regional boards nor the Board would relish participating in a public squabble, so appointments are settled through behind-the-scenes discussions.

When one party to those discussions is as prestigious and dominating a figure as Paul Volcker, the role of the boards, already vestigial, tends to be insignificant. Since Volcker became chairman in 1979, presidents have been appointed at six banks. Two of them—Anthony M. Solomon in New York and E. Gerald Corrigan in Minneapolis—clearly were hand-picked by Volcker. Solomon had served in the Treasury when Volcker was Under Secretary of the Treasury for Monetary Affairs, and Corrigan was a senior officer of the Federal Reserve Bank of New York when Volcker was that bank's president and served briefly as his special assistant when he was appointed chairman.

The other four presidencies share a common characteristic in that, with one exception, their occupants—William F. Ford in Atlanta (succeeded, after his resignation in 1983, by Robert P. Forrestal), Silas Keehn in Chicago, Theodore H. Roberts in St. Louis, and Karen N. Horn in Cleveland—had little professional background in monetary policy issues prior to their appointment. The exception was Ford, who had been chief economist at Wells Fargo Bank.

That hardly means that the role of the boards in their selection was significant, however. Certain members of the Reagan administration were known to be supporting monetarist candidates—economist Jerry L. Jordan, a former member of the Reagan administration's Council of Economic Advisers, was widely mentioned as a candidate—and the ultimate selection of neutral presidents probably was a victory for Volcker.

On balance, it seems fair to say that the selection process for bank presidents tends, in practice, to enhance the standing and authority of the chairman. That does not make the process any more democratic, of course. But by providing 14-year terms for Board members,

Congress clearly intended to distance the Fed somewhat from the usual political give-and-take, and that insulation is probably not greatly augmented by the process of appointing presidents. In any event, would-be critics should focus their attention on the Board—the chairman, in particular—and not so much on the regional boards and bank presidents.

Once bank presidents are appointed, they are potentially subject to another, far from subtle, form of influence. Their budgets are subject to review by the Board. Thus their staffing levels, as well as their salaries, are subject to Board approval. How much impact this source of influence has is difficult to evaluate, and in any event, it probably would vary from one president to another. One bank president told the author that another bank president had become less outspoken in Federal Open Market Committee meetings while trying to gain Board approval for construction of a new bank building. At the same time, however, he assured the author that such considerations never affected *his* decisions to agree or disagree in FOMC meetings. Suffice it to say that the case is not proved, and given the inherently subjective nature of such influence, it probably never could be.

If the regional banks have long since lost their power to set policy, what function do they serve? In addition to the operational responsibilities discussed earlier, the regional banks actually do enhance the diversity of policy recommendations considered by the FOMC. The banks are clearly in closer contact with developments in their regions than the Board of Governors ever could be, and the information thus acquired surely benefits the policy process to some degree. In particular, the boards of the banks, as well as the boards of the 25 bank branches, typically are made up of prominent local citizens, and many of their members feel a personal responsibility for keeping the Fed informed about local business developments.

Moreover, the board memberships provide the Fed with a presence in localities all over the country that can be extremely useful in garnering public support for its objectives.[9] But from a larger perspective, by far the most important contribution of the regional banks is in the area of economic policy research.

In comparison to the predictable uniformity of research and policy recommendations emanating from many governmental agencies, the Federal Reserve System is a hotbed of diversity. It is not at all uncommon for one regional bank to be circulating research results or policy recommendations that clash with those of some other regional bank or even with those of the Board of Governors itself.

In fact, one of the more significant ways the banks and their presidents influence policy is through the research they sponsor. In the past several years, the most significant contributions have tended to be made by the staffs of the Federal Reserve Banks of Boston,

New York, Kansas City, St. Louis, and San Francisco. As a rule, the first three of these have tended to have somewhat more confidence in the effectiveness of fiscal measures in economic policy while questioning the degree of reliance that should be placed on achieving numerical targets for monetary aggregates. In contrast, San Francisco and especially St. Louis have been strongly supportive of such targets, and researchers at St. Louis have repeatedly questioned whether fiscal measures have any but the most ephemeral effects on economic performance.

One should not, however, exaggerate the degree to which diversity is tolerated in the Federal Reserve System. During the last several years, there have been a number of instances in which research results generated by staffs of the regional banks were either suppressed completely, or else published only after being larded with caveats at the insistence of senior members of the Board staff (who can be assumed to have acted in accordance with the views of the Board, especially the chairman, to whom the staff directors report directly). Nevertheless, it is clear that the Fed does encourage a great diversity of internally circulated research, in all likelihood, much more than any other governmental agency.

Whether this multiplicity of research effort is beneficial is an inherently subjective judgment. On balance, though, it probably is quite valuable. Since none of the contending theories has a monopoly on wisdom, diversity can serve to alert policymakers to the blind spots that all simplified theories contain. In any event, there is no doubt that a high-quality research staff has the potential to augment a regional bank president's expertise and prestige, both within the FOMC and without. However, that potential is not always realized.

As a practical matter, the Board staff dominates policy discussions. One reason for that is simply its size and quality. It is one of the largest economic research staffs in the country, and it includes many economists and statisticians of a very high professional caliber. Another reason is of a more practical nature. The Board staff serves as the staff of the FOMC and prepares the briefing materials and analyses of policy alternatives used by the FOMC members in formulating policy decisions. A regional bank may have fine economists on its staff, but their access to the crucial decision-making forum cannot approach that of the senior members of the Board staff.

Some might argue that research is not the *only* way in which the regional banks affect policy. The primary example probably would be the Federal Reserve Bank of New York. It implements monetary policy on a daily basis through operations of its Domestic Open Market Desk, while its Foreign Desk carries out operations in foreign exchange markets, if any, at the direction of the Treasury. The managers of the Desks at the New York Fed generally have a role in FOMC meetings on a par with that of senior members of the Board staff. But this channel of influence does not really lead from the bank to the FOMC. The managers are members of the FOMC staff, in addition to being officers of the bank. Even in this instance, then, there is little identifiable influence of the bank itself on policy.

For policy formation, then, the FOMC is usually all that matters; the banks (except for the fruits of their research) do not.

Running the FOMC

The Federal Open Market Committee meets about eight times a year in the spacious board room on the second floor of the Eccles building in Washington, D.C.[10] At the first meeting of the year, typically in late January or early February, annual targets are adopted formally. At the July meeting, those targets are reviewed and targets for the following year are adopted provisionally. In addition, the committee formulates a directive to the Federal Reserve Bank of New York to guide the implementation of committee objectives through open market operations.

That the FOMC ever gets anything done at all is certainly one of the more remarkable features of the whole policy process. The committee has 12 members—7 Board members and 5 bank presidents. In addition, the other 7 bank presidents attend meetings and participate fully in discussions, though they may not vote. That makes 19 participants—12 voting and 7 nonvoting. With a group of that size, over an hour and a half is required merely to permit each participant to speak for five minutes! Moreover, the FOMC members are not by any means the only participants in the meetings; senior staff members also take part.

A typical meeting might proceed as follows.[11] First, the manager of the New York Fed's Foreign Desk presents a report on international developments since the last meeting. That usually takes about 10–15 minutes, longer if there are questions and discussion. Next, the manager of the Open Market Desk reports on open market operations and conditions in the domestic financial markets. That takes another 10–15 minutes or so, with more time required for questions and discussion.

Then a member of the Board's senior staff discusses recent economic developments and presents a summary of the Board's economic forecast. An extensive written description of the forecast which—dubbed the "green book" in reference to the color of its cover—will have been distributed to committee members in advance of the meeting.[12] The presentation consumes another quarter hour or so, plus discussion time.

Next the policy discussion gets underway, as the staff director

for monetary policy reviews the policy options that the staff has prepared for the committee's consideration. The options, depicting several
alternative short-run target paths for the monetary aggregates, are doc-
umented in the "blue book." This book is also available to members
in advance of the meeting. The presentation typically requires about
15–20 minutes, with discussion accounting for perhaps another half
hour or more.

The chairman then calls for general discussion. This is the opportunity for each of the 19 members to state his or her views. In order
to avoid prolonging the meeting indefinitely, the time allotted for this
purpose is usually only about five minutes or less per member, just
about enough time to state briefly which way one thinks the economy
is going and which of the staff's policy options, if any, one prefers.
Even so, the "roundup," as it is called, consumes something on the
order of another hour and a half.

At the end of the roundup, the chairman can generally suggest
a policy stance that will command majority support. If necessary, straw
votes are taken before a formal vote in order to clarify further the
dimensions of a possible consensus. The chairman himself frames the
terms of such votes and thus can use them to elicit information from
the members as well as to influence the direction of discussion. Finally,
the formal vote is taken to endorse either one of the staff's options
or a modification put forward by Volcker or perhaps another FOMC
member.

Thus, the business of a routine FOMC meeting can be transacted
in half a day. Meetings may last substantially longer, however. If special
presentations are to be heard, if the chairman wishes to allow additional
time for discussion (for example, a roundup on national and regional
economic developments), or twice a year, when a review of the annual
aggregates target ranges is conducted, additional time is required. In
particular, two-day meetings are the norm when aggregates targets
are reviewed.

While a group as large as this might seem prone to factiousness,
in practice, members rarely dissent in policy votes, and then, only if
strongly held views prevent them from joining the majority. A spirit
of collegiality is one of the FOMC's most outstanding characteristics.
Most members take their responsibilities seriously. They feel, no doubt
correctly, that the Fed's credibility is greatest when it speaks with a
unified voice. They feel that policy differences are best resolved through
discussion and compromise.

In that process, the chairman naturally plays the leading role,
along with a small number of other members. Those members who
have little background in the technical complexities of monetary policy
tend to align their vote with a member, quite possibly the chairman,
who does have such a background and whose judgment they trust.[13]

Volcker's mastery of the subject makes his views carry great weight and helps him guide the formation of a consensus.

Another reason for this impressive degree of unity surely lies in the role of the staff. As the procedure of FOMC meetings makes clear, staff assessments establish the baseline analysis for both the economic and financial outlooks, and a substantial amount of the committee's time is given over to their presentation and discussion. Not only that, but the Board staff's economic and financial forecast, incorporated in the green book, and its analysis of policy options, contained in the blue book, are circulated to all the committee members a few days prior to the meeting. In contrast, a dissident committee member has only a few minutes to argue his views in the formal meeting, plus whatever he can achieve during impromptu discussions in the hallway or over lunch.

Moreover, those committee members who possess a high degree of professional expertise concerning the properties of the economic models underlying the staff analysis almost inevitably assume a more prominent role in the discussions than members who lack such a background. In a technical discussion of economic policy, solid professional economic training is largely indispensable to anyone who would hope to influence the outcome; for the most part, those who don't have it tend to rely on the judgment of those who do.

Under these circumstances, the relative unanimity of the group, briefed by the staff (which is, of course, primarily responsible to the chairman) and under some pressure not to fracture the consensus assembled by the chairman, is not altogether surprising.

In any event, by the end of each meeting, the FOMC has formulated a directive to the New York Fed indicating how the manager of the Open Market Desk is to translate the committee's objectives into monetary conditions. The precise construction of that operating procedure has assumed great significance in its own right in recent years. However, the repeated, and occasionally heated, discussion of operating procedures that has taken place during the last couple of decades cannot be understood in isolation from the historical evolution of the Fed's conceptual view of money, credit, and monetary control. That is a topic for the next chapter.

Notes

1. These days, it would be a rare individual who has even heard of "par banking"—which is simply the practice of banks undertaking to pay 100 cents on the dollar (i.e., the par value) for checks drawn on other banks. Thanks to the Federal Reserve Act, par banking has been virtually universal in this country for decades, though a very few nonpar banks remain to this day. Prior to this reform, writing a check (or,

more typically in those days, paying in private bank notes) was hampered by the difficulty of knowing precisely what the check or notes might be worth when discounted in another town or state.

"Elastic currency" referred chiefly to the ability or, prior to the act, the *in*ability of the money supply to expand temporarily to meet seasonal needs. Around the turn of the century, the U.S. economy was still overwhelmingly agricultural. Not surprisingly, the most frequent contemporary example of the need for elasticity was the seasonal requirement for currency to facilitate agricultural transactions around harvest time, when interest rates would rise as demands for a relatively fixed supply of currency mounted. Farmers (and many others) were not pleased. At present, the best example of currency "elasticity" in this sense is the provision of additional supplies of currency during the holiday season at the end of the year. Even in our electronic, credit-card age, the Fed each year provides during November and December something on the order of $5 billion in extra currency to accommodate holiday shoppers, most of which is withdrawn during the following January. From time to time, certain economists have protested that such a policy constitutes an unjustified intrusion in the workings of the marketplace. It is true, of course, that if interest rates rose high enough, some of us would revise our holiday plans and celebrate Christmas in July, but we would rather not. To the extent that anyone thinks about the subject at all these days, most regard an elastic currency as a self-evident good thing, not worth serious dispute.

2. It would be more logical to call this activity the advance function or loan function rather than the discount function. The Federal Reserve Act grants the Fed power to purchase, or discount, certain kinds of commercial securities. As a practical matter, though, this power has not been used for many years. Instead, the preferred technique is to make loans to banks secured by appropriate collateral. That has major administrative advantages, because the Fed avoids having to administer and collect on what would be a bewildering variety of commercial obligations. It also facilitates short-term lending, which accounts for by far the largest portion of the Fed's advances. Nevertheless, just as the lending function continues to be misnamed, the rate charged on advances is still referred to as the discount rate.

3. For an excellent, brief account of the political maneuvering that preceded the passage of the original Federal Reserve Act, see Roger T. Johnson, *Historical Beginnings . . . The Federal Reserve* (Boston: Federal Reserve Bank of Boston, 1977).

4. H. Parker Willis, *The Federal Reserve: A Study of the Banking System of the United States* (Garden City, N.Y.: Doubleday Publishing, 1915), p. 68.

5. The story of that episode, which lies outside the scope of this book, has been told well many times before. Perhaps the best description is provided in Milton Friedman and Anna J. Schwartz, *A Monetary History of the United States, 1867-1960* (New York: National Bureau of Economic Research, 1963), chapter 7.

6. The most recent suggestion along these lines is contained in the 1983 *Monetary Policy Report* of the House Committee on Banking, Finance, and Urban Affairs.

7. For details on the background of this prohibition, see Friedman and Schwartz, *A Monetary History*, p. 446.

8. A grotesque example of the irrelevance of the boards' votes in formulation of policy occurred in 1983. All during that year, the discount rate was maintained unchanged at 8½ percent. During the first 11 months of the year (as of this writing, the latest period for which public records are available), the Board deferred or denied no fewer than 92 separate requests for changes. Assuming that the boards kept proposing while the Board kept disposing, about 100 requests must have been overruled during the year as a whole without a single one being accepted! For details, see H. Erich Heinemann and Charles Lieberman, "Economic Research: Prospects" (New York: Shearson/ American Express, April 6, 1984).

9. For example, in some instances the boards were apparently quite helpful in making certain that their local congressmen understood the need for and importance of the Monetary Control Act of 1980.

10. In addition, from time to time the chairman may decide to hold a committee meeting on a telephone conference call. Such consultations are generally focused on a limited number of questions and are much shorter than regular meetings.

11. For an unsurpassed description of the procedure of the Federal Open Market Committee and the Open Market Desk, see Paul Meek, *U. S. Monetary Policy and Financial Markets* (New York: Federal Reserve Bank of New York, 1982). The discussion in this book has benefited greatly from Meek's detailed account. For a unique insider's view of FOMC proceedings during the 1960s and early 1970s, see Sherman J. Maisel, *Managing the Dollar* (New York: W. W. Norton, 1973). Another very interesting analysis of the committee's operation is Thomas Mayer, "Federal Reserve Policy in the 1973–1975 Recession: A Case Study of Fed Behavior in a Quandary," in *Crises in the Economic and Financial Structure,* ed. Paul Wachtel (Lexington, Mass.: D. C. Heath, 1982), pp. 41–83.

12. Another document—previously known as the "red book" by virtue of its red cover but now clad in a beige cover— is compiled from reports submitted by the regional banks covering primarily local business conditions. It is prepared two weeks or so before FOMC meetings and is also made available to Congress.

13. Sherman Maisel noted the same phenomenon during his membership on the Board in the 1960s and 1970s. See Maisel, *Managing the Dollar,* chapter 6.

3

FEDERAL RESERVE POLICY AND THE MONETARIST CHALLENGE

All of the Volcker Fed's most important policy initiatives had major antecedents in the concepts of previous years. While the Fed's policy changed in a number of respects during the 26 years from the end of the Korean War to 1979, certain persistent features stand out. One is the traditional importance that policymakers have ascribed to credit and terms of lending as an economic indicator. A second, and closely related, aspect is the preference given to interest rates as a device for implementing policy. Those two features, given theoretical expression early in the 1950s through the credit availability view, have endured throughout the entire postwar period.

Beginning in the early 1970s, however, a new focus was introduced as the Fed gradually modified its strategy to give monetary aggregates a central, though far from dominant, role. That shift of emphasis, though hardly a total break with the past, was largely attributable to growing acceptance of monetarist views about the proper role of monetary policy.

This chapter traces how these divergent intellectual crosscurrents prepared the conceptual backdrop for the Volcker Fed's most remarkable policy departures.

Credit and credit availability

Credit—especially credit extended by banks—was a key focus of the Federal Reserve from its inception. The concept of an elastic currency, capable of meeting the "needs of trade," necessarily implied a notion of a relatively stable relationship between expansion of credit and expansion of business activity.

During the Fed's early years, adherence to this idea, formalized by economists as the "real bills doctrine," was so absolute that little attention was given to any independent influence of the money supply. The attitude was, in essence, that if credit expansion were limited to the needs of trade, which in practice usually meant avoidance of lending for "speculative" purposes, then the money supply would take care of itself.

During the early 1950s that attitude began to change somewhat. In its annual report for 1952, the Fed for the first time described its objectives as providing for expansion of bank credit and money appropriate to meet the needs of a growing economy. Money was admittedly in second place, but at least it was deemed worthy of independent mention.[1]

That statement of objectives followed closely on the celebrated March 1951 "Accord" between the Treasury and the Federal Reserve, which freed the Fed from an obligation to support prices of Treasury debt, i.e., to peg the interest rates on Treasury notes and bonds.[2] The process by which rates had been pegged was quite simple. If, for example, rates were under upward pressure, the Fed bought Treasury securities in amounts sufficient to hold rates (and thus bond prices) approximately stable. When the Fed paid for such purchases, it posted credits to the reserves accounts of banks, and added to the volume of reserves available to the banking system. (The ability to create reserves in this fashion is the distinguishing characteristic of a central bank.)

If the upward rate pressure had been occasioned merely by some temporary distortion of banks' needs for reserves, the operation did no harm. On the contrary, it probably had some distinct benefits. But if rates were tending to rise due to an inflationary boom, as was the case during the Korean War, an attempt to prevent them from rising and thus restraining spending would compound the inflationary pressures.

Serving as an adjunct of Treasury finance had thus deprived the Fed and monetary policy of any meaningful role in economic stabilization. In form at least, the Accord restored the Fed's independence, and with it, the basis for an independent monetary policy. In principle, the Fed could now vary interest rates over whatever range might be required in order to achieve its objectives. As a practical matter, however, the actual exercise of this new power, illustrated in Chart 3–1, was quite restrained, at least by the standards of recent years.

There were several reasons for this. One was the then fashionable view that interest rates, though theoretically important, were in practice of little significance to macroeconomic policy. The Keynesian

CHART 3–1
Nominal Interest Rates Were Quite Low throughout the 1950s

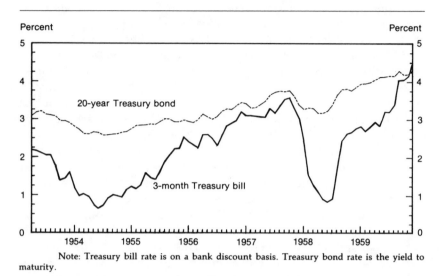

Note: Treasury bill rate is on a bank discount basis. Treasury bond rate is the yield to maturity.

notion of a "liquidity trap," a situation in which the public's demand for money is so sensitive to changes in interest rates that monetary policy can have little effect on the levels of income and employment, provided a convenient rationale. In addition, a variety of surveys of business decision-making practices seemed to suggest that business firms typically paid little heed to interest rates when formulating their investment plans. Consequently, fiscal policy was widely assumed to be the major, if not actually the only, effective instrument for economic stabilization.

This view was not unanimous, however. Some economists argued that the real stock of money balances was a determinant of consumption spending, though few felt confident of the size of its impact.

An alternative, and, for many within the Federal Reserve, a more intuitive and appealing rationale for the Fed's independent policy role was provided by the availability theory. Reduced to essentials, the theory held that a modest increase in interest rates could affect business investment by causing banks to reduce the availability of loans for such purposes.[3]

The key to this result was the fact that the higher rates would produce capital losses in banks' portfolios of Treasury securities, losses that would have to be realized (and reflected directly in bottom-line earnings) in order to accommodate business demands for loans. Banks' understandable reluctance to take such losses would, so the story ran, prompt them to restrict the availability of loans. The most articulate exponent of this view was Robert V. Roosa, who at different times during the 1950s was a senior member of the research department at the Federal Reserve Bank of New York and domestic Desk manager.[4]

The availability theory did indeed have intuitive appeal, though critics pointed out that it left unanswered a number of questions about the logical consistency of banks rationing credit on the basis of criteria other than profitability. Those and related questions were the subject of a fair number of articles in economic journals during the ensuing decade and a half. But well before all of the loose theoretical nuts could be tightened, the availability view had a major attraction for Fed policymakers, for it implied that small changes of interest rates could have disproportionately large impacts on economic activity, despite businesses' apparent insensitivity to interest rates, on the one hand, and the hypothesized liquidity trap, on the other. Consequently, the Fed did have an important policy role (thus confirming what many had believed all along), and implementation of its policy need not involve large adjustments of interest rates.

That last implication was of major significance in view of a political consensus that was overwhelmingly averse to high interest rates. Throughout the 1950s and 1960s, no matter what the stage of the business cycle, congressional committees routinely grilled Federal Reserve Chairman William McClesney Martin about what were allegedly excessively high interest rates.

The Federal Reserve is, of course, a creation of Congress, and accountable to that body. Thus it required no stretch of the Fed's imagination to foresee a hostile reaction, possibly culminating in a substantial reduction of the Fed's independent authority, if interest rates were allowed to vary too freely. The availability view appeared to provide a way to avoid that eventuality while implementing a responsible monetary policy.

The predominant view of Federal Open Market Committee members was broadly in line with the availability theory, since it accorded well with their practical experience in financial affairs. However, no one ever succeeded in quantifying the role of availability effects in transmitting monetary policy to the economy at large. Thus no one really knew how much availability impact would follow from a given change of interest rates, or how fast that impact would take place.[5]

However, the lack of such knowledge was not considered a major problem. The FOMC operated with only the most imprecise notion of the economic relationships underlying its policy decisions. In part that reflected an intuitive sense, particularly on the part of Chairman Martin, but shared in greater or lesser degree by other members as well, that such relationships were not readily susceptible to quantification. (Also, prior to the general availability of high-speed computers, preparing such estimates would have been extraordinarily time-consuming.)[6] Instead, the Fed tried to "lean into the wind"—a phrase repeated frequently by Chairman Martin—by easing interest rates when business conditions seemed to be weakening and raising them when inflationary pressures were building.

Under these circumstances, it was only natural that in implementing its policy objectives, the Fed relied on adjustments to market conditions, i.e., on small changes in interest rates induced either by variations in banks' access to reserves or by changes in the Fed's discount rate. In addition, from time to time "open-mouth operations," exercises in moral suasion or simply venting of the Fed's desires, played a role. And since interest rates were the trigger for credit availability effects, the specific technique for implementing a policy change was vastly less significant than the reflection of that change in market interest rates.

Despite the Fed's repeated affirmation during the 1950s of the significance of credit *and* money, variations in the money stock were of little independent concern, either theoretically or operationally. Indeed, prior to 1944, the Fed had not even bothered to collect and publish reasonably comprehensive monthly data for the money stock, and it was not until 1955 that this data was reported routinely in a seasonally adjusted form.

Nevertheless, despite what now appear to have been rather crude policy procedures, the money stock grew at a relatively modest trend rate—at an annual average of about 2 percent for M1—during the 1950s (see Chart 3–2). Growth was far from constant, however. Writing in the early 1960s, economists Milton Friedman and Anna J. Schwartz remarked of this period that the Fed's growing "confidence in the efficacy of monetary policy in the 1950s was inversely related to monetary stability."[7]

While the period from the end of the Korean War through the early 1960s was marked, on the whole, by very stable prices and a respectable rate of economic growth, all was not tranquil. In particular, the 1958 recession was sharp, and the rise in the unemployment rate, from 3.7 percent in March 1957 to 7.5 percent at its peak in July 1958, produced a storm of criticism of the Fed for pursuing an unduly restrictive—or, as Friedman charged, an erratic—policy. Through it all, though, policy was implemented by means of what were, in retrospect, very modest variations in interest rates.

Or were they? Reckoned in percentage changes, rate movements were quite large, even by the standards of recent years, simply because the prevailing levels of rates were so low. For example, a rise of one percentage point may seem small in absolute terms, but during much of the 1950s, such a change would have doubled rates on Treasury bills. Indeed, during mid-1959, bill rates, pushing the 3 percent level, were almost *three times* as high as they had been a year earlier. Not

CHART 3–2
M1 Year-Over-Year Percentage Growth Rate

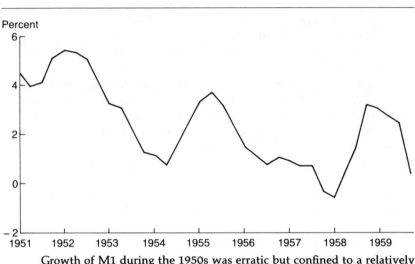

Percent

Growth of M1 during the 1950s was erratic but confined to a relatively low trend.

even the rate volatility in the early 1980s approached that standard.

Percentage changes of rates are potentially important for one reason. Most economists view consumer wealth as a major determinant of spending decisions, and the rate of change of wealth is in principle closely related to percentage changes of interest rates, particularly long-term rates. Long-term rates were far less variable than bill rates during the 1950s, but year-to-year changes on the order of 20 percent or more, comparable to changes observed in the early 1980s, were fairly common. Consequently, even minor absolute changes in interest rates may have had significant impacts on spending behavior.

There were probably three important features of the 1950s that allowed monetary policy to be effective, if not universally applauded. One was the extremely cautious fiscal policy pursued during the Eisenhower administration. Conditioned as Americans now are to seemingly perpetual, multibillion-dollar deficits, it is difficult to appreciate just how restrained that policy was.

Perhaps the best illustration is that during the 1952–60 period, the federal debt as a portion of GNP declined from 64 percent at the end of 1951 to 47 percent at the end of 1960, while federal expenditures were roughly stable at about 19 percent of GNP (Chart 3–3) compared to about 25 percent in recent years. Deficits and surpluses in the federal budget were rather small, and for the eight-year period as a whole, the cumulative budget deficit was $12 billion, equal to a minuscule

0.2 percent of GNP. That compares to deficits of about 5 percent of GNP in recent years. The absence of any strong fiscal stimulus meant that the Fed could exert a sufficiently restrictive effect on the economy without more than a modest nudge of interest rates.

In addition, it is quite possible that inflation expectations were significantly different during the 1950s than they are now. Consumers, their memories of the massive deflation of the 1930s still fresh, tended to respond to an increase in the inflation rate by restraining their purchases and lifting the overall saving rate. Such responses were the exact opposite of the "buy now, it'll cost more later" attitude prevalent during the 1970s.[8] Any such tendency toward reining in spending in reaction to the emergence of price pressures clearly made the Fed's economic stabilization job that much easier.

Finally, if the availability theory ever had a chance of success, it was surely in context of a relatively simple financial structure like that of the 1950s. Banks, functioning as essentially passive recipients of deposits, were the overwhelmingly dominant suppliers of short-term credit to business, while money markets, with the obvious exception of the Treasury bill market, were relatively undeveloped. As long as banks were the central conduit for short-term business credit, the capital losses that rising interest rates would create in their investment

CHART 3–3

Federal Expenditures and Budget Position as a Percentage of GNP

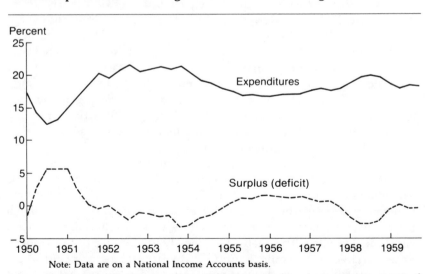

Note: Data are on a National Income Accounts basis.

Following the Korean War, federal expenditures as a percentage of GNP declined gradually, while the federal budget was roughly in balance until the end of the 1950s.

portfolios might well have some impact on their willingness to finance business spending.

However, the financial structure changed. Banks developed means of managing their deposits so that capital losses on investments did not have to be realized in order to accommodate loan demands. In addition, increasingly sophisticated markets for various kinds of short-term business borrowing provided a channel by which credit flows could circumvent banks altogether. In the new financial environment, the key preconditions of the availability view were no longer well satisfied, and it would have been surprising, indeed, if modest changes in interest rates could have achieved the desired effects.

Twilight of the credit availability view

Several developments during the 1960s and 1970s radically altered major features of the earlier environment. The first significant change was the introduction in 1961 of negotiable certificates of deposit (CDs) paying a market rate of interest. CDs had been around for decades, but two features were new. The first was the willingness of large banks to pay market rates on corporate deposits (which had often been considered too volatile to justify payment of any interest). The second was the all-important quality of liquidity, achieved through securities dealers making markets in CDs, i.e., standing ready to buy and sell them at quoted rates.[9]

Walter B. Wriston, until recently chairman of Citicorp, is generally credited with the innovation of modern CDs, an innovation that was crucial to the continued success of large banks. CDs enabled them to tap the corporate cash that was increasingly being channeled into other money-market instruments (for example, Treasury bills) by ever more yield-sensitive corporate treasurers. Once such investors could obtain a slightly higher rate on CDs without sacrificing liquidity— i.e., the ability to sell out the investment quickly, at little or no loss, to meet an unexpected cash need—bank deposits became a highly competitive short-term investment outlet.

CDs were banks' first true instrument of liability management. Admittedly large banks had borrowed regularly in the federal funds and repurchase agreement markets,[10] but such borrowings were predominantly in very short maturities that did not allow banks much discretion in managing their interest-rate exposure. In contrast, CDs were time deposits with a maturity typically in the three to four-month range. A large bank could issue CDs to fund loans or could allow them to run off if the funds were not needed. Once the market matured and banks realized the full potential of liability management, a rise in interest rates no longer forced them to realize capital losses on their long-term investments. Instead, they generally preferred to issue CDs (or later, some other liability-management instrument) as needed to fund their loans. Thus a critical link in the availability theory was severed, at least for the larger banks, whose credit standing gave them ready access to the CD market.

There was just one problem: the Fed imposed ceilings on the rates of interest that could be paid on time deposits, including CDs. When market interest rates rose to levels above those banks could legally pay, it would become impossible for banks to sell new CDs to replace maturing issues. Accordingly, funds would flow out of CDs (and thus out of the banks that had issued them) and into other money-market instruments.

That situation could create severe problems for a bank depending on CDs for a significant portion of its funds. Initially, the Fed was fairly accommodating in periodically adjusting the ceiling rates to facilitate banks' continued access to the market. Later on, however, maintenance of rigid ceilings came to be viewed by many in the Fed as a possibly helpful device for reinforcing its control over credit availability, which the development of CDs appeared to have weakened.

More than theoretical niceties impelled the Fed to this view. The politically powerful homebuilding and thrift institution lobbies, among others, raised a steady clamor against high interest rates. For practical reasons, there were strong motives for deploying a policy instrument that showed promise for delivering maximum restraint on spending with minimum pressure on interest rates.[11]

But it didn't work. It failed because investors were becoming much more sophisticated. Regulators' attempts to close off existing channels for short-term investments merely shunted activity into new channels, with little net effect on business spending. The most dramatic instance occurred in 1969. During that year, market rates soared far above the rates that banks were permitted to pay on CDs. The result was that large banks lost about 50 percent of their CDs during the year, which of course set off a frantic scramble for funds to replace those lost. The largest banks began to raise substantial amounts of funds in the unregulated Eurodollar market, where market rates could be paid without restriction. The availability of such rates naturally attracted some investors who previously had placed funds in the CD market.

In addition, banks developed a number of other devices for minimizing the impact of the rate ceilings, such as loan participation certificates (which made the erstwhile depositor a part-owner of a specific loan) and commercial paper issued by bank holding companies (which "downstreamed" the proceeds of the paper issue by purchasing loans from the subsidiary bank). The Fed predictably reacted to these innovations by clamping on new restrictions as quickly as the loopholes could be detected, analyzed, and fitted out with regulations.[12]

However, banks and their customers had another card up their collective sleeve against which the Fed's proliferating regulations were almost powerless. The market for commercial paper, unsecured corporate IOUs with very short maturities, had existed for years, but now it began to surge. Paper issued by nonfinancial business firms almost doubled during 1969 alone, reaching in December what was then a record $5.4 billion. Financial companies, including the consumer finance companies that traditionally had dominated the market, were not far behind. Their outstandings ballooned 24 percent to end the year at $22.9 billion. And banks, or more precisely, bank holding companies, stormed into the market as well, lifting their paper from negligible amounts to $4.3 billion by December. Overall, the size of the paper market increased by more than half during the year.

Many of the new entrants to the market, especially the nonfinancial issuers, had never before been sufficiently motivated to go to the expense and trouble of setting up arrangements with a dealer to market their paper, having it rated by a rating agency, and so forth. Now they had a powerful motive, for by issuing their own paper, they could secure access to funds which banks, subject to the CD rate ceilings, could provide only with difficulty, and possibly not at all.

Banks, for their part, also found the arrangement attractive. By providing "back-up" lines of credit for their customers' paper issues, the banks earned fees without having to fund the credits themselves. Investors, of course, found commercial paper an attractive outlet for short-term placements, especially since CDs paying market rates were practically nonexistent. Thus there was something for everyone in the commercial paper market, and large banks rushed to assist their largest and best customers—those of sufficient credit standing that their paper would be acceptable to investors—to gain access to it.[13] As the market grew, the flow of business credit increasingly circumvented the banks, thus once again undermining a key precept of the availability theory.

As banks' role in extending short-term business credit was diminished, however, the character of the risk assumed by investors in private money-market instruments also changed. Commercial paper is the sole obligation of the issuer. The commitment of the bank providing the back-up line generally may be withdrawn if the issuer's creditworthiness changes. Under those circumstances, investors, who may be placing funds needed shortly to pay taxes, dividends, or other essential commitments, are understandably skittish about exposing themselves to credit risk in the paper market. Most such investors probably would have felt more comfortable investing in CDs of major banks, but that option was obviously foreclosed. Consequently, credit flows were being channeled into a market increasingly populated by new issuers and fickle investors, in which a disruption could have widespread repercussions.

The disruption occurred on June 21, 1970, when the Penn Central Transportation Company, with $82 million of paper outstanding, filed for bankruptcy. Investors immediately began to shun the paper of all but the very strongest issuers. Insolvency suddenly was a real prospect for many firms, which clearly would not be capable of replacing maturing paper with new issues. Nor would the banks necessarily be capable of providing assistance through back-up lines, since their access to funds through the CD market was severely limited. The story of what the Fed did to prevent the Penn Central crisis from becoming a full-blown financial crisis is a topic for Chapter 10, but for present purposes, the crucial event was the suspension of ceilings on CD rates. Though the ceilings were not abolished (they remained on longer-term CDs until 1973, for example), it was clear, even within the Fed, that attempts to restrain business spending by restricting the availability of credit were likely to be disruptive and self-defeating.

While policies designed to create availability effects returned in 1979–80, as we shall see in the next chapter, the objective then was vastly different from what it had been in the 1950s and 1960s. Instead of achieving restraint on spending with minimal effects on interest rates, the later measures were intended, in large part, to augment the impact of higher interest rates by temporarily fostering disruption. Thus Penn Central marked the end of any serious policy role for the availability view.

The monetarist challenge

The monetarist challenge to the Fed's credit-oriented policy had its origin in Milton Friedman's 1956 restatement of the quantity theory of money.[14] Prior to that time, the quantity theory, which related the general price level to the money stock, had been little more than a tautology. Friedman's unique insight was to derive the demand function for money from a generalized theory of wealth allocation and to make the connection between money and income an empirically testable hypothesis.

This approach prompted relatively little controversy among professional economists, most of whom agreed that the demand for money should logically be contained within the same basic theoretical framework they used to analyze consumers' demand for other goods.

Also, Friedman's emphasis on the individual's wealth allocation process contributed to a reorientation of economists' views about the determinants of consumption spending. The earlier view that consumption was influenced primarily by current income was quickly supplanted by general agreement that wealth, whether measured by Friedman's "permanent income" variable or in some other fashion, was the main determinant. When Friedman received his Nobel prize in 1976, his contribution to the theory of consumption behavior was cited prominently.

Controversy, however, centered on Friedman's empirical conclusion—that the demand for money was, in practice, a stable function of a relatively small number of variables (though in principle the number of factors affecting the wealth-allocation process was acknowledged to be almost uncountably vast). That was in sharp contrast to the liquidity-trap notion, in which the public's craving for money was so sensitive to small changes of interest rates as to swamp any relation between changes in money and changes in income.[15]

The policy implication of the monetarist challenge was fundamental: by expanding the money supply at some constant rate (Friedman thought a rate of about 4 percent would be appropriate) growth of income could also be stabilized. Income growth from year to year would not be completely uniform, of course, for the lags from money to spending (and thus to income) were long and variable. Also, a myriad of minor factors had necessarily been omitted from the estimated empirical relation. Nevertheless, a constant rate of growth of money seemed to provide a fundamental guidepost for a policy intended to insure long-run stability of the price level.

The contrast between the theoretical policy prescription and actual practice could hardly have been greater. For Friedman and other monetarists, the theoretical structure of the credit availability view was almost irrelevant. In their opinion, the reality of policy was much simpler: the Fed, even after the Accord, attempted to stabilize interest rates to resist rate increases during cyclical expansions and rate declines during recessions, thus amplifying the swings of the business cycle.

Naturally, no one inside the Fed seriously defended rate stabilization for its own sake. But the availability view suggested that small changes of interest rates might have disproportionately large economic consequences. Thirty years later, it may seem hard to believe, but Treasury bill rates were only about 2 percent when the economy peaked in July 1953, while a small decline to about ¾ percent was enough to initiate a recovery in June 1954. The following cycle was marked by a peak rate of about 3 ½ percent, which, when prolonged for several months after the onset of recession in August 1957, contributed to a very sharp contraction in economic activity. Under those circumstances, the economic potency of small changes in interest rates, which were, as noted earlier, large percentage changes, was altogether credible.

In addition, some felt that any attempt to stabilize the growth of money during the onset of a recession would lead to a build-up of liquid balances in the economy that would be hard to reverse later on. Such a policy, it was feared, would do little to shorten the duration of recessions while doing a great deal to exacerbate the strength, and potentially inflationary consequences, of the ensuing recovery. This concern essentially reflected the availability view: a moderately paced business expansion would be jeopardized by large movements of interest rates in either direction.

Moreover, many in the Fed felt, not without some justification, that the peculiar institutional structure of U.S. financial markets meant that large changes in interest rates could threaten the very existence of the markets and thus the Fed's ability to implement any policy at all. Probably of greatest concern in this regard was the fact that most securities firms operated with very little capital relative to the amounts of securities that they positioned, i.e., held in inventory. Losses caused by small rate changes potentially could erode their capital and eventually put them out of business. A substantial reduction in the number of dealers, in turn, would cause those remaining in business to be much less willing to make markets for securities by standing ready to buy and sell.

Such a reduction in market liquidity quite possibly could lead to wider financial and economic repercussions as well. This perspective and the availability view obviously shared a common theme in that small changes of interest rates were felt to have major consequences for both financial markets and the economy. Nevertheless, the two were quite distinct, and the later eclipse of the credit availability view did not preclude continuing concern about the possible fragility of financial markets.

For many monetarists, one of the major attractions of the apparent stability of the money demand function was that it made possible the formulation of a relatively simple rule to guide the Fed's acitivities. In contrast, the Fed, for reasons discussed below, has always insisted on the essential role of judgment in formulating policy.

To many monetarists, however, that view was, and is, almost perverse. In their opinion, the major obstacle to economic stabilization is monetary policy's tendency to amplify the economy's cyclical movements—a bias implicit in attempts to stabilize interest rates. That bias could be countered only through some sort of quantitative criterion for evaluating policy. Without such an objective criterion, there could be no assurance either of the short-run cyclical appropriateness of policy or of its long-run consistency with price stability. As for the alleged fragility of financial markets, the dominant monetarist attitude was, and is, that such concerns were greatly exaggerated.

During the 1960s and 1970s, monetarists and many others devoted a great deal of time and effort to criticizing the Federal Open

Market Committee's procedure for instructing the Desk manager at the New York Fed to carry out the Committee's policy intentions through open market operations. What was at issue was the day-to-day "operating target" for guiding provision of reserves (about which more in subsequent chapters). Prior to 1966, in fact, the written directive adopted at the end of each FOMC meeting did not give the Desk manager any quantitative guidelines for adjusting the provision of reserves during the period between FOMC meetings. As a result, it was largely up to him to decipher the Committee's intentions, to cast them into operational terms, and to justify these actions at the following meeting. In 1966, in order to guide the Desk manager in making policy adjustments in the interval between FOMC meetings, the "proviso clause" was incorporated into the directive. It typically instructed the Manager to maintain net free reserves— i.e., excess reserves held by banks less their borrowings at the discount window—at a stipulated level, provided that growth of the bank credit proxy was not excessive.[16]

The proviso clause remained in the directive until 1970, when it was supplanted by explicit short-run targets for several monetary aggregates. In 1972, reserves available to support private deposits (RPDs) briefly entered the directive. However, in practice the federal funds rate had been a key reference point all along, and shortly afterward, the FOMC dropped RPDs in favor of the simpler expedient of specifying a narrow range for the funds rate thought to be consistent with the targeted growth of the monetary aggregates. Thus, after a decade and a half of spirited discussion and repeated modifications to the directive, the operational focus of monetary policy was still "market conditions" as embodied in the funds rate.

Actually, framing the directive to ensure that the Desk manager acted in accordance with the committee's wishes during the intermeeting period was only a minor part of the problem. After all, the FOMC met at intervals of only a few weeks, and policy would not have been greatly different if the Manager made no changes whatever in response to new information obtained between meetings.[17] Instead, the crux of the issue was the unwillingness of the FOMC itself to tolerate large changes of interest rates, either by ordering them in its directive or by achieving them indirectly through stipulating growth rates for some reserves measure.

For more than two decades, monetarists pursued their criticism of the Fed's policy approach, converting to their views a substantial number of members of Congress as well as academics, financial market participants, and personnel within the Fed itself. Yet the Fed's procedures remained remarkably resistant to substantive change. The adoption of internal targets for growth of monetary aggregates in 1970 produced no major changes, as actual growth routinely departed from the target ranges.

In 1975, monetary aggregates targets were made formal and public in response to a congressional resolution. But the targets were adjusted every calendar quarter in a fashion clearly designed to minimize any possible discrepancies between actual and targeted growth. Not a few critics observed that the targets appeared to be chasing after the aggregates instead of serving as a serious guide to policy.

The most visible change in policy procedures occurred in 1978, when the Humphrey-Hawkins Act (formally, the Full Employment and Balanced Growth Act) mandated annual targets for money and credit, together with semiannual reports to Congress concerning the Fed's performance in hitting the targets. But this change also was more apparent than real. The federal funds rate continued to be the Fed's key operating variable, while the aggregates routinely grew at rates outside the targets. The act was indeed effective in putting an end to the quarterly shifting of the targets mentioned earlier, but it did little, in itself, to create substantive change in the Fed's policy, which continued to give substantial weight to stability of interest rates.

Probably the act's most important impact was on Congress itself. The semiannual monetary policy oversight hearings before the House Banking, Finance, and Urban Affairs Committee and the Senate Banking Committee provided a convenient forum for excoriating the Fed chairman. But similar opportunities had existed in the past. The oversight hearings made a fundamental break with the past by changing the congressional focus from interest rates to the growth rates of monetary aggregates. Since few in Congress were conversant about the technical details of targeting monetary aggregates, the new focus left the Fed Chairman occupying the high ground in policy disputes, and tended to insulate the Fed from political concerns over interest rates.

Admittedly, some members of the congressional committees continued to prod the Fed to engineer both lower interest rates and lower aggregate growth rates. But there was a growing realization that in the short run—and with two-year terms, most congressmen are condemned to live perpetually in the short run— the combination of lower rates and slower money growth was a logical impossibility, even though monetary restraint (and higher rates) now might lead to lower rates later on.

The high irony is that the adoption of the monetary policy provisions of the Humphrey-Hawkins Act appears to have resulted, not so much from congressional infatuation with monetarist principles, as from traditional congressional concern that the Fed represented a major power center beyond its practical scrutiny. That, presumably, is why the mandate for annual aggregates targets emanated from the same committees which, from time to time, pushed a variety of other proposals having not even the slightest supportive relation to aggregates targeting.

If monetarists had strange bedfellows in Congress, there was clearly one common ground which they did share: a predisposition toward rules. Congress, after all, produces masses of legislation, and its natural inclination is to achieve results through rules with the force of law. Many monetarists, though not all, were also inclined to adopt rules for monetary policy, to prevent what they viewed as the Fed's perverse exercise of discretionary authority. But despite this sympathetic attitude, the Humphrey-Hawkins Act provided no enforcement procedures in the event that the targets were not achieved, which was frequently the case. Almost any other regulatory agency could be sued if it violated its legislative mandate, but the only enforcement provided to back up the monetary mandate was congressional chastisement. And many members of Congress clearly preferred it that way. They may have had a predisposition toward rules, just as many monetarists did, but they also harbored a concern that something might go wrong, that Congress was not well placed to pass judgment on the details of monetary policy. That, after all, had been the original argument for the Fed's semiautonomous status.

Furthermore, preserving discretionary authority left Congress free to castigate the Fed for whatever policy failures might occur. Because Congress did not "get out in front" by mandating a rigid monetary growth target, it could duck the responsibility, as well as the attendant political heat, associated with such an approach.

And so it came to pass that Congress subjected *itself* to semiannual monetary policy oversight hearings involving details of aggregate growth rates, operating procedures, and a myriad of other technicalities that few of its members were competent to discuss. Thus, the Humphrey-Hawkins Act had little impact on the Fed's policy approach, but a major, wholly unintended, impact on the effectiveness of congressional criticism of high interest rates.

Consequently, despite monetarists' persistent efforts, congressional action (or inaction) failed to produce substantive implementation of their agenda for monetary policy. That left the Fed itself as the only authority capable of doing much to put monetarism into practice. And the Fed, despite the presence on its staff of a fair number of able economists who were in substantial agreement with monetarist views, remained obdurately opposed. Three principal reasons largely explain why the Fed was so resistant to monetarist ideas.

First, despite the fact that the economics profession in general recognized the procyclical bias latent in interest-rate targeting, a large number of economists still remained unconvinced that rigid monetary targeting was the best possible policy.

Many were skeptical of the alleged stability of the demand for money, especially in the short run. Since monetarists never produced any convincing evidence to suggest that variations in money growth that did not accumulate beyond a span of six months or so had any systematic impact on spending, and since measurement problems are severe during short time periods, many economists concluded, and still do, that tight control of monetary growth was neither feasible nor desirable. In contrast, monetarists argued that short-run disturbances would average out over time. Moreover, their first priority was long-run stabilization, and they argued that short-run fine tuning would compromise that objective.

Furthermore, as economists began to appreciate that in a world in which every economic relationship must be estimated statistically, with an unavoidable residual of imprecision attached to all parameter estimates, they abandoned arguments framed in terms of perfectly stable (i.e., perfectly predictable) money demand functions. They opted, instead, for a more general analysis in which all of the relevant economic relationships were subject to uncertainty. It turned out that monetarist prescriptions were an optimal policy approach in such an analytical framework, but only when the uncertainty attached to money demand was less than that attached to estimates of aggregate spending behavior, and not always, even then.[18]

On the one hand, if the strength of spending, and in particular, its sensitivity to interest rates, were highly uncertain, while the relation of income to money was fairly predictable, then targeting the money stock in general would provide more assurance of achieving the desired level of spending than would targeting an interest rate. On the other hand, if spending were fairly predictable, but money demand highly unpredictable, as might be the case during a financial crisis or during a rapid change in the institutional structure of assets regarded as "money," then an interest rate target might be preferable. The analysis also suggested that in general, though not always, some combination policy giving weight to both money and interest rates was superior to sole reliance on either one.

Consequently, many monetarists were willing to concede that in principle rigid adherence to a monetary growth rule might not always be appropriate. Nevertheless, they contended that, as a practical matter, most economic information is so unreliable that in the great majority of circumstances, such an approach was the best possible.

But many economists strongly disagreed with that view. The professional consensus was that rigid monetary control was probably not desirable during periods shorter than six months or so, due to a formidable host of short-run slippages and measurement problems (discussed in some detail in Chapter 5). This concession, especially given conflicting evidence concerning the longer-run stability of money demand, weakened the appeal of the monetarist agenda.

Second, personalities played an important role in the Fed's resistance to monetarism. The monetarists were largely from academic backgrounds and tended to display a crusading spirit utterly alien to many within the Fed and other financial institutions. In many respects, monetarists were actually quite constructive in their policy recommendations and analyses, going to considerable lengths to spell out how they could be implemented within the framework of existing institutions.

Nevertheless, to many in the Fed and elsewhere, monetarists appeared to be "true believers" from whom experienced policymakers and financial market participants almost instinctively recoiled. That probably was not entirely the fault of the monetarists. Entrenched institutions, especially bureaucracies, of which the Fed is one, tend to display a bunker mentality that makes them resistant to criticism, especially criticism from those perceived to be outside the organization or nonsupportive in some way.

But senior Fed officials also differed fundamentally from monetarists in their attitude toward the risks involved in disturbing financial markets. For monetarists, the greatest imaginable disturbance was latent in what they saw as the inflationary bias of the Fed's policy approach. All else was quite secondary. The Fed naturally questioned whether its approach contained any bias toward inflation and emphasized what it considered to be the obvious facts of fragile financial markets. Perhaps the best concise public expression of this view was given by Alan R. Holmes, who was Desk manager during much of the 1960s and 1970s:

> Some exponents of the monetary school . . . seem to imply that interest rate variations make no difference at all—somehow the market is supposed to work everything out. It seems to me that there are serious risks in the assumption that the financial markets of the real world—in contrast to the markets of a theoretical model—can readily handle any range of interest rate variation. Pushing too hard on money supply control in the face of rapid interest rate adjustment could wind up by destroying the very financial mechanism which the monetary authority must use if it expects to have any impact on the real economy. Psychology and expectations play too great a role in the operations of these markets to permit the monetary authority to ignore the interpretations that the market may place on current central bank operations.[19]

To the monetarists' reforming zeal, then, the Fed instinctively countered that "something might happen."

Finally, the monetarists and the Fed appear to have had a systematically different appraisal of the political setting in which monetary policy must operate. It was one thing to argue, as monetarists did, that interest rates should be more freely variable, that ceilings on interest rates paid on consumer deposits should be abolished, and so forth. It was another thing altogether to devise a political strategy that, once those measures were adopted, would preserve them by disabling the political clout of, for example, the thrift institutions and housing industry lobbies. Beyond doubt, the Fed could have done much more to arrest the rising inflation trend, especially during the 1970s. But monetarists themselves were very quiet about the political dimension; one of the attractions of monetary rules was the illusory prospect of entirely removing political interference from monetary policy. Many in the Fed would have replied that getting from here to there was the greater part of the problem.

As it happened, though, the accelerating trend of inflation during the 1960s and the 1970s was galvanizing the political consensus that ultimately allowed the Volcker Fed to undertake a policy blitz on a scale unthinkable but a few years earlier.

Notes

1. See Milton Friedman and Anna J. Schwartz, *A Monetary History of the United States, 1867–1960* (New York: National Bureau of Economic Research, 1963), pp. 627–29.

2. For a discussion of why the Accord was perhaps less of a policy shift than might appear, see Friedman and Schwartz, *A Monetary History,*, p. 625.

3. In the language familiar to economists (but few others), this meant that monetary policy could affect the location of the IS curve, even if it was relatively powerless to shift the LM curve.

4. Roosa's initial publication of the availability theory was "Interest Rates and the Central Bank," in *Money, Trade and Economic Growth* in honor of John Henry Williams (New York: Macmillan, 1951), pp. 270–95. Not so incidentally, Paul Volcker was a junior member of the New York Fed's research staff during the time Roosa was articulating the theory.

5. These days, most economists would answer these questions, respectively: none (or close to it), and who knows (or cares)?

6. The Fed staff first routinely prepared a consistent macroeconomic forecast for use by the Open Market Committee in 1966.

7. Friedman and Schwartz, *A Monetary History,* p. 638.

8. This point has been highlighted by Michael K. Evans, "Macroeconomic Forecasting in the 1980s," *Business Economics*, September 1983, pp. 5–10.

9. The early development of the CD market is described in William C. Melton, "The Market for Large Negotiable Certificates of Deposit," Federal Reserve Bank of New York *Quarterly Review*, Winter 1977–78, pp. 22-34; reprinted in *Current Perspectives in Banking: Operations, Management, and Regulation*, 2d ed., ed. Thomas M. Havrilesky and John T. Boorman (Arlington Heights, Ill.: Harland Davisdon, 1980); and in *Bank Management: Concepts and Issues*, ed. John R. Brick (Houston: Dame Publications), 1980.

10. The federal funds market is discussed in more detail in Chapter 6.

11. Congress, the Fed, and other responsible government agencies also responded to the pressures from the thrifts and the housing industry in a variety of other ways. These included the extension of interest-rate ceilings to thrifts (at a fixed differential above rates banks were permitted to pay) in 1966, and raising the minimum purchase in weekly auctions of Treasury bills from $1,000 to $10,000 in 1970. The interest of consumers in receiving a market rate of return on their savings was not well represented

until 1980, when the Depository Institutions Deregulation Act mandated a phasing out of limits on interest rates on consumer-type accounts.

12. While special reserve requirements were the Fed's preferred instrument for dealing with banks' proliferating funding devices, other techniques were employed as well. On July 21, 1975, Chairman Arthur F. Burns sent a letter reaffirming the Fed's policy that banks should not "solicit or encourage the placement of deposits by United States residents at their foreign branches unless such deposits are placed to serve a definite, necessary purpose outside the United States." In essence, banks were expected to withhold information about the burgeoning Eurodollar market from any investors who were not already participants. This attempt at muzzling the free flow of financial information—almost comical in retrospect—certainly had only the most minimal effects on the ability of investors to find profitable short-term outlets for their cash.

13. The best description of this process is John P. Judd, "Competition Between the Commercial Paper Market and Commercial Banks," Federal Reserve Bank of San Francisco *Economic Review,* Winter 1979, pp. 39–53.

14. Milton Friedman, "The Quantity Theory of Money—A Restatement," in *Studies in the Quantity Theory of Money,* ed. Milton Friedman (Chicago: University of Chicago Press, 1956), pp. 3–21.

15. More formally, economists would have characterized a liquidity trap as a situation in which the demand for money was infinitely elastic at some positive level of the interest rate; that notion was reproduced for years in introductory textbooks in macroeconomics. On an empirical level, however, the size of the interest elasticity was not really the main issue. Rather, the money demand function's stability, or predictability, was the focus of dispute. More on that topic later.

16. The bank credit proxy itself symbolizes the priority which the Fed continued to give to credit versus measures of the money supply. The proxy was simply the total deposits of banks that were members of the Federal Reserve System (at that time the Fed received reasonably timely data only from member banks). It was, thus, close in value to the total of credit extended by these banks. Nevertheless, "total *deposit* proxy" would have described its composition more clearly.

17. As Alan R. Holmes, Desk manager at the time, put it:

> we are fairly cautious about over-interpreting any short-run wriggle in the credit proxy. While forecasts of the proxy have generally proved to be more stable than money supply forecasts . . . they, too, have proved to be somewhat undependable on a week-to-week basis. Thus we have felt it desirable—particularly early in the month when firm data are scant—to wait for some confirmation of any suggested movement of the proxy before beginning to shade operations toward somewhat greater firmness or ease.

Alan R. Holmes, "Operational Constraints on the Stabilization of Money Supply Growth," *Controlling Monetary Aggregates,* Federal Reserve Bank of Boston, 1969, p. 70.

18. This statement conveys the spirit, but not the detail, of the analysis of choice of policy instruments under uncertainty. For the original exposition, see William Poole, "Optimal Choice of Monetary Policy in a Simple Stochastic Macro Model," *Quarterly Journal of Economics,* May 1970, pp. 197–216. Further refinements are provided in Stephen F. LeRoy and David E. Lindsey, "Determining the Monetary Instrument: A Diagrammatic Exposition," *American Economic Review,* December 1978, pp. 929–34.

19. Holmes, *Controlling Money Aggregates,*

4

THE SATURDAY NIGHT SPECIAL

The Federal Reserve's decision on October 6, 1979 to abandon numerical targets for the federal funds rate as its preferred technique for controlling money growth in favor of a reserves-oriented operating procedure was easily its most important policy departure in decades. The decision introduced a qualitatively new element of uncertainty into financial markets, as stabilization of interest rates ceased to be a dominating constraint on policy. Instead, turning back the rising tide of inflation assumed pride of place among the Fed's policy objectives. In a fundamental sense, the decision was born of the Fed's realization that in a highly inflation-prone economy stabilization of interest rates is at best an ephemeral objective.

Prelude

Since we are now some years removed from the events of 1979, it is easy to forget the turmoil of that year, to forget in particular, how close the United States was to a full-fledged flight from financial assets. For more than a decade prior to 1979, inflation had been on an accelerating trend. Numerous analysts and investors had noted that each succeeding inflation peak was higher than the last, while each recession-induced inflation slowdown left the rate higher than the previous trough (Chart 4–1).

The seeming inevitability of the pattern was reinforced by the political environment, which evidenced little willingness to come to

CHART 4–1

The Inflation Trend: Consumer Price Index Year Over Year Percentage Change

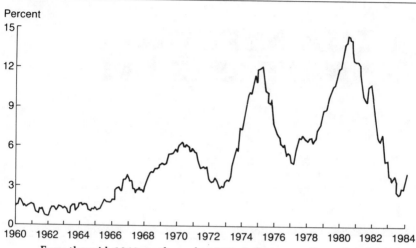

Percent

From the mid-1960s to the early 1980s, inflation accelerated and decelerated cyclically around a steadily rising trend.

grips with the situation. Economic policy in the decade of the 1970s had been a continuing succession of ineffective measures that resolutely avoided attacking the root of the inflation problem.

The Nixon administration's woefully ill-conceived program of price controls (promptly abandoned as its failings became manifest), was followed by a highly stimulative monetary policy in the middle of the decade. To the cynical, that policy appeared to have much more to do with the 1976 presidential election than with any well-thought-out strategy for dealing with the inflation problem. Even those who contested the attribution of such motives—pointing to the moderate expansion of M1 during 1975–76, for example—could not deny that the observed result, intended or not, was inflationary.

The Carter administration's "voluntary" wage and price guidelines were hardly better. Periodic attempts in Congress and in the executive branch to "jawbone" interest rates did little more than to demonstrate politicians' sensitivities. It did not require much imagination to conclude that the pattern on the chart, repeated in Republican and Democratic administrations alike, would probably persist for a long time.

In particular, the Fed's part in the pattern appeared very well established. The Fed, after all, had pursued a policy so stimulative that, in 1975, it drove interest rates well below the inflation rate and held them there for over a year.[1] As the protracted economic recovery gained momentum during the second half of the decade, the Fed allowed the federal funds rate to rise, but always by grudgingly small amounts, leaving investors with little doubt about the importance monetary policymakers attached to inflation relative to other economic objectives.

However, by its nature, this pattern of ever-accelerating inflation could not be sustained. Inflation, as everyone knows, is a form of tax. But it is a tax that can be escaped if one avoids holding nominal financial assets—e.g., cash, deposits, bonds—that depend for their value on the value of the monetary unit in which they are denominated. The most dramatic events leading up to 1979 were, at root, a reflection of the efforts of more and more investors to avoid the inflation tax. Everyone would avoid the burden only when financial assets, including money, for all practical purposes ceased to circulate. In other words, the efforts of individuals and businesses to insulate themselves from inflation contained the seeds of financial collapse.

Participants in foreign exchange markets may be the investors most acutely sensitive to inflation. It is only natural that it should be so, since they must form a daily judgment as to the value of different currencies relative to one another. If they expect to lose purchasing power by holding one currency, they can trade it for another with better prospects for retaining its value. In the process, the former will tend to lose value relative to the latter. This is just what happened to the U.S. dollar during the late 1970s. The United States was the first of the major industrial economies to emerge from the recession that followed the 1973 oil shock. Thus its imports ran well ahead of exports, leaving foreigners with ever larger dollar balances. At the same time, with dollar interest rates well below the U.S. inflation rate, foreigners were being asked to accept a continual erosion of the real purchasing power of those balances. The result, predictably enough, was sustained downward pressure on the foreign exchange value of the dollar.

Foreign central banks, however, had an interest in forestalling an abrupt loss of value by the dollar. Appreciation of their own currencies against the dollar would tend to undermine the competitiveness of their countries' exports to the United States, as well as their ability to compete against U.S. exports in world markets. The fact that the United States was leading the world economic recovery only increased the desire not to have their domestic economies be left behind in the revival of world trade. Accordingly, foreign central banks, conspicuously those of Germany and Japan, engaged in massive dollar purchases in an effort to counter the dollar's weakening foreign exchange value. In both 1977 and 1978, foreign central banks bought about $30 billion of U.S. Treasury securities in this way.

Foreign monetary authorities were not terribly happy about picking up the tab for a large share of the U.S. Treasury's deficit. The Europeans especially proffered pointed advice concerning the need for improved fiscal discipline in the United States. But they supported the dollar because they felt that was their only viable course. Undoubtedly these operations did moderate the decline of the dollar somewhat, but they were not large enough to alter the fundamentals of the problem. The foreign central banks merely replaced the private sector as the holder of depreciating dollar assets. In November 1978, the United States launched a major effort to prop up the dollar, relying on higher interest rates as well as massive intervention in the foreign exchange markets. Initially, the rescue package seemed to work, but as inflationary pressures continued to mount, the dollar resumed its decline.

Increasingly pessimistic sentiment abroad had a domestic counterpart, of course. The pessimism encompassed portfolio managers' wariness about committing to long-term bonds as well as the growing "survivalist" movement. The latter, in its many forms, offered many solutions, ranging from buying gold to buying ammunition and freeze-dried food. But they all addressed a common concern that the progressive inflation spiral was unsustainable, and that an ultimate financial collapse was not only conceivable but probable.

In one form or another, this spirit animated many of the most dramatic developments of the late 1970s. The booming housing market, fueled by the conviction that real estate was an unparalleled inflation hedge, spurred a proliferation of mortgage financing devices that would have seemed fanciful but a few years earlier. Consumers, more and more, borrowed to make purchases before prices increased. Interest in precious metals and antiques skyrocketed. It seemed as though investors would consider anything—except, of course, traditional financial investments.

My most vivid memory of the period is an incident that took place one evening in a course I taught for M.B.A. students covering the structure and performance of financial markets. Most of the students worked during the day in financial firms in lower Manhattan and were, on the whole, far better informed about financial markets than most people would be. In 1979, during a lecture about the functions and investment characteristics of equities, I took a poll of the class to determine the students' preferred investments. I had taken such polls in earlier years, and they routinely turned up a scatter of preferences including owner-occupied housing, bonds, and stocks. This time it was different.

While a sizable contingent still favored housing, large numbers felt that the single best investment for them was in precious metals or art objects or similar inflation hedges. Out of a class of approximately

60 students, exactly 2 votes were cast for stocks, none for interest-bearing securities. I had never seen anything like it.

I launched into a fairly stern admonition on the theme that, historically, the only way nations have been able to pull themselves up out of the mud was to save via financial assets that channel funds to productivity-raising investment. My class, in contrast, clearly was almost totally uninterested in buying anything that a business firm might be able to sell in order to finance productive investment! After I had finished with my impromptu oratory, the class was silent for a moment. Then a fellow sitting toward the rear of the class raised his hand and in a hesitant, confused tone said, "I understand what you are saying, but it just doesn't make any sense."

The week before

On September 29, Paul Volcker, not quite two months into his term as chairman of the Federal Reserve Board, and Treasury Secretary G. William Miller met in Hamburg with Chancellor Helmut Schmidt and their German counterparts in one of a series of consultations stemming from the 1978 dollar support package. Financial markets were clearly troubled. Despite five increases of the prime rate during September, gold had risen to a new high of almost $400 per ounce only the day before, an increase of about $100 in six weeks (Chart 4–2). The dollar had fallen to a new low of $0.57 against the German mark, about the same as its level prior to the massive dollar support operation in November 1978. Many thought it would soon go lower. The decline had occurred despite a protracted series of gradual increases in U.S. interest rates that had at length raised short-term rates close to the previous records set in 1974. But the financial markets were focusing on the unchecked pace of U.S. monetary expansion and the apparently unhindered acceleration of the inflation rate, already not much below the level of short-term interest rates. At the Hamburg meeting, the Germans reportedly made clear their unwillingness to participate in another dollar rescue plan, as long as the United States was unwilling to address its inflation problem.

Volcker had been thinking about precisely that problem for some time. It seemed to him that a major part of the inflation process was psychological—a widespread perception that the inflation trend was accelerating, as the Fed invariably reacted ineffectually and only after the event. Banks and other lending institutions also seemed to Volcker to be caught up in the process. They appeared to feel that as long as they indexed their lending rates to the rates they paid on their CDs and other funds sources, they were operating in an essentially risk-

CHART 4–2
Price of Gold
London Afternoon Fixing, End of Month

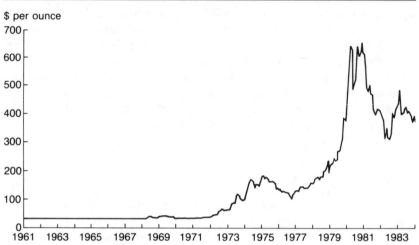

The price of gold, which had been on a rising trend during the 1970s, skyrocketed in 1979 and the early 80s.

free world, where traditional standards of prudent lending could be relaxed. The psychology that propelled the "buy now, pay later" syndrome assumed that the terms on which payment would be made were attractive to borrowers. Financing costs would be relatively low, especially when compared to the rate at which prices were advancing.

The key to changing that psychology was to invalidate the prevailing assumptions about the Federal Reserve and monetary policy, especially with respect to the level and stability of interest rates. In the Hamburg meeting, Volcker outlined several steps that he proposed to take, including an idea he had entertained for some time: permitting substantial variability in the federal funds rate rather than closely restricting its day-to-day movements as the Fed had done for decades. After a brief appearance the next day at a meeting of the International Monetary Fund in Belgrade, Volcker returned to Washington.

Discussion of possible improvements in policy implementation had been underway within the Federal Reserve System for years. Several members of the Board staff, for example, had argued internally that some form of reserves targeting had substantial practical and theoretical advantages over the use of the federal funds rate as an operating target. The monetarist-oriented Federal Reserve Bank of St. Louis had also pushed that point of view.

However, the prevailing attitude within the System had been

that such refinements, even if meritorious (and not everyone agreed that they were), were hardly urgent. But attitudes were changing. Now, as Volcker instructed the senior staff to review policy options in light of the emerging financial crisis, the context in which earlier proposals had been considered was suddenly altered in the most fundamental way. The chairman was willing to tolerate qualitatively more interest rate volatility. He wanted more caution among lenders and borrowers, not the prevailing comfortable expansiveness, and he wanted to demonstrate to all that conventional assumptions about monetary policy were no longer valid. Proposals that in some cases had been broached 10 or 20 years earlier now began to receive their first serious consideration as viable policy options.

In the financial markets, the week was marked by growing apprehension. Many expected that the Fed might tighten its policy stance another notch in the not too distant future. And on a more fundamental level, the accelerating inflation rate, the absence of meaningful attempts to rein in federal spending, and the consequent battering of the dollar's foreign exchange value were points of concern. As if that were not enough, toward the end of the week, the markets were buffeted by (unfounded) rumors that Volcker had threatened to resign.

But despite the undercurrent of tension, the markets continued to function more or less normally. The federal funds rate, for example, traded during the week in a very narrow band around 11¾ percent, with a slight declining tendency. Reflecting the growing tension, other money market rates rose substantially over the week—by about 60 basis points for three-month Treasury bills. Yields on long-term Treasury bonds rose gradually, ending about 10–15 basis points higher than the week before, but the cautious mood did not prevent business from being done in the long-term bond markets.

For example, in its first-ever public offering of long-term debt securities, IBM came to market with an issue of 7-year notes and 25-year debenture bonds totaling $1 billion. It was the largest public borrowing by a private corporation in U.S. financial history. The underwriting syndicate, managed by Salomon Brothers and comanaged by Merrill Lynch, included 225 other firms, with all of the Street's most prestigious investment banking firms represented.

Reflecting the underwriters' confidence, the notes and bonds were priced very aggressively and offered to the public on Wednesday, October 3. But by the end of the week, a large portion was still in the hands of the underwriters. Despite the attractiveness of IBM's high credit quality, many investors were apprehensive about interest rates, which were rising almost from the moment the offering began. On Thursday, the Treasury auctioned $2.5 billion of four-year notes at an average yield of 9.79 percent—17 basis points (i.e., 0.17 percentage points) more than the slightly longer maturity IBM notes. The IBM bonds continued to yield more than comparable-maturity Treasuries, but not much. That made the IBM securities highly unattractive to investors. Nevertheless the underwriters decided not to "break" the syndicate to allow the price of the securities to decline (thus raising the yield) to find its own level. That would have meant immediate financial losses to them, and the incremental risk of continuing to try to sell the securities in the following week seemed tolerable. All previous experience suggested that conditions in the financial markets next week would not be much different from conditions in the week just ended. That was the way the Fed worked!

Saturday

As staff members proceeded to work out the operational details of a new policy approach, Volcker decided to call a special meeting of the Federal Open Market Committee for Saturday, October 6. On Friday, the bank presidents were notified by wire, and they traveled immediately to Washington, where they were quartered in different hotels so as to avoid attracting public attention.

When the meeting got under way on Saturday morning, there was a great deal of discussion, but little dissension. All members realized that extraordinary measures were required, and the only prepared plan for action was that which had been evolving during the week. As Lawrence K. Roos, then president of the monetarist Federal Reserve Bank of St. Louis, recalled later: "All the people who had opposed monetary aggregates targeting before were now for it."

To demonstrate its resolve, and to achieve the maximum psychological impact, the Fed made use of every policy instrument at its disposal. Reserve requirements were increased.[2] The discount rate was raised. And provision of reserves through open market operations would henceforth be less sensitive to the federal funds rate.

The first of these actions, in isolation, might easily have been ignored by all financial market participants save the banks, for whom it constituted a de facto tax increase. The reason is that, in the past, the Fed had supplied whatever reserves were necessary to meet reserve requirements, since to do otherwise would have caused the funds rate to diverge from its targeted level. Without a change in the funds rate target, a change in reserve requirements was mostly a nonevent. Similarly, a change in the discount rate had generally had little more than symbolic significance. For a given funds rate target, changing the discount rate merely altered the extent to which reserves were provided through open market operations or through discount window lending. Thus, in isolation, the discount rate change, like the change in reserve requirements, would also have had little enduring impact on the markets.

But neither of these measures was implemented in isolation. Instead, they were given force by the Fed's decision to abandon funds rate targeting.

That afternoon, Volcker held a press conference to announce the decisions that had been reached. As intended, the announcement hit the financial community like a bombshell. Yet amid all the confusion, the break with the past was less than at first appeared. Indeed, the most vivid illustration of that point was the first page of the press release issued at the press conference.

> The Federal Reserve today announced a series of complementary actions that should assure better control over the expansion of money and bank credit, help curb speculative excesses in financial, foreign exchange and commodity markets and thereby serve to dampen inflationary forces.
>
> Actions taken are:
>
> 1. A 1 percent increase in the discount rate, approved unanimously by the Board, from 11 percent to 12 percent.
>
> 2. Establishment of an 8 percent marginal reserve requirement on increases in "managed liabilities"—liabilities that have been actively used to finance rapid expansion in bank credit. This was also approved unanimously by the Board.
>
> 3. A change in the method used to conduct monetary policy to support the objective of containing growth in the monetary aggregates over the remainder of this year within the ranges previously adopted by the Federal Reserve. These ranges are consistent with moderate growth in the aggregates over the months ahead. This action involves placing greater emphasis in day-to-day operations on the supply of bank reserves and less emphasis on confining short-term fluctuations in the federal funds rate. It was approved unanimously by the Federal Open Market Committee.

Pride of place was given to the two policy instruments that normally would have had little more than symbolic impacts. Almost as an afterthought, it seemed, notice was given in the next-to-last sentence that much of what financial market participants had taken for granted about the Fed and interest rates had changed. The Saturday Night Special (as it irreverently came to be called) ended an era.

Figuring it out

What on earth did the Fed mean by "placing greater emphasis in day-to-day operations on the supply of bank reserves"? Over the weekend, that question was on the mind of practically everyone involved in financial markets. They could be excused for feeling less than certain about the specifics, for the explanation provided in the remaining four and one-half pages of the press release included a mere half page of generalities about the new policy approach. And the Fed could be excused, perhaps, for not providing any details. Only a few Board members and a small number of senior members of the Fed's staff, almost all of them at the Board in Washington, had been actively involved in working out the details of the new approach. Only they were in a position to explain it with any clarity. In addition, they recognized that the very newness of the approach meant that changes might have to be made in light of practical experience.

Nevertheless, some additional clarification was obviously necessary, and over the weekend, a decision was made to present a basic outline of the new approach at a meeting at the Federal Reserve Bank of New York on Tuesday afternoon. In keeping with established practice, only the so-called "primary" dealer firms were invited to send representatives, though of course the new policy affected virtually all financial market participants. That was because of the special relationship between the Fed and the primary dealers, with whom it conducted open-market operations.

On Sunday, Peter D. Sternlight, the Desk manager, telephoned several of his fellow Desk officers and asked them to come to the New York Fed on Monday to review the rationale of the new approach and its implications for the functioning of the securities markets. Much of the discussion was also devoted to going over what Sternlight would say to the dealers on Tuesday.

When the rest of the Desk staff arrived the following morning, "the new procedures" (as they were called) were something of a mystery. I can personally attest to this point. At the time, I was an economist on a rotating assignment to the Desk, and I was just as confused as anyone else. The confusion in the Street was understandably much greater, and took the form of trauma in the financial markets.

That morning I took a phone call from a friend at a securities dealer firm who opened the conversation by saying, "Welcome to the free-fall market! There are no bids on the screens!" What he meant was that none of the government securities dealers was sufficiently certain of what was happening to be able to say what a proper interest rate *was* for a Treasury bill or a government bond, and in those circumstances, they did not want to own any. Hence the video screens that display bid and ask quotations in the Treasury securities market— the most liquid of all the world's securities markets— were devoid of bids, amid proliferating offers.

The Tuesday afternoon meeting was a classic case of communication difficulties. Sternlight did a creditable job (I thought) of presenting a rough outline of the new procedures, a sketch which, even after the passage of a few years, still provides about the best concise prose description of both the logical structure as well as the spirit of the procedures.

The dealers' reaction was awful. When Sternlight duly noted that the specific details of the procedures were "still very much experimental," a dealer sitting behind me snapped to his companion, "Here's one lab rat who has just dropped a million bucks!"

But if the new procedures remained somewhat mysterious to many, Sternlight's presentation made one point absolutely clear: "Needless to say, but I'll say it anyway, the obligation to show some reasonable-sized bids, at prices you deem appropriate, goes for Treasury financing operations as well as System go-arounds." In other words, the obligation of the primary dealers to underwrite auctions of Treasury securities, i.e., to bid in size great enough to purchase the entire offering if necessary, was in no way to be relaxed by the mere fact that dealers no longer could count on stability of short-term financing costs.

That was apparently too much for one member of the audience, affiliated with a firm which had, at that time, a substantial unhedged position in the IBM underwriting. When Sternlight asked if there were questions, the dealer was quickly on his feet complaining loudly about the unreasonableness of expecting dealers to underwrite Treasury auctions when they could have no confidence about the level of their financing costs. Within his own frame of reference, he was right, of course. For decades, the Fed had gone to considerable effort to maintain relatively unchanged conditions in money markets during Treasury financings. Now that security blanket had been abruptly withdrawn.

Over the course of the week following the Saturday Night Special, markets remained thin and illiquid, while bond rates, which had jumped an unprecedented 30 basis points over the weekend, continued to rise. One day that week, I watched senior Desk personnel call each of the 30-odd primary dealer firms to chat briefly—and to remind them of their obligation to underwrite an auction of Treasury notes. They did so, but the markets remained tense and confused. It was easy to see why: the funds rate, formerly the focal point of the Fed's cautious concern for interest-rate stability, was now changing 50 to 100 basis points—or more!—per day.

And what of the IBM deal? The underwriting syndicate finally broke up on Wednesday, October 10. The deal was a spectacular disaster for the underwriters and original purchasers, who together may have lost $40–50 million as bond prices plunged. But that was merely the loss on the IBM offering. The "lab rats" in the aggregate lost vastly more.

What the Fed did

With the aid of hindsight, it is easy to identify the key change, the abandonment of strict funds rate targeting, which marked the fundamental divide between monetary policy before October 6, 1979, and afterward (Chart 4–3). However, the differences between old and new can sometimes be exaggerated. Certainly anyone who listened carefully to Sternlight's presentation could not have failed to note his statement that:

> We don't plan to be rigid or mechanistic in pursuit of reserve targets. This may cause some die-hard monetarists to subdue their elation at our change in approach and recall their congratulatory messages. But we are too much aware of slippages of various kinds in the short run to be really rigid.

But not everyone attended that meeting. And a press conference held immediately afterwards did not greatly improve communication. An article in the October 22, 1979, issue of *Time* magazine reported: "The Fed is now saying that, within broad limits, interest rates can go where they will because the Federal Reserve Bank of New York will instead be concentrating on cutting down the supply of money directly." Only the first part of that statement was accurate. Similar errors of interpretation appeared in virtually all of the media. The general failure to notice the continuity between the new and the old is even more remarkable

CHART 4–3
Interest Rates Around October 6, 1979

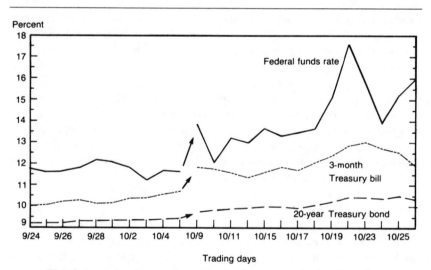

The federal funds rate became much more volatile after October 6, 1979, as did other rates.

in view of the fact that the reserves-oriented procedures were but one component of the program.

For example, the Saturday press release gave pride of place to the marginal reserve requirements on managed liabilities. They were intended to penalize banks that expanded their reliance on funds raised through repurchase agreements, CDs, Eurodollars, and so forth, beyond a specified base level by increasing substantially the cost of such funds. The objective was to exert a direct impact on the willingness of banks to extend credit, a policy approach strongly reminiscent of that pursued, though Regulation Q ceilings on deposit interest rates and other stopgap measures, in 1969–70. Thus, the credit availability view, though badly battered, was alive after all!

In addition, the new procedures themselves were not so different from previous practice as they initially appeared. As Sternlight made clear, they were *not* the monetarists' ideal of total reserves control (about which more in Chapter 6). That approach abjured any concern with interest rates and sought to maintain a tight link between expansion of reserves and expansion of money.

In contrast, the new procedures were merely reserves-oriented. They employed a growth path for nonborrowed reserves as a device for (more or less) automatically changing the pressure on banks to borrow from the discount window as money growth diverged from its target. In turn, the change in borrowing pressure would change interest rates, and that would affect the demand for money.

This convoluted procedure was anathema to monetarists, though ironically enough it was Allan H. Meltzer, a leading monetarist, who (as far as the author has been able to determine) first proposed operating procedures like those adopted.[3] In essence, the new system was simply funds-rate targeting reborn with a semiautomatic pilot that promptly revised the target funds rate in response to deviations of money growth from its target rate.

Since the new procedures would have done Rube Goldberg proud, and since they are still a key reference point in the Fed's current, but slightly modified, operating procedures, it is worthwhile to spend a moment reviewing their mechanics.

The annual growth targets for monetary aggregates were the fundamental reference point for the new procedures. In general, the targets, formally adopted early each year and reviewed shortly after midyear, provide for growth from the fourth-quarter average of the previous year within a specified range of growth rates. For example, the M1 target for 1984, illustrated in Chart 4–4, contemplated growth in a 4 to 8 percent range.

At each FOMC meeting, the Committee adopts short-run growth targets thought to be consistent with the annual targets. As an illustration, if M1 were tracking under its target, the FOMC might

CHART 4–4
1984 M1 Target Range

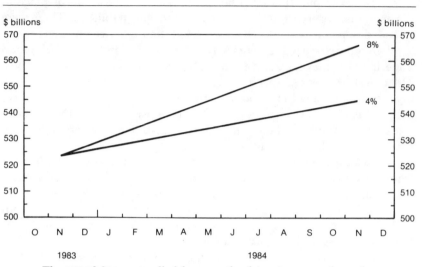

The 1984 M1 target called for growth of 4 to 8 percent from the average level in the fourth quarter of 1983.

adopt a short-run target designed to return it to the middle of its target range within some time period, for example, three months.

Since reserve requirements are calculated (in a complex fashion) as a fraction of deposits, a short-run target growth path for a monetary aggregate necessarily implies a growth path for required reserves.[4] As a practical matter, the monetary aggregate that mattered most in computing the required reserves path was M1, the transactions aggregate (which we will discuss more in the next chapter). The broader aggregates M2 and M3 were generally far less important, for two reasons. In the first place, most economists believe that M1 is theoretically and empirically more closely related to spending behavior that the others, so that it should be given greater weight in policy formulation. In addition, since reserve requirements on the checkable deposits included in M1 are fairly high (about 12 percent), while the reserve requirements on other items in M2 and M3 are either zero or very low, changes in required reserves naturally reflect changes in M1-type deposits fairly closely.

The relationship between the M1 target and the required reserves path is illustrated in a stylized form in Chart 4–5. Of course, in reality, the calculation of the path for required reserves is not simple. For example, a change in the composition of M1 between currency (which has no reserve requirement) and deposits (which do) will naturally

CHART 4–5
M1 Target and a Derived Target for Required Reserves

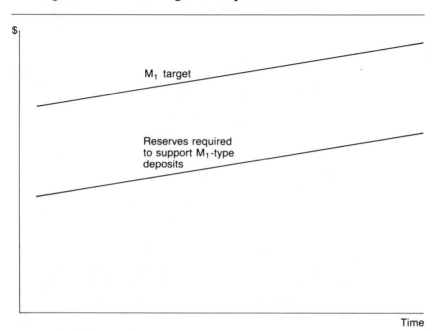

Note: This illustration assumes that reserves necessary to accommodate the public's demand for currency and non-M1 deposits are fully provided.

Through a complex calculation, a target path for required reserves can be derived from a short-run growth target for a monetary aggregate.

alter the required reserves path associated with the M1 target path.

Given the path for required reserves, an associated path for total reserves is easily calculated by adding to required reserves the estimated amount of excess reserves which banks will hold. The computation is illustrated schematically in Chart 4–6. It remains to determine *how* those reserves will be provided to banks.

The total of reserves supplies is composed of nonborrowed reserves and borrowed reserves. In this context, borrowed reserves are identical to short-term "adjustment" borrowings from the Fed's discount window. So-called extended credit advanced to institutions faced with longer-term liquidity problems is considered part of nonborrowed reserves. Under the old procedures, the division between nonborrowed and borrowed reserves was of no great significance, for the Fed generally sought to add or drain reserves in whatever amounts were necessary to hold the funds rate close to its target.

In contrast, in the new procedures, the interplay between the two categories had major implications for the level of the funds rate.

CHART 4–6
Total Reserves Target

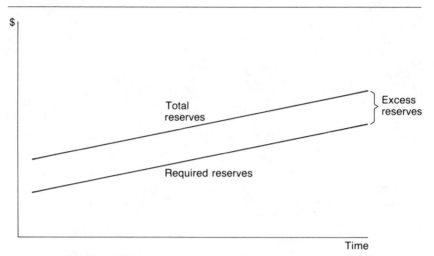

A target for total reserves is calculated by adding to the required reserves target an assumed amount of excess reserves held by banks and other depository institutions.

CHART 4–7
Nonborrowed Reserves Target

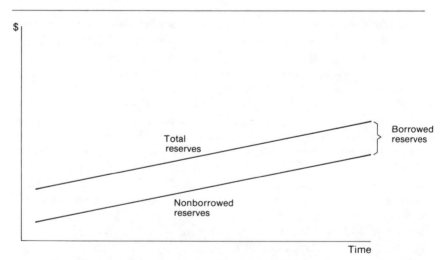

A nonborrowed reserves target is calculated by subtracting from the total reserves target an assumed amount of borrowed reserves.

The Fed's approach was to subtract from the total reserves path a constant amount of borrowed reserves. The result was a path for nonborrowed reserves running parallel to the total reserves path and below it. Chart 4–7 illustrates these paths. (Typically, the amount subtracted corresponded to the level of discount window borrowing in the period immediately preceding an Federal Open Market Committee meeting. However, adjustments have been made when that amount seemed distorted.)

Now suppose that growth of the monetary aggregate begins to track faster than its target. That implies that banks' required reserves (and thus total reserves) will rise faster than the total reserves path in Chart 4–8. Since the Fed is limiting its provision of nonborrowed reserves to that called for by the nonborrowed reserves path, the difference between that and banks' total reserves demand must be made up through borrowing reserves from the discount window. As also shown in Chart 4–8, continued monetary growth at above-target rates results in steadily increasing dependence on discount-window borrowing.

CHART 4–8
Deviation of Discount-Window Borrowing from Original Level

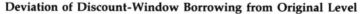

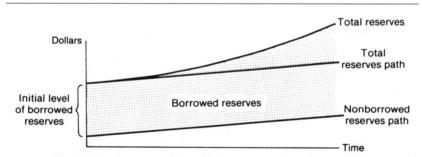

If monetary growth is faster than targeted, the nonborrowed reserves targeting procedure causes the amount of discount-window borrowing to rise.

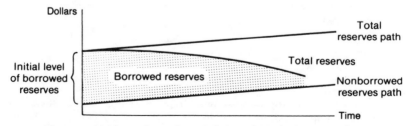

If monetary growth is slower than targeted, the procedure causes borrowing to decline.

That, in turn, implies upward pressure on the funds rate. Chart 4–9 illustrates the process that generates the pressure. In contrast to earlier diagrams, which represented paths for various reserves measures over time, Chart 4–9 pictures the reserves market during a single reserves maintenance period.[5]

During the period, the amount of nonborrowed reserves is constant, determined by the Fed's open market operations. Otherwise expressed, the supply of nonborrowed reserves is independent of the funds rate. However, the quantity of reserves supplied through discount-window borrowings is related to the funds rate, or more precisely, to the difference between the funds rate and the discount rate. The reason is that banks' reluctance to be dependent on the good

CHART 4–9
Equilibrium in the Reserves Market

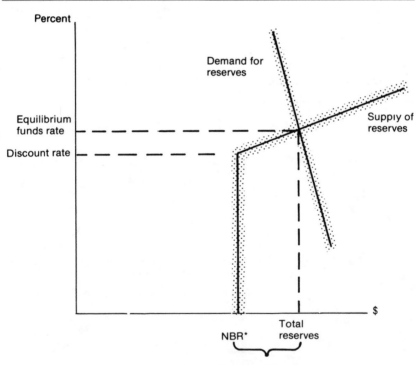

* Path target for nonborrowed reserves (actually path target plus a small, frictional amount of borrowed reserves).

Equilibrium in the reserves market requires that banks' demand for reserves (the sum of required reserves and excess reserves) equal the total supplied as nonborrowed and borrowed reserves.

graces of the discount window makes them bid more aggressively for funds as the volume of their borrowing rises.[6] That raises the federal funds rate and puts upward pressure on other interest rates as well.

Given the Fed's supply schedule for reserves, i.e., the line relating the sum of nonborrowed and borrowed reserves to the funds rate, the funds rate is determined by the location of banks' reserves demand schedule. As noted earlier, their total demand for reserves includes required reserves, which are related to their deposits by fractional reserve requirements, and excess reserves.

If deposits grow faster than targeted, as in the earlier example, banks' reserves demand increases (shifts to the right), while the supply schedule does not shift at all. The result is a higher level of discount-window borrowing and a higher funds rate. However, that is not necessarily the end of the story. If the Fed desired to force money back to its target faster than might be achieved via the higher funds rate, it might depress its supply of nonborrowed reserves. In terms of Chart 4–9, that would shift the supply schedule to the left, raising both the funds rate and borrowed reserves and the funds rate still higher. Alternatively, the Fed could achieve much the same effect by increasing the discount rate. Such a move would shift the supply schedule up vertically, raising the funds rate and reducing borrowed reserves.[7]

If instead deposits grow slower than targeted, banks' reserves demand decreases (shifts to the left), and discount-window borrowing declines, as does the funds rate. However, once borrowing has been reduced to zero or close to it, the stage is set for a free-fall plunge of the funds rate. Should reserves demand decline still further, the demand function would intersect the vertical portion of the reserves supply schedule. In other words, with total reserves held constant (equal to nonborrowed reserves), any decline in required reserves must be offset, at least initially, by an equal increase in banks' holdings of excess reserves. As banks attempted to disencumber themselves of the excess, the funds rate would drop sharply. However, the Fed almost certainly would not allow such a situation to arise. Instead of allowing discount-window borrowing to decline to zero, the discount rate would be lowered, while some pressure on banks to borrow would be maintained by simultaneously reducing the supply of nonborrowed reserves (shifting the reserves supply schedule to the left). That approach would allow the funds rate to decline without a free-fall developing.

In essence, then, the new procedures—termed nonborrowed reserves targeting by economists—boiled down to a link from the monetary target to the nonborrowed reserves path, and from there to interest rates via banks' reluctance to borrow from the Fed. Interest rates in turn were the link to control of money growth. Moreover, the structure of the procedures meant that they could not be expected to work automatically, as in a hands-off, rule-based approach. Discretionary changes in provision of nonborrowed reserves and periodic adjustments to the discount rate were an inherent part of the system.

More credit emphasis

During the weeks immediately following October 6, 1979, it had seemed to Volcker and other FOMC members that the new program was well received, domestically as well as abroad, and that inflation psychology was starting to abate. But by early 1980, those gains appeared to be unraveling as shocking reports of huge, double-digit inflation rates—the consumer price index rose at a record rate of 18.7 percent in March 1980—eclipsed even the previously undreamed of levels of interest rates. Money and credit continued to expand, as did economic activity. And in another sinister development, gold reached its all-time high price of $850 per ounce on January 21, 1980 (though within a week it dropped back to $624—which was, nevertheless, about three times its level a year earlier).

Inside the Fed in early 1980, it was a common understanding that Volcker was highly irritated at the way banks had been able to continue expanding their lending despite the new marginal reserve requirements on managed liabilities. Those reserve requirements had been intended to increase banks' costs of funding new loans, and to reduce their confidence of being able to fund any amount of future commitments. But once banks understood details of the new reserve requirements, they turned out not to be so onerous as originally feared. In any event, the commercial paper market was still a potent mechanism for rechanneling short-term business credit flows.

At the same time, some of the most prominent economists in the financial community, notably Henry Kaufman of Salomon Brothers and Albert M. Wojnilower of First Boston, were speaking out for still further measures to stem the growth of credit. Perhaps the most dramatic was Kaufman's statement on February 21, 1980, that the government should "declare a national emergency to deal with inflation."[8]

And last but not least, the Carter administration, fully cognizant of the sensitivity of economic issues in a presidential election year, resolved that it must do something about inflation. Monetary policy did not appear to be working, at least not quickly enough. Measures to reduce the stimulus provided by the federal budget deficit would also take time to work, even on the unrealistic assumption that the administration could maneuver them through Congress. Obviously what was required was some kind of policy initiative already within the administration's existing authority, which would achieve its effects quickly and, it was hoped, with minimum electoral pain.

As it happened, the hitherto little-noticed Credit Control Act of 1969 gave the president sweeping powers to restrict and allocate credit administratively. No congressional consent was required to invoke the act, and it might just provide the swift antiinflationary cure so ardently sought. Moreover, with some of Street's leading lights urging such a course, the initiative could count on at least some positive response.

The Federal Reserve played a major role in designing and implementing the Special Credit Controls program, as was to be expected. The Fed was, of course, the only governmental agency routinely involved in regulating banks and receiving reports from many of the nonbank providers of credit. In addition, Lyle E. Gramley, the member of the Council of Economic Advisers most directly involved with the program, had been a member of the Board staff prior to joining the Council. (He was later appointed to the Board of Governors, where as of this writing he still serves.) And last but not least, it was only logical that the Fed, frustrated with the lack of results from the special reserve requirements introduced in October, should attempt to achieve some refinements.

Thus it came to pass that on March 14, 1980, the "special measures of credit restraint" were announced. No one could say the program was not comprehensive. It extended, in one way or another, to banks, thrift institutions, finance companies, money market mutual funds, credit card companies, and retail providers of credit. Its designers were aware that the program had, as Volcker later put it, "zero economic appeal," so that there never was any intention that it should be other than temporary. Nevertheless, the feeling was that measures were needed which would have a certain shock value.

That the program did indeed provide, though in ways for the most part unintended by its designers. For example, the politically sensitive administration specifically exempted credit provided for the purchase of autos or housing—how very ironic, then, that those sectors were among the most severely affected! All in all, confusion was the most tangible product of the program, within and without the Fed.

The administrative responsibilities the Fed assumed were immense, and there had been no prior planning or staffing. As a result, everything was improvised, as staff members pitched in to shoulder responsibilities for various aspects of the new program while continuing to cover their routine assignments. In addition, the new regulations had to be interpreted and applied to the many special cases that existed in the real financial world. And that spawned a steadily growing body of official interpretations.

If the program created chaos inside the Fed, confusion was all the more palpable on the outside. Consumers, admonished to put away their credit cards, did just that, and paid down their installment borrowings at a frenzied pace. And, in the process, they jarred the Fed by rapidly drawing down their demand deposit accounts, which caused M1 to go into a nosedive during April and May. Volcker later remarked that for consumers the program turned out to be an immediate "psychological bust."

Perhaps the greatest irony of all, however, was that the economy had begun to contract (according to the National Bureau of Economic Research, generally regarded as the arbiter in such matters) in February, a month before the announcement of the program. There was no way the program's designers could have known that, although the Board staff was forecasting an imminent slowdown, and it might not have mattered if they had. After all, the objective of the program was to a high degree psychological and not quantifiable in conventional economic terms.

Beyond a doubt, the controls greatly amplified the sharpness of the emerging economic slowdown, and in the second quarter, real GNP dropped at a 9.6 percent annual rate, one of the most abrupt quarterly declines on record. Indeed, in late spring, it appeared that the bottom was falling out of the economy. The unemployment rate soared a full percentage point during April and May, while sensitive commodity prices plunged. M1 entered a nosedive that swiftly carried it far below its target range, and the federal funds rate dropped a stunning 10 percentage points in the space of only two months. Other rates declined commensurately.

In that environment, the Fed moved quickly to terminate the program, as many market participants had expected it to do all along. In response to the termination, and probably more important, in response to the much lower levels of interest rates, the economy rebounded promptly in the third quarter. Commodity prices shot up once more, and broad-based measures of inflation, hardly missing a beat, continued to increase at very high rates.[9]

Indeed, even in terms of its psychological objectives, the credit controls produced questionable results. There is no evidence that they contributed to any lasting change in inflation psychology. In any event, if such an effect did exist, it was swamped by the plunge of interest rates during the second quarter. Moreover, the absence of any discernible improvement in the inflation trend was compounded by the revival of cynicism about monetary policy.

Indeed, the credibility of monetary policy—the degree of public confidence it could command—was arguably the most important influence on inflation psychology. If confidence in monetary policy were attainable only through a demonstrated willingness to maintain bone-crushing levels of interest rates until a slowing inflation trend was well established, then the plunge of rates prompted by the program's economic chaos surely undermined the Fed's credibility.

If, instead, confidence depended on a continuing commitment to slowing the expansion of money—and for many economists and financial market participants that was by far the most important gauge—the program was also a setback, for the plunge of the money stock in the second quarter was followed by a bulge that many found appalling but all too believable.

Internally, the Fed vowed never to repeat the policy errors of 1980—in particular, to avoid letting interest rates decline to levels at or below the inflation rate. Precisely that had occurred in June before policy shifted to block further rate declines. In sum, then, the credit controls program was a psychological bust in more ways than one.

In the financial markets, apprehension was widespread that Fed policy was a vassal to political expediency. In the months before the election, many anticipated that the Fed would aggressively inject reserves to try to bring interest rates down in time to help Carter's election campaign. Though such views were far from being universally held, no one laughed.

Backing off

The Fed confounded such skeptics by making policy progressively tighter as the economy rebounded. Interest rates promptly retraced their earlier declines and marked new records, with predictable consequences for Carter's reelection campaign. Henceforth, inflation would be combated through a continuing policy of monetary restraint—with no gimmicks.

That did not, however, mean that the new monetary control procedures introduced with such fanfare in October 1979 were inviolate. Indeed, Sternlight had put the financial markets on notice at the outset that implementation of the procedures would not be rigid. If anything, that proved to be a considerable understatement. Late in the second quarter of 1980, for example, the Fed blocked any further declines of the funds rate despite the fact that M1 was several billion dollars below its target range.

Later that year, when the extraordinary (and unexpected) sharp rebound in economic activity was becoming apparent, and when M1 was threatening to overshoot its target range, the increased levels of discount-window borrowings generated by the new procedures were not reflected (so the Fed thought) in fully commensurate rises in the federal funds rate.

Rather than accept those interest-rate levels, the FOMC voted to depress provision of nonborrowed reserves, thus increasing discount-window borrowing still further and stepping up the pressure on the funds rate. The discount rate was increased several times. In addition, in November, a surcharge was applied to frequent borrowers from the discount window and subsequently increased. These measures produced the intended effect as the funds rate soared to new highs by year-end.

Thus, 1980 provided plenty of evidence that the Fed could and would use its own judgment when necessary to override or to reinforce the policy adjustments emanating from the new procedures. If this was not the mechanical, hands-off approach that many had thought—despite Sternlight's clear statements—was introduced in October 1979, the Committee's willingness to allow rates to adjust quickly still constituted a radical departure from the past.

During 1981, the FOMC continued to use its judgment, supported by staff analyses, to modify the procedures. In part, that decision was unavoidable. At the start of the year, NOW accounts (discussed further in Chapter 5) became available nationwide, and balances in such accounts soared. No one had any clear idea of how much additional balances the new accounts would attract from sources not included in M1.

For that reason, the M1 target, the bedrock of the new procedures, was largely inoperable, and so were the procedures. By mid-year, it seemed clear that most, if not all, of the shift of funds into the new NOW accounts had been completed, so that in principle the procedures could have been restarted. But that did not happen. In fact, M1, whether or not it was adjusted for estimated shifts of funds, tracked under its target range during virtually all of 1981. The Fed responded to the shortfall with cautious, measured easing steps, since the broader aggregates were growing above their target ranges, while inflation showed only tentative signs of deceleration. The easing reduced the funds rate from about 19 percent in early summer to a bit more than 12 percent in December.

Toward the end of 1981, however, M1 growth began to accelerate sharply, so that by early 1982, it was already well above the top of its target range, while the broader aggregates were also growing at the top of their ranges. Reserves availability was tightened in response, sufficiently to propel the funds rate back to a 14–15 percent range. The M1 bulge in the first half of the year was overwhelmingly due to continued rapid expansion of NOW accounts. Since NOW accounts tend to be used less actively for spending than demand deposits, the relation of M1 to GNP began to change markedly. Other factors, discussed in Chapter 5, may also have contributed to the impact. Whatever the case, growth in the conventional measure of the link between money and income—M1 velocity—began to nosedive (Chart 4–10). The Board staff's initial reaction was that the abnormal movement would be self-reversing, just as it was in 1980, so that M1 would return to its target range without major additional steps to tighten

CHART 4–10
M1 Velocity
Year Over Year Percentage Change

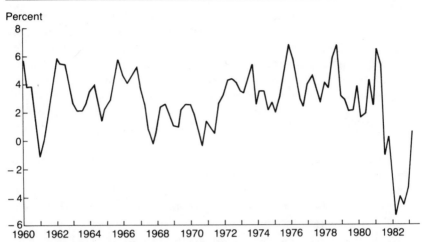

Percent

From late 1981 until early 1983, M1 velocity was in a plunge without precedent in several decades of monetary experience.

policy. Accordingly, market interest rates remained at high levels even while the Fed overrode the significant tightening moves that rigid adherence to the reserves-oriented procedures would have produced.

As it turned out, that cautious approach was rewarded. The expected business recovery did not occur during the summer of 1982. In addition, the crisis facing many international borrowers exploded in August when Mexico announced that it would be unable to meet scheduled debt payments. That situation would have been greatly exacerbated had the Fed attempted to pare back money growth quickly during the first half of 1982, by allowing the reserves-oriented procedures to force rates higher.

By late June, M1 showed signs of a deceleration that might return it to its target range. At the same time, it was becoming increasingly clear to the Fed that the plunge in M1 velocity was not self-reversing as many had thought earlier. If anything, it was gaining momentum. Economists produced a variety of possible explanations—explored in the next chapter—but few felt very confident about the course of developments in the year ahead.

In contrast, there was abundant evidence of the continued weakness of the economy, the now very apparent slowdown in inflation, and the worsening international credit situation. Consequently, the Fed began the first of several steps toward a less restrictive policy stance which culminated by late 1982 in an 8½ percent discount rate (down from 12 percent in June) and a funds rate a bit less than 9 percent (compared to over 14 percent in June). In large part due to the declines of interest rates produced by this policy shift, the economy finally began its recovery in December.

Starting in late summer, when only limited easing steps had been put in place, M1 growth accelerated again and continued to grow strongly for the rest of the year. The Fed chose to ignore that development altogether, and formally set aside its M1 target at the October FOMC meeting. The weak condition of the economy, the continuing plunge of inflation, and what was by now referred to as simply "the debt crisis" scarcely seemed to merit the substantial tightening moves that rigid adherence to the reserves-oriented procedures would have required.

During 1983, the procedures were almost totally neglected, in favor of a policy approach that made only small adjustments to the volume of discount-window borrowing forced on banks and thus to the funds rate. During the year, the funds rate rarely traded lower than the 8½ percent discount rate and seldom exceeded 9½ percent— a pattern of stability that contrasted strikingly with the past few years. In part, the decision to back off from the new procedures reflected the uncertainty connected with the introduction around the beginning of the year of new types of deposit accounts on which interest rates were deregulated. But more fundamentally, the decision recognized that velocity was continuing to decline, while no one could confidently predict when its behavior would return to a more normal pattern.

In terms of the graphic analysis presented earlier, the supply of nonborrowed reserves adjusted to whatever level was needed to preserve the quantity of borrowed reserves about unchanged. Critics promptly pointed out that if this were not funds-rate targeting, it was a close cousin. They were correct, and yet there were significant differences from the way funds-rate targeting had been practiced in the old days.

One difference was largely technical and chiefly apparent to professional participants in financial markets. The funds rate was allowed to vary quite a bit from day to day—unlike the old days— and the Fed rarely entered the market to supply and drain reserves during the same reserves maintenance period.[10] As a result, market participants' notions of where the funds rate ought to trade were far more approximate than they had been prior to October 1979.

The second, and more important, difference was that real interest rates continued at historically almost unprecedented levels (Chart 4–11). Though the differences are somewhat less dramatic when real rates are measured on an after-tax basis, the contrast with the expansiveness of the mid-1970s is still vivid.

CHART 4–11
3-Month Treasury Bill Yields:
Nominal, Real, and Real After 40% Tax Rate

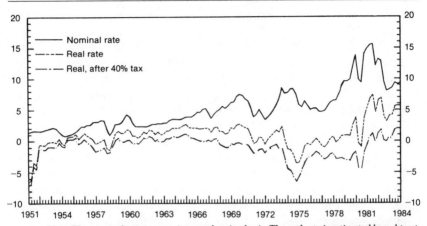

Note: The nominal rate is on an interest-bearing basis. The real rate is estimated by subtracting from the nominal rate the inflation rate as measured by the year-over-year percentage change of the personal consumption expenditures deflator. The real, after-tax rate is estimated by multiplying the nominal rate by one minus an assumed 40 percent tax rate and then subtracting the inflation rate.

While nominal yields on 3-month Treasury bills in the early 1980s were at their highest levels in decades, real, after-tax yields were not much higher than they had been between the end of the Korean War and the mid-1960s.

Volatility and credibility

If there was almost universal agreement that the Fed's policy was restrictive, critics continued to deplore the erratic short-run movements in money. Clearly, improved precision of monetary control—which many had taken for granted would result from the new procedures—was not achieved. Instead, growth of M-1 appeared to become substantially more volatile than it had been prior to October 1979, despite its slowing trend.

What accounted for this qualitatively greater volatility? It is unlikely that the new procedures themselves were the cause, as interest rates did indeed respond rapidly to deviations of monetary growth from its target. The operating procedures could have been structured to produce still tighter control of monetary growth, and, naturally, still more volatile interest rates. But no one would have expected that the replacement of a sluggish funds rate targeting procedure by the nonborrowed reserves target system would, by itself, have produced more erratic money growth rates. Rather, the answer appears to lie in the rapid introduction and growth of new types of deposit accounts during the period, the disturbances to established credit and deposit behavior produced by the credit controls program, as well as the changing character of the payments system itself. These effects are discussed in Chapter 5.

Though the dramatic deterioration of the short-run precision of monetary control was dismaying to many in the Fed, and positively appalling to monetarists, it did not preclude a continuing policy of disinflation. By early 1983, the inflation rate had plunged to the lowest level in over a decade, so that inflation-adjusted interest rates remained only slightly lower than the postwar record levels established but a few months before. Policy was clearly restrictive.

As a result, though the controversy over the proper implementation of monetary policy continued as lively as ever, the Fed's credibility as a force for disinflation increased enormously. Credibility is, of course, an intangible and highly subjective concept. But several developments bear witness to the change.

Since ridicule and credibility have an almost opposite emotional content, one of the most telling indications is that whatever else they might think about the wisdom of its policy, almost no one any longer bothered to tell stories about the Fed being a vassal to political expediency.[11]

Another bellweather was that financial assets took on a new attractiveness as inflation fears began to abate, while prices of "hedge assets" intended to serve as a personal inflation defense took a pounding. In a sense, the mirror image of the Fed's newfound sense of commitment was the marked deterioration in the fortunes of those who earlier had profited on inflation fears.

Gold was far and away the outstanding symbol of that fall from grace. By the time policy began to shift toward ease in late June 1982, the price of gold had sunk to $296.75 per ounce, a whopping 65 percent decline from the frenzied peak in early 1980. In the course of that plunge, many goldbug and survivalist newsletters vanished as quickly as they had sprung up before. Even the report of the presidentially appointed Gold Commission was allowed to fade into obscurity almost as soon as its ink was dry.

Finally, the professional respect accorded Volcker and the Fed had never been higher. So great was that respect, in fact, that in June 1983, Volcker was appointed by President Reagan to serve a second four-year term as chairman, despite being a holdover appointee of President Carter, and despite the intense opposition of monetarists within the administration. Many factors entered into that decision. High on the list reportedly was Volcker's expertise in defusing the debt crisis (about which more in Chapter 11).

But two other important considerations surely were that Alan Greenspan, chairman of the Council of Economic Advisors under President Ford, chairman of the National Commission on Social Security Reform, and himself a leading candidate for the job, also endorsed Volcker, while a survey of sentiment among financial decision makers showed overwhelming support for reappointment.[12]

In December 1983, the same survey asked respondents to list the two most important causes of high long-term interest rates. A mere 2.4 percent thought volatile money growth was important. An even smaller 1.4 percent thought that recent easy monetary policy—a reference to the bulge in M1 during the second half of 1982 and the first half of 1983—played a significant role.[13] Thus, the record was fairly clear on the point: short-run volatility of money growth need not stand in the way of a credible monetary policy.

Notes

1. Ironically, that policy did not appear so stimulative when gauged in terms of M1 growth. M1 grew only 4.9 percent during the year—a pace little different from the 4.4 percent growth in 1974, a year of sharp recession. In contrast, M2 growth exploded to 12.6 percent in 1975, after rising only 5.5 percent in 1974. The reasons behind this curious behavior are discussed in the next chapter.

2. Reserve requirements are fractional amounts of deposits (and sometimes other liabilities as well) that financial institutions must maintain in the form of acceptable reserve assets (chiefly deposits in reserve accounts at Federal Reserve Banks). All other things equal, an increase of reserve requirements reduces the ability of banks to extend credit.

Reserve requirements and reserve accounts are discussed in more detail in Chapter 7.

3. The occasion was a 1969 conference sponsored by the Federal Reserve Bank of Boston. In essence, Meltzer proposed, as a first step toward what he viewed as a more satisfactory system, that the "proviso clause" directive (discussed in Chapter 3) then in use be reversed so that the Desk manager would be instructed to achieve a certain targeted growth of reserves provided that the funds rate did not trade outside a specified range. Meltzer also suggested that that range be gradually widened and ultimately eliminated. In form, if not intent, this proposal contained the key elements of the new procedures. See *Controlling Monetary Aggregates* (Boston: Federal Reserve Bank of Boston, 1969), p. 99.

4. The monetary target involved would be the short-run target, not the annual target.

5. A reserves maintenance period is the period of time during which banks must maintain reserves to meet their reserve requirements. Chapter 7 describes the current, two-week reserves maintenance period.

6. This process is discussed further in Chapters 6–7.

7. One reason why such an action might be desirable relates to the statistical properties of econometric estimates of the borrowing function. Unlike the simple schematic representation in Chart 4–9, the uncertainty attached to the borrowing function is likely to be much greater for high levels of borrowing, which have occurred relatively

seldom in the past. Consequently, the estimated impact on the funds rate of a change in borrowing will probably be more reliable at modest levels, say in a range of $500 million to $2 billion. Consequently, increasing both the discount rate and the level of borrowing would probably have a more predictable impact on the funds rate than would trying to achieve the same effect solely by pushing borrowing to extremely high levels.

8. Striking though such a statement was, the "New York view" associated with Kaufman and Wojnilower was hardly new. As noted in Chapter 3, belief in the efficacy of quantitative restrictions on credit availability and the relative impotence of interest rates in controlling a business expansion had figured prominently in much of the Fed's postwar policy. The best chronicle and exposition of this view is Albert M. Wojnilower, "The Central Role of Credit Crunches in Recent Financial History," *Brookings Papers on Economic Activity,* 2 (1980), pp. 277–326.

9. Wojnilower later claimed that this result was to be expected due to the premature dismantling of the controls. He continued to feel they should have been made permanent. See Wojnilower, "Central Role of Credit Crunches."

10. In terms of Chart 4–8, the reason was the Fed's desire to prevent the reserves demand schedule from intersecting the vertical part of the reserves supply schedule at any time during the reserves maintenance period, so as to avoid even a temporary plunge of the funds rate.

11. For a vivid exception, see Maxwell Newton, *The Fed* (New York: Times Books, 1983).

12. Richard B. Hoey and Helen Hotchkiss, "Decision-Makers Poll" (New York: A. G. Becker Paribas, Inc., June 2, 1983). Specifically, 76.9 percent of the 702 survey respondents had "most confidence" in Volcker; no one else was supported by more than 5.8 percent, while the top-drawing monetarist was Milton Friedman with 5.5 percent.

13. Hoey and Hotchkiss, "Decision-Makers Poll" (New York: A. G. Becker Paribas, December 21, 1983).

5

MEASURING AND ADJUSTING MONEY

Noneconomists sometimes are astonished to learn that monetary economists have been engaged since the 1950s in a spirited debate over the fundamental properties of the empirical, as well as the ideal theoretical, measure of money. Not only are the arguments now pretty much what they were two decades ago, but at almost any professional economic conference touching on the subject of monetary policy, many of the speakers will be the same ones who played active roles in similar debates two decades ago.

In part, that is testimony to the longevity of the predominantly young economists who opened new avenues of inquiry into monetary policy issues during those years. But it also testifies to the fact that many of the disputes are difficult, if not impossible, to resolve by empirical investigations alone, since one's appraisal of "the data" is influenced considerably by adherence to several theoretical concepts.

Concepts and definitions

One source of disagreement is the concept of money itself. Almost everyone agrees that money serves two principal roles, as a medium of exchange and as a store of value, but there are wide differences between groups of economists in the degree of emphasis which they assign to them.

For example, those who emphasize the role of medium of exchange view money as the critical element in the process by which individuals and other economic agents conduct the myriad of transactions underlying the income and product flows of an advanced economy. From there, it is generally but a short intellectual step to the view that the preferred empirical measure of money is one that includes liquid assets that perform a transactional role to a high degree—like currency and checkable deposits—while excluding others that are judged either not to serve such a function or else only to a relatively minor extent. In another small step, many economists try to explain the demand for such "transactions balances" with a theoretical model that views the stock of balances as essentially an inventory held to facilitate transactions. However, the amount of money inventory desired depends on the returns available on other highly liquid investments. Higher returns will induce individuals to try to get by with less money balances per dollar of transactions than they otherwise would. In this concept, the returns that matter are those available on bank deposits and money market instruments. Yields on stocks and bonds, which are clearly far less liquid investments, are viewed as irrelevant to the money inventory.[1]

In contrast, other economists emphasize money's role as a store of value. That naturally leads to an empirical measure which includes "near-money" assets that possess a high degree of liquidity without necessarily performing a major direct role in transactions. For this more inclusive concept, it is only reasonable that the menu of assets that may substitute for money is plausibly much larger than in the transactions-oriented view.

Finally, a relatively limited number of individuals maintain that the complex and shifting collection of assets that make up "money" is unknowable, so that no satisfactory empirical measure can be constructed to guide monetary policy.

Clearly, with such a variety of concepts lurking in the background and coloring economists' views about what is an acceptable money measure, continuing dissension is almost inevitable. Yet the actual degree of conflict should not be exaggerated. Most economists incline to the transactions-oriented money concept and view the existence of alternative, highly liquid assets as primarily relevant to the definition of the opportunity costs (e.g., the interest income foregone) of holding money balances.

Measuring money

Once an economist has settled on what seems to be an appropriate concept of money, the next problem obviously is to relate available data on currency and deposits to the theoretical magnitude. Two kinds of problems are involved in putting empirical flesh on the bare theoretical bones of the money concept. The first is the identification of the assets that should be included, and the collection of data. That sounds quite straightforward, but it's not. Without exception, the economic theories that have been constructed over the years to explain the role of money in the economy regard money as an *asset* held by individuals and firms for various purposes. However, in practice, the data collection procedures that underlie the actual measurement of the money stock almost exclusively measure certain *liabilities* of various types of financial institutions.

In principle, that is no problem at all, since as any beginning accounting student knows, one person's liability must be someone else's asset. In practice, however, what individuals and other economic agents *perceive* as their money assets probably corresponds imperfectly to what is measured in the form of liabilities of financial institutions. The goal of perfect correspondence obviously can never be achieved, since different individuals may view the same type of asset as having different qualities of "moneyness."

That consideration leads to the second basic problem of empirical money measurement: how to add together the various component assets to form one composite measure of money? The traditional approach— which is still the established procedure—is rather austere: an asset is either money (in which case it is included) or it is not (in which case it is excluded altogether). Furthermore, there is no differentiation between components chosen for inclusion, so that a dollar of currency is taken to have a moneyness property identical to that of a dollar of demand deposits, and so forth. In recent years, this procedure— occasionally referred to somewhat derisively as the "simple sum" or "all or nothing" approach to monetary aggregation—has come into question.

An alternative approach, developed primarily by economist William A. Barnett, formerly on the staff of the Board of Governors and currently a professor at the University of Texas at Austin, employs the economic theory of index numbers to determine what weights to use in summing the components.[2] Provided that a number of conditions are met, it turns out that the weight assigned to each component is inversely related to the rate of return on that component. The theoretical result is clear enough, but the success of practical application is obviously sensitive to the quality of measurement of the component rates of return.

Currency, for example, clearly has a return, even though it pays no interest—otherwise, who would want it?—but quantification is difficult. The same is true for demand deposits, on which explicit payment of interest is prohibited, as well as other kinds of deposits subject to interest rate ceilings. Accordingly, the appeal of Divisia monetary aggregates, so named for the French economist who first formulated the

index-number theory used in Barnett's work, is linked crucially to
one's confidence in the estimated rates of return.

Another alternative approach to weighting the components in
a monetary aggregate is aptly dubbed "money is as money does." The
key idea, developed by Paul A. Spindt, an economist on the staff of
the Board of Governors, is that the moneyness of any component
should be reflected directly in the frequency with which it is used
for transactions.[3] In this view, the proper weights to use in aggregating
components are their respective turnover rates, defined as the dollar
volume of transactions during a given time period, divided by the
average balance during the period.

The practical problems in estimating such weights, while perhaps
less formidable than those of the Divisia approach, are daunting nonetheless. For example, no one has a very firm estimate of how many
times per month currency turns over. Turnover data is available for
demand deposits, NOW accounts, and savings deposits. But another
problem arises: how to separate the transactions in essentially financial
assets from all the rest.

Such a separation is important, since it is the link from money
to income-generating transactions that is of special interest, not the
myriad of intermediary exchanges among financial assets themselves
(e.g., swaps of currency for demand deposits, demand deposits for

CHART 5–1
Money Supply Velocity Measures
Year over Year Percent Change

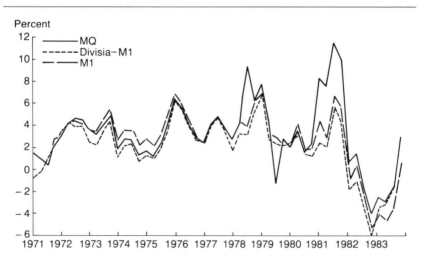

Monetary velocities calculated with alternative measures of transactions
money all showed broadly similar sharp declines during the early 1980s.

NOW accounts, and so forth). Unfortunately, almost no data exist that shed light on such a breakdown. Estimates of the weights are thus highly provisional, involving a large judgmental input.

As it turns out, velocities defined using both Divisia-M1 and MQ (Spindt's quixotic mnemonic for his turnover-weighted aggregate) behave quite similarly to the velocity of M1. In particular, the spectacular plunge of M1 velocity that occurred during 1982 is present in at least equal degree for the other two (Chart 5–1).[4]

As of this writing, there appears to be little prospect that simple-sum M1 will be replaced by either Divisia-M1 or MQ, although the Board has expressed enough interest to ensure that estimates of both continue to be prepared on a monthly basis by the Board staff and are used as an aid in analysis of questionable behavior in the conventionally defined aggregates. However, probably the greatest contribution of these alternative measures of money is to show how heterogeneous this thing called "money" actually is, and to underscore how sensitive its measurement can be to an essentially arbitrary process of adding up its parts. As we will see shortly, that is very important to keep in mind whenever the relative composition of M1 is changing significantly.

Innovations

The late 1970s and early 1980s were marked by a proliferation of various types of accounts that served transactions purposes in greater or lesser degree. In contrast, the 1960s and early 1970s witnessed almost nothing that could be regarded as a significant change in the payments system. No major new transactions accounts were introduced. About the only important modification to the structure of existing accounts was periodic tinkering with the rates of interest permitted to be paid on savings and time deposits. Meanwhile, Congress and the regulatory authorities took steps to ensure that consumers would not be able to enhance their returns by utilizing alternative means to effect their payments and to accumulate liquid savings. Even the development of certificates of deposit (CDs), described in Chapter 3, produced no identifiable impact on corporate transactions accounts. But CDs and a number of other innovations facilitated ever more efficient management of money balances, and thus surely contributed to the approximate 3–4 percent trend growth rate of M1 velocity during much of the postwar period.

Not surprisingly, the 1960s and early 1970s were the golden years of the money-demand relationship, or so it now appears with the aid of hindsight. In 1972, Princeton University economist Stephen M. Goldfeld published statistical results that were generally regarded as the state of the art in the empirical application of monetary theory.

They suggested that a very stable relationship existed between income and a narrowly defined monetary aggregate consisting of currency and demand deposits.[5]

Unfortunately, within a couple of years, Goldfeld and others were trying to pin down what was going wrong in the money demand function, for starting in 1974, the estimated relationship wobbled off course in a highly uncharacteristic fashion and began to overpredict actual money demand by substantial amounts, amounts often referred to by monetary economists as "the missing money." To understand why that might have happened, consider some of the institutional changes that got under way in the mid-1970s.

Corporate cash management techniques

One of the more significant innovations of the 1970s was the development of corporate cash concentration and investment systems that permitted corporate treasurers to make their payments with far less cash on hand than would have been required previously. In concept, such techniques are simple. Since a large corporation typically has accounts at many banks, the key to managing the total cash position is to monitor payments being made and then to amass any and all surplus cash in the various accounts into one account, which can then be invested overnight or for whatever time period seems reasonable. Obviously, this process presupposes a sophisticated system for monitoring account balances and effecting balance transfers quickly.

As computer technology improved during the 1970s, such systems became a reality, and banks began promoting them to their largest customers, who obviously had the most to gain from reducing average levels of uninvested cash. Smaller firms also began to take steps to improve their cash management practices. This was feasible because even in the absence of expensive balance monetary systems, much could be done to speed up receipts without, of course, speeding up disbursements.

For example, a firm with sales in several geographic regions may find it advantageous to arrange for lock boxes in several cities dispersed throughout the regions. A lock box is merely a numbered post office box from which a bank, not the firm itself, regularly collects mail. The bank deposits the checks immediately and forwards any additional correspondence to the firm. The result is generally a substantial reduction of the time required for checks to travel through the mail and be deposited. Anyone who regularly pays bills to a retail chain store or similar firm probably noticed long ago that the address on the remittance envelope is little more than a post office box—a telltale sign of the ubiquitous lock box!

Another trend that gathered momentum during the late 1970s and early 1980s was the practice of firms paying for bank services (loans, account maintenance, etc.) by explicit payment of interest and fees, rather than by keeping agreed-upon "compensating balances" in noninterest-bearing deposits as was traditional. In principle, it might not matter much whether payment is explicit or only implicit (interest income foregone on the compensating balances). As a practical matter, however, it mattered a great deal. For one thing, interest rates were on a rising trend during this time. Whatever a corporate treasurer initially might have thought he was paying in the form of balances, the actual cost later turned out, more likely than not, to have been higher. That experience did not make treasurers wildly enthusiastic about implicit payments. Another factor surely was that the whole idea of unpredictable compensation flies in the face of the logic of most of the other cash management activities of corporate treasurers, which reduce costs through reducing uncertainty.

How much impact did improved cash management techniques have on the demand for money? No one claims to know for sure, but several members of the staff of the Board of Governors have investigated the issue and reached some plausible conclusions.[6] First, corporate cash management seems to have accounted for the bulk of the missing money. That is not surprising, given that nonfinancial corporations own about two-thirds of all demand deposits.

The second main conclusion was that the introduction of cash management techniques appeared to be spurred by peaks of interest rates. For example, the high interest rates of 1974 appear to have prompted some corporations to make the investments and staff modifications necessary to manage their cash effectively, changes that stayed in place when interest rates later declined. Subsequent interest rate peaks appear to have brought forth a similar additional response. Indeed, anyone reading the advertisements in banking journals during the last several years could not have failed to be impressed by the number of large banks aggressively marketing their cash concentration systems. Such ads may well have promised more than the banks could deliver in some circumstances, but the new systems surely contributed to a palable reduction in the average level of corporate cash balances.

Improved cash management techniques altered the relationship between spendable balances and actual transactions by permitting a much higher volume of transactions per dollar of balances. But, at the same time, it was becoming more difficult to say what, exactly, constituted corporate balances. As Albert M. Wojnilower has pointed out, business credit lines expanded rapidly during the 1970s, and the *unused* portion of those lines—which most firms would regard as immediately spendable funds—was comparable to the volume of corporate demand deposits by the end of the decade.[7] The link between the *concept* of money as freely spendable balances and the *measurement* of money as currency and checking account balances was becoming looser.

Consumer accounts

While corporations were rapidly improving their cash management practices, consumers and their banks were not far behind. As usual, the driving force behind the innovations was the interest of economic agents in minimizing their loss on noninterest-earning cash held during a period of high interest rates.

Chronologically the first innovation of the period was the Negotiable Order of Withdrawal (NOW) account. Since 1933, it has been illegal to pay interest on demand deposits. However, in the early 1970s, savings bankers in New Hampshire and Massachusetts saw an opportunity to gain a competitive advantage over their commercial bank rivals by providing an account that was, in all but name, an interest-paying checking account.

The commercial banks predictably howled with indignation, but the state banking and judicial authorities permitted the accounts to be offered.[8] Confronted with such a potent competitive threat, the banks demanded that they, too, be allowed to offer the new accounts. Thus two states out of 50 permitted interest on consumer-type checking accounts by 1974. Within months, banks in the other New England states were complaining about the unfair advantage enjoyed by institutions just across the state line, and by 1976, all six of the New England states were authorized by federal legislation to offer NOWs.

As anyone capable of reading a roadmap would predict, New York and New Jersey were the next focus of complaint, and they received their NOWs in November 1978 and December 1979, respectively. Clearly the bandwagon was rolling, and Congress, evidently weary of the constant bickering among the contending lobbies, simply authorized NOWs nationwide effective at the end of 1980.

From the standpoint of money measurement, the growth of NOWs presented a problem of adjusting the money measure for the expansion of a new type of transaction account. While the adjustment was simple conceptually, in practice it was a bit more complex than simply adding the NOWs to currency and demand deposits. This was because there were strong grounds to believe that at least some portion of the NOW balances was likely to be savings balances rather than transactions balances—remember, it was savings banks that started the whole thing—and the influx of savings balances into the M1 aggregate would distort the growth of the total of currency, demand deposits, and NOWs. The Fed coped with this distortion by simply estimating the portion of NOW balances derived from savings accounts and adjusting the total accordingly.

Unfortunately, no one really knew how much of the influx of funds into NOW accounts represented savings balances. At the time, the Fed thought that about 22.5 percent of the NOW flows in January came from savings, with about 27.5 percent coming from that source in February and subsequent months. More recent research has suggested that a portion less than 20 percent may have been more accurate.[9]

About two years later, a similar problem arose when two new deposit accounts totally free of interest-rate restrictions were authorized. These money market deposit accounts (also referred to as MMDAs and super savers) introduced December 14, 1982, and the super NOW accounts, introduced January 5, 1983, caused huge shifts of funds between deposit categories.

The growth of MMDAs was astounding. Spurred by above-market interest rates offered by banks as a temporary promotional device, they garnered almost $300 billion in the first two months of their existence. These accounts were excluded from M1 owing to limitations on checking privileges and included only in the broader aggregates. The super NOWs, included in M1, were much less spectacular. Banks did not promote them actively. Unlike the MMDAs, they had no restrictions on the number of account withdrawals and carried a stiff 12-percent reserve requirement to boot. As a result, they grew only about $26 billion in their first two months—not bad performance by any means, but very small potatoes compared to the MMDAs.

When they were introduced, all of these accounts—NOWs, super NOWs, and MMDAs—created uncertainties about the pace of "true" monetary expansion. But that impact was of relatively short duration, and could be coped with by making (necessarily imprecise) adjustments. Eventually, the Board staff's best estimate was that inflows to super NOWs from outside M1 just about offset the outflow of balances shifted from M1 to the super savers. The more fundamental problem was that as a progressively larger portion of M1 came to earn interest at approximately market rates, the behavior of money demand (not just its measurement) might be affected significantly. We will return to that point in a moment.

From the standpoint of money measurement, the most important, and most intractable, development in consumer banking is arguably the overdraft (line of credit) account, together with its plastic cousin, the credit card. These accounts developed as a logical response to pressure to reduce the costs of consumer lending, and they almost certainly have had a major impact on consumers' holdings of money balances.

Consider for a moment the economics of consumer lending. From the lender's standpoint, extensive paperwork and credit evaluation are involved every time a loan is made. And the interest rate charged on the loan must be comparatively high if the lender is to cover the processing cost as well as his or her cost of funding the loan. That is obviously unattractive to borrowers and also is unattractive to any lender concerned with building up a loyal customer base. The big advantage of overdraft accounts is that the paperwork and credit evaluation costs are incurred only when the credit line is established or enlarged. Thereafter, the customer can take out a loan (by drawing on the credit line) and pay it back any number of times without adding to such costs. Credit cards operate the same way. The only real difference is that they are acceptable for payment in situations when payment by check would be inconvenient.

Unfortunately, in the process of streamlining consumer lending procedures, the notion of balances, which is absolutely fundamental to money measurement, has been altered. To see how, consider Chart 5–2. In the top panel, a plot of a hypothetical account balance is displayed. It is assumed that the consumer owning the account borrowed $3,000 initially, spent some of it, deposited some checks, spent some more, and so forth. One thing that the consumer was careful not to do is to overdraw the account. In the diagram, the region of negative deposits is labeled NSF—bank jargon for "insufficient funds," meaning that your check bounced. No one wants that to happen, so the hypothetical consumer is careful to keep the deposit balance positive.

Now let's replace the $3,000 loan with a $3,000 credit line. The consumer now can keep essentially nothing in his deposit account, being careful only to avoid exceeding the credit line. Accordingly, the NSF region is the area below negative $3,000 in the bottom panel of the diagram. In this illustration, the consumer may well be conducting several thousand dollars of transactions per month through the account, but the balance is only rarely different from zero. That is, the balance of the demand deposit account, which would be included in the measured money stock, is zero. Obviously, the credit line is only partially utilized, and the unused portion constitutes the "balance" as far as the consumer is concerned. In other words, it is the amount that the consumer can spend immediately, at his sole discretion.

At this point, the reader may well think it makes sense to include such credit-line balances in demand deposits. However, that is not done. Most of the deposit data are created, ironically, as a spinoff from data required to compute reserve requirements. Negative demand deposits are not considered demand deposits at all, but are treated as loans, which are not subject to reserve requirements (nor should they be). The upshot is that hardly any data are collected by the Federal Reserve or anyone else concerning overdraft lines. That's a pity, for the growth of overdraft checking may well have played a major role

CHART 5–2
Balances in a Consumer Checking Account

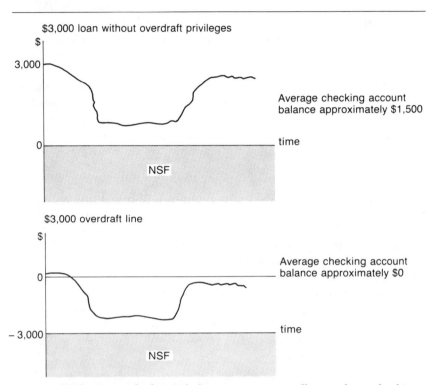

$3,000 loan without overdraft privileges

Average checking account balance approximately $1,500

$3,000 overdraft line

Average checking account balance approximately $0

Without overdraft priviledges, a consumer will try to keep checking account balances strictly positive.

With overdraft priviledges, the average deposit balance may well be zero, even though the consumer is conducting the same transactions as before.

in altering the transactions characteristics of consumer checking accounts in recent years.

Beyond a doubt, one of the most spectacular developments in consumer banking, if not necessarily the most important for money measurement, was the innovation of money market mutual funds. Money funds grew slowly for some time after their introduction in 1974, but began to grow explosively in 1978 and subsequent years. At their peak in November 1982, their assets (excluding those of money funds that cater exclusively to institutional investors) totaled $191 billion. In concept, a money fund is simplicity itself: it is a mutual fund that invests in short-term money market instruments. The major difference between a money fund and a regular mutual fund (and the key to the success of the money funds) is that most allow share owners to write checks on their share balances. That makes balances in a money fund just as accessible as balances in a demand deposit or NOW account, with one hitch—most funds do not permit checks to be written for amounts less than $500 or so. This is because money funds have to pay banks to clear checks for them, and most have no desire to pay for high volumes of such activity.

From the consumer standpoint, money funds had one paramount advantage: they paid market interest rates while regulations prevented banks and thrift institutions from doing likewise. However, the introduction of accounts free of such interest-rate restrictions put banks and thrifts on an equal—in some respects, more than equal—footing in the competition for consumer-type balances. The most dramatic evidence of that fact is the plunge of money-fund assets that followed the introduction of the MMDAs in December 1982. Within six months, the assets of consumer-type money funds had plunged $50 billion, more than a quarter of their level in early December. Moreover, under the terms of the Monetary Control Act of 1980, all restrictions on consumer deposit interest rates are due to be phased out by 1986. Thus, the heyday of money funds is clearly past.

Studies have shown that most money-fund account holders rarely write checks on their accounts, though a small number utilize them very actively. At a large money fund with which the author is familiar, the rule of thumb is that 10 percent of the accounts generate 90 percent of the drafts.

The emergence of the money funds raised in spectacular fashion an old issue in measuring money: what do you do when only some portion of a deposit type is perceived by its owners as constituting money and not the rest? Do you include all or a portion of it in the definition of money, or do you exclude the whole thing? The Board staff's approach was the traditional one described earlier: money funds are *not* properly included in transactions balances like currency and checking-type accounts.

While several reasons were put forth for this view, two considerations were apparently critical.[10] First, the turnover rate of the money funds is very similar to that of savings accounts. In plain English, the volume of withdrawals from money funds, relative to average balances, is similar to that for savings accounts. The turnover rate for demand deposit accounts is vastly higher. The second consideration was that nobody could say with any confidence what portion of the money funds should be considered transactions-related. At the time the issue was being debated (1979 and early 1980), money funds were growing so rapidly, at a rate of about 300–400 percent annually, that if anything other than a very minuscule portion had been included in M1, its growth rate would have been raised palpably. That would have forced the Federal Reserve either to raise the M1 growth target (and thus to face criticism that it was relaxing its monetary control objectives), or to tighten its policy stance sharply to stem the growth. Both seemed rather unsavory alternatives, especially since the evidence to that point suggested that the higher interest rates produced by a tighter policy would, at least initially, increase the growth of money funds still further.

Turning over

One of the real mysteries of the last several years is just why the turnover rate of deposits has increased so enormously. By 1983, the average demand deposit account at banks outside New York City was turning over about 240 times per year— i.e., on average, total balances in demand accounts were withdrawn about once every business day during the year! That rate was roughly 2½ times as fast as it was five years earlier. Furthermore, the increase in turnover was not confined to demand deposits. Turnover rates for other checkable deposits (chiefly NOW accounts) and savings deposits also increased about 2½ times during the five year period, though they remained far below the turnover of demand deposits. Undoubtedly, cash management practices, overdraft accounts, money funds, and heaven only knows what else have played an important part in raising turnover, but the precise mechanism of their impacts is unfortunately still unknown.

In an environment where the utilization of transactions-type assets—or their "moneyness"—is changing so rapidly, a turnover-adjusted money measure such as Spindt's MQ holds special appeal. It provides a reasonable alternative to the traditional all-or-nothing approach to monetary aggregation, which seems hopelessly inadequate in a world of proliferating near-money assets. Also, MQ is probably the only aggregate that can consistently incorporate the expanding role of overdraft checking accounts into the definition of money. Perhaps further research will provide some relief from the data problems that make MQ, despite its fascinating qualities, still but a prototype of what a new M1 could be.

Alternatives to redefining money:
Sophisticated models of money demand

In principle, one can cope with the problem of changing moneyness created by financial innovation in two different ways. One is to alter the weights on various components of the money measure so as to maintain the aggregate's moneyness unchanged. As the preceding discussion has shown, that is a tall order. The other approach is to refine statistical models of money demand to capture the impacts of the kinds of events that would make simple-sum M1 diverge from the ideal transactions concept. It is this second approach that has received the greatest attention from economists in recent years.

Not only is there substantial uncertainty about the appropriateness of the weights used to define MQ or Divisia-M1, but the task of forecasting those weights so as to be able to forecast money demand seems quite intimidating to many economists. In principle, the same set of factors that affect turnover rates, for example, should affect the demand for M1, and many researchers find it statistically simpler, and more fruitful for policy analysis, to estimate their influence on M1 directly. At present, three quite different analytical approaches have been made in that spirit.

One is the approach of a number of economists on the staff of the Board of Governors. They have concentrated on refining measures of the interest sensitivity of demand for M1-type balances. One example is the interest-rate ratchet model employed to explain corporations' investments in staff and techniques used to minimize their idle cash balances. Another innovation is to allow the interest sensitivity of demand for transactions accounts to rise as the level of market interest rates increases, the logic being that higher rates induce depositors to surmount all manner of costs and inconveniences that make active management of M1-type balances "just not worth it" at lower rate levels.[11]

An entirely different approach has been taken by economists at the Federal Reserve Bank of San Francisco. They have emphasized an interaction between activity in the bank loan market and departures of the actual money stock from its desired level. Though the elaborate interest-rate variables incorporated in the Board staff's models are absent from the San Francisco model, the estimated interest sensitivity of money demand is quite high in comparison to empirical results common a decade or so ago.[12]

A third significantly different approach is the model developed by Michael J. Hamburger. One of Hamburger's key, and somewhat controversial, assumptions is that the money demand equation should be represented in terms of velocity (actually the inverse of velocity, the money stock divided by GNP). That means that all other things being equal, a 1 percent rise in income will be associated with a 1 percent rise in money demand. In addition, Hamburger assumes that the demand for money is sensitive to yields in the bond and equity markets, an assumption consistent with his portfolio view of money but at variance, as noted earlier, with the inventory view.[13] Hamburger's results also suggest a significant sensitivity of money demand to bond rates and to yields on equities, but *not* to short-term interest rates.

One of the few features these models share in common is a considerable sensitivity of money demand to financial yields, though naturally they disagree enormously with regard to which yield. That sensitivity is the reason why they all achieve some success in explaining (in the statistical sense) the 1982 velocity plunge.

The common story, reduced to essentials, is that as financial yields dropped during the period, individuals and firms desired to hold more of their financial assets in the form of M1-type balances. Therefore, money growth during an adjustment period of several quarters' duration was rapid relative to spending growth—so that velocity plunged. The adjustment was basically a one-shot affair, however, so that barring another large change in yields in the future, velocity growth should resume a more normal pattern.

These results, of course, are not necessarily ironclad. Indeed, econometric models tend to have rather large "decay rates" over time. Nevertheless, the fact that they provide similar implications on the basis of considerably different methodologies offers some hope that the conclusion may hold.

Unfortunately, the very success of the models in explaining the velocity plunge calls into question the Fed's practice of setting annual targets for the money stock. Suppose, for example, that financial market participants were to adjust their expectations of future inflation downward sharply. If nominal interest rates did not decline commensurately, real rates would rise and probably would cause economic activity to contract. That would reduce money demand, and the Fed would allow interest rates to decline in order to return money growth to its existing target range.

But the models indicate that the demand for money would then increase relative to income, so that if the Fed did not wish to exacerbate a recession, it would be forced either to let M1 expand faster than targeted, or else to reset the target at a higher level. Neither course of action could be expected to sit well with advocates of rigid rules for monetary control.

There is, however, a possibility that such effects may become less important in the future, so that M1 takes on a simpler relationship to spending. Some economists have argued that after deposit interest deregulation is fully implemented, disparities between rates paid on M1-type balances and market interest rates will be reduced, and that the two will tend to move together.[14] The resulting relatively stable rate differential would reduce the incentive for depositors to switch funds back and forth between M1 and other assets. Presumably, it would allow the demand for transactions balances to dominate the behavior of M1 much more than it does now. But it is too early to judge the extent to which this possibility will be realized in practice.

The elusive seasonal adjustment

Any definition of the money stock presents the Federal Reserve with a problem of how to provide the data to the public in a seasonally adjusted form. The reason is fairly straightforward. In their raw form, data on currency and deposits routinely display very large changes during the course of a week or two. Some of the largest of these changes are periodic. They occur every year and merely reflect normal seasonal changes in financial flows. But the Fed is concerned, quite properly, that individuals who are unaware of the periodicity in the data, or merely incapable of estimating its pattern very well, might receive a wholly misleading impression of monetary developments if the data were published only in their raw form.

Nonetheless, misleading impressions of short-run money growth rates abound, even in the seasonally adjusted data. For example, during 1983, the largest change from one month to the next in the monthly growth rate of M1 as originally reported was the 29.0 percent acceleration registered between April (−2.7 percent) and May (26.3 percent). Financial markets reacted sharply to what appeared to be a major strengthening of money demand. But after the seasonal factors had been re-estimated in early 1984, the acceleration was a considerably less jarring 17.4 percent, from positive 3.6 percent in April to 21.0 percent in May.[15] Subsequent revisions will probably pare back the acceleration still further.

In general, because of the way the Fed calculates and recalculates seasonal factors, one may confidently expect that the volatility of M1 as initially reported in any year will be substantially reduced during the following three years, rather like the way a rock thrown in a pool makes waves that gradually subside.

Unfortunately, by the time that happens, the Fed may have already reacted to spurious movements in the money stock produced by inadequate seasonal adjustments. After all, those who favor close control of monetary growth necessarily express a willingness to risk responding to such potentially misleading signals. The issue is no pipe-dream. A careful study of the Fed's policy responses during the 1970s concluded that "the combination of inadequate adjustment of preliminary M1 figures for seasonality plus the Fed's reaction to these preliminary figures has been the major cause of observed seasonal variations in interest rates during the 1970s."[16]

In essence, then, for a protracted period of time, the Fed's adjustment procedure failed to cope with an emerging pattern of seasonal variations in M1, and the Fed, for whatever reason, did not see fit to ignore completely the spurious volatility. The result was that the remaining seasonality was transmitted into the federal funds rate and other interest rates. The funds rate was depressed to about $\frac{9}{10}$ of its annual average early in the year and lifted to about $1\frac{1}{10}$ of the average during the late summer months—a very sizable impact. For example, if the funds rate had averaged 10 percent during a year, this effect would have caused a 2 percentage point rise from the seasonal low to the seasonal high.

Apparently, no comparable study has been done for the period after October 1979. But it would not be surprising to find a similar pattern. To understand how a dull, unexciting statistical technique can give rise to such baleful consequences, one must understand just what seasonal adjustment is.

The notion of seasonal variation is almost intuitive to most people. Everyone is familiar with seasonal changes in temperature, daylight hours, and so forth. Seasonal movements in the money stock are similar to those kinds of changes, but the pattern is strongly influenced by holidays, dates for federal disbursements, and tax payment dates, as well as by the Fed's long-standing policy of making the money supply sufficiently "elastic" to accommodate routinely such temporary jumps in money demand.

Chart 5–3 shows the monthly average levels of nonseasonally adjusted and seasonally adjusted demand deposits and currency for the three years 1981–83. The seasonality is readily apparent. Currency rises during the summer vacation season as well as around the holidays toward the end of the year. The reasons for that pattern should be obvious to anyone who has ever taken a vacation or gone Christmas shopping. Demand deposits also move up as the holiday season approaches, then decline, only to rise again around the April income tax payment date, and so forth. Overall, what is striking about Chart 5–3 is the high degree of regularity in the patterns.

Now consider Chart 5–4, which displays the weekly changes of seasonally adjusted and nonseasonally adjusted demand deposits and currency for the period 1981–83. It is clear that the Federal Reserve's seasonal adjustment process has removed almost all of the seasonal variation in the series, so that the adjusted series are far smoother than the raw data. Looking at the diagram, it seems hard to believe that one of the unsettled issues in the monetary policy field concerns precisely the inadequacy of the Fed's seasonal adjustments.[17]

Before turning to the points in dispute, it is worthwhile to reflect for a moment on what seasonal adjustment procedures do. In principle, seasonal adjustment removes from a data series all of the variation that is traceable to periodic (i.e., seasonal) influences. Thus, the adjusted series will contain only the variation produced by trend and cyclical

CHART 5–3
Demand Deposits and Currency Adjusted and Nonadjusted

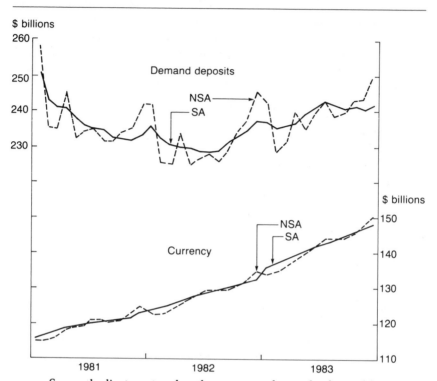

Seasonal adjustment makes the patterns of growth of monthly average demand deposits and currency much smoother than they are in the raw data.

influences, as well as whatever "noise," i.e., random, unexplainable movements, may be present.

The best way to see what is going on is to take an example. Consider housing starts. It is difficult to pour concrete, nail on shingles, and so forth in ice and snow (though it *can* be done!). Consequently, more houses tend to be built in July than in January. When statisticians seasonally adjust the housing starts data, they "fudge up" the January number to allow for the average amount by which January is lower than the annual average and "fudge down" the July numbers to allow for the average amount by which July exceeds the annual average.[18]

But keep in mind that the calendar months, strictly speaking, do not cause housing starts to vary. They mainly represent the influence of the weather. (Perhaps that is why someone once said that after seasonal adjustment, there is never any ice in the Great Lakes.) Otherwise expressed, seasonally adjusted housing starts are adjusted for the

CHART 5–4
Weekly Changes in Demand Deposits and Currency Adjusted and Nonadjusted

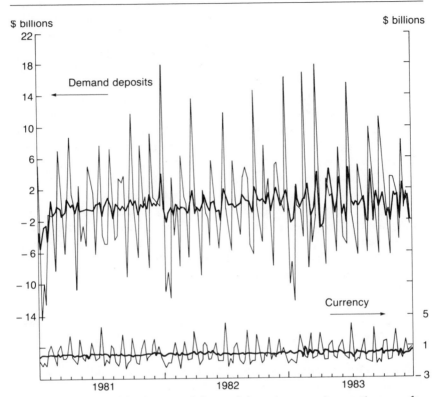

$ billions $ billions

Demand deposits

Currency

1981   1982   1983

    Though weekly changes of demand deposits are quite erratic even after seasonal adjustment, the adjusted data for demand deposits and currency show far smaller weekly changes than the raw data show.

average weather in different months. What about the *actual* weather? In principle, there is no reason why one could not use statistical techniques to prepare a housing starts series from which the influence of the actual weather had been removed. In fact, for some purposes, that series might be more useful than the usual seasonally adjusted data. But the key to understanding conventional seasonal adjustment is to remember that only the average influence observed in any given month is being rinsed out.

    With that in mind, let's review the procedure by which the Federal Reserve adjusts the money stock data. First, the adjustment procedure is applied separately to each major component. That is an intuitively attractive approach, since as we saw earlier, the pattern of currency seasonality is dramatically different from that displayed by demand deposits, for example.[19]

For each component, monthly averages of the data are computed. The monthly average data series is adjusted using a variant of a statistical computer program called Census X–11.[20] It produces a set of monthly seasonal factors, i.e., a set of amounts by which the different months are greater or less than the (detrended) annual average.

Analysts at the Fed then break down the monthly factors into weekly factors, all the while enforcing the condition that the seasonal influence allocated to the various weeks in a month must add up to the seasonal impact which X–11 assigned to that month. While some statistical routines assist in this task, the ultimate factors derived for the weeks are, to an important degree, based on the judgment of analysts intimately familiar with the money stock data. They do not have free rein, however, for whatever weekly factors they come up with must conform with the overall monthly factors produced by X–11.

This procedure has significant advantages. First, X–11 is generally considered be close to the state of the art of seasonal adjustment, and the Fed's factors are grounded on the X–11 output. Another advantage of X–11 is that its output is reproducible, so that anyone who feeds the money data into the program will come up with the same set of monthly factors that the Fed comes up with.

That is an important consideration in view of the potential for politically inspired criticism of the Fed for "massaging" the money data if it were to use a less objective technique. Nevertheless, there is still scope for an experienced analyst to assist in constructing the weekly factors (which X–11 was never designed to do). All in all, the procedure has quite a bit to recommend it.

Unfortunately, the X–11 methodology has some drawbacks, of which two stand out. One is that when the pattern of seasonality is changing from year to year, the preliminary, or year-ahead, factors produced by X–11 will tend to misestimate the true pattern. (This is probably a major source of the defective preliminary M1 adjustments that were discussed earlier.) As a result, the preliminary factors will tend to be revised significantly in subsequent years. The Fed uses an X–11 variant that corrects this problem to some extent, but there probably will never be a perfectly satisfactory technique for coping with changing seasonal patterns.

The second difficulty is that X–11 cannot take account of interactive effects, except in a very limited way. This is important, since there are strong grounds for believing that variation in the money stock is influenced by such effects. To take the simplest example, in computing the weekly average money stock data, balances on Friday are given a weight of three-sevenths, as is appropriate since they also remain on deposit during Saturday and Sunday. What this means is that whenever some periodic payment happens to land on Friday, it can potentially exert a thrice-magnified influence on the weekly average data.

Additional interactive effects are produced by holidays and other events. If these kinds of effects always occurred on the same date in the same month, then X–11 would capture their influence implicitly, but the Gregorian calendar ordains otherwise. Consequently, a fair portion of the predictable variation of the money stock data is not captured by X–11's monthly factors and thus is simply not available for Fed analysts to allocate to the weekly factors.

As an illustration, consider the notorious "social security week" phenomenon often cited by analysts to explain, in part, the variability of the weekly money stock. Typically, social security payments are disbursed by the Treasury so that they will be in the hands of recipients on the third day of the month. However, if the third falls on the weekend, the payment date is advanced to the preceding Friday. If Friday happens to be a holiday and the Treasury is closed, payment is moved up to Thursday. Since monthly social security payments are quite substantial, this sets the stage for a sizable interactive effect. However, the phrase "social security week" is in reality a misnomer. First of all, a variety of other payments, such as those for payrolls and various kinds of monthly bills, also take place at about the same time as the social security payments, and these are most likely involved in the process. Then, too, electronic funds transfer has been playing an increasing role in all federal payments and independently accentuates whatever interactive effect may already exist.[21]

Do not imagine for a minute that the Federal Reserve is unaware of this phenomenon, even if no one knows for sure what produces it. One may also take for granted that the Fed would dearly love to purge it out of the adjusted money data. But reflect on the constraints which the Fed's adherence to the X–11 methodology imply, and the persistence of the bizarre quality should become easier to understand.

Inadequate seasonal adjustment of the money stock data provides bread and butter for quite a few market participants. Specifically, almost all Fedwatchers routinely prepare forecasts of weekly money stock changes. Almost without exception, their forecasts are based solely and exclusively on their subjective corrections of the Fed's seasonal factors. In other words, fancy stuff like income, employment, inflation, and interest rates has virtually no role in forecasting the weekly money number. It's a seasonal adjustment game.[22] In brief, a Fedwatcher will proceed by comparing changes observed in similar weeks in previous years to form a notion of what the seasonal movement actually is after allowing for the various special interactive effects mentioned earlier. Once the Fedwatcher has produced a reasonable estimate of the change in the nonseasonally adjusted data, he adjusts

it with the Fed's (previously published) seasonal adjustment factors—
et voila! the forecast of the seasonally adjusted money number results.
There are, of course, harder ways to earn a living.

Naturally, no Fedwatcher's forecasts are unerringly accurate, but
many do achieve a fair measure of success in predicting the weekly
data. That degree of success is perhaps the most convincing evidence
that further refinement in the Fed's seasonal adjustment procedures
is a reasonable objective. But note a paradox: as one succeeds in incorporating all kinds of special, and possibly bizarre, effects into a model
explaining the variation of the raw money stock data, the notion of
what actually is the seasonal variation becomes less clear.

Are the social security week effects seasonal in nature? Some
would note that the existence of such effects is possible only because
of the Fed's willingness to accommodate them through a relatively
flexible monetary control procedure. Were control more rigid, the seasonality would be transferred from the money data to market interest
rates.[23] Others would argue that while they may be predictable, they
are no more seasonal than worse-than-average weather and thus are
properly regarded as part of the "cyclical" or "irregular" components.
This highlights an important feature of X–11: there is little or no theoretical structure. Basically, X–11 is merely a statistical program that
works satisfactorily in its own frame of reference, which is isolating
periodic monthly (or quarterly) variation. And that is seasonal adjustment—no fancy stuff involved, and the program always gives you a
precise number representing the seasonal influence. The price of explaining the variation more adequately may well be that one loses
the ability to be comparably precise about what seasonality is, so that
adjustment becomes inherently a subjective process (as it is with most
Fedwatchers).

In sum, seasonal adjustment of the money stock seems destined
to remain a permanent quandary.

Notes

1. As is explained in more detail in Chapter 8, liquidity is the ability to buy
or sell a large amount of a good without significantly affecting its price. By extension,
liquid assets have substantial certainty of cash value.

2. For a concise overview of this approach, see William A. Barnett, Edward
K. Offenbacher, and Paul A. Spindt, "New Concepts of Aggregated Money," *Journal of
Finance,* May 1981, pp. 497–505.

3. Paul A. Spindt, "Money Is As Money Does: A Revealed Production Approach
to Monetary Aggregation," Special Studies Paper, Board of Governors of the Federal
Reserve System, June 1983.

4. Barnett and his colleagues have argued that the Divisia aggregate with the
most desirable properties is Divisia-M3. The velocity of that measure is indeed slightly

more stable than the velocity of conventionally defined M3, but both also plunged sharply in 1982.

5. More recently, researchers have questioned whether the money-demand relationship estimated by Goldfeld was, in fact, so stable and reliable as was generally thought when Goldfeld's results were published. For details, see John P. Judd and John Scadding, "The Search for a Stable Money Demand Function: A Survey of the Post-1973 Literature," *Journal of Economic Literature,* September 1982, pp. 993–1023.

6. For a review of these findings, see Judd and Scadding, "Search for a Stable Money Demand Function," pp. 998–1001.

7. Albert M. Wojnilower, "The Central Role of Credit Crunches in Recent Financial History," *Brookings Economic Papers 2,* 1980), pp. 277–326.

8. The reasoning was, in essence, that since the savings banks legally could require 90 days' notice before permitting withdrawals from the accounts, via NOWs or otherwise, account balances were not payable on demand and thus were not subject to the prohibition of interest on demand deposits. The fact that the savings banks had not exercised that legal option for decades was deemed to have no bearing on the matter.

9. Barbara A. Bennett, "Shift Adjustments to the Monetary Aggregates," Federal Reserve Bank of San Francisco, *Economic Review,* Spring 1982, pp. 6–18.

10. The Board staff's reasoning is presented in Thomas D. Simpson, "The Redefined Monetary Aggregates," *Federal Reserve Bulletin,* February 1980, pp. 97–114.

11. Thomas D. Simpson and Richard D. Porter, "Some Issues Involving the Definition and Interpretation of the Monetary Aggregates," in *Controlling Monetary Aggregates III* (Boston: Federal Reserve Bank of Boston, 1980), pp. 161–234; and Flint Brayton, Terry Farr, and Richard Porter, "Alternative Money Demand Specifications and Recent Growth in M1," Board of Governors of the Federal Reserve System, processed, May 27, 1983.

12. John P. Judd, "The Recent Decline in Velocity: Instability in Money Demand or Inflation?" Federal Reserve Bank of San Francisco *Economic Review,* Spring 1983, pp. 12–19.

13. Michael J. Hamburger, "Recent Velocity Behavior, the Demand for Money and Monetary Policy," *Monetary Targeting and Velocity* (San Francisco: Federal Reserve Bank of San Francisco, 1984), pp. 108–128.

14. See, for example, John P. Judd and John L. Scadding, "Financial Change and Monetary Targeting in the United States," *Interest Rate Deregulation and Monetary Policy* (San Francisco: Federal Reserve Bank of San Francisco, 1982), pp. 78–106.

15. Not all of the reduced volatility in this example was due to revised seasonal factors; a small portion was produced by revisions to the originally reported raw data.

16. Thomas A. Lawler, "Federal Reserve Policy Strategy and Interest Rate Seasonality," *Journal of Money, Credit and Banking,* November 1979, pp. 494–99.

17. The Fed has been conducting research on seasonal adjustment procedures for years. Most recently, the Bach Commission considered the problem of definition, measurement, and adjustment of the monetary aggregates, while in 1981, the Committee of Experts focused solely on the adjustment issue.

18. This extremely terse description is an oversimplification of statistical seasonal adjustment techniques, but it does convey the essence of the process. For an excellent, brief description of the state of the art of seasonal adjustment, see *Seasonal Adjustment of the Monetary Aggregates: Report of the Committee of Experts on Seasonal Adjustment Techniques* (Washington, D.C.: Board of Governors of the Federal Reserve System, 1981).

19. And, of course, the seasonality of savings deposits is different from that of demand deposits—and therein lies an interesting story. As noted earlier in this chapter,

in early 1981, the Fed was "shift-adjusting" M1-B (now known simply as M1) to try to correct for the influence of inflows of savings balances into NOW accounts. However, the NOW accounts included in M1-B initially were *not* seasonally adjusted, on the grounds that since nationwide NOW accounts were a new phenomenon, there were no historical data to use in preparing seasonal adjustment factors. While that was strictly correct, a better solution to the problem was pointed out by Edward P. Foldessy, a columnist for *The Wall Street Journal.* Foldessy reasoned that since the Fed was already estimating the portions of NOW accounts coming out of demand deposits and savings deposits, it made sense to adjust the NOW accounts with a seasonal factor composed of the same portions of the demand deposit seasonal factor and the savings deposit seasonal factor. Eventually, the Fed agreed and adopted Foldessy's procedure. *Moral:* the Fed may have one of the largest economic research staffs in the country, but that doesn't mean it can't be shown a thing or two from time to time by a smart guy with a sharp pencil.

20. Strictly speaking, the X–11 adjustments are further refined with a so-called ARIMA technique, but that does not greatly affect the description given here.

In addition, the Fed recently began publishing monthly M1 data seasonalized using an experimental, "model-based" procedure that employs statistical regression techniques to capture periodic effects that may elude more conventional seasonal adjustment procedures.

21. The phrase "electronic funds transfer" in this context primarily refers to the practice of the Treasury providing banks with computer tapes of periodic payments including—but not confined to—social security benefit payments, veterans' benefit payments, and so forth. On the appropriate day, the tapes are read by a bank's computer, funds are credited to the proper accounts, and the bank's reserve account at the Federal Reserve is also credited—all without recourse to expensive and cumbersome paper checks. Next time you see a reference to "direct deposit" on some kind of check, you'll know that's a polite way of referring to EFT.

22. A minor qualification is in order. While seasonal adjustment is overwhelmingly the major factor in Fedwatchers' forecasts of the weekly money supply, during the week preceding the weekly data release, a number of Fedwatchers routinely survey a sample of banks to learn what the changes in their deposits actually were, and adjust their forecasts accordingly. Needless to say, the Fed could easily put such analysts out of business overnight by releasing the deposits data more or less as it is received. However, since the unedited data could contain errors that might mislead the public, such a prompt release is anathema to the Fed. The result, of course, is a small, hothouse industry composed of Fedwatchers who survey banks and sell the survey results—the quality of which is surely considerably worse than any unedited data the Fed might provide.

23. Milton Friedman has advocated a rule-based monetary control procedure that would not accommodate any kind of seasonal pattern in the demand for money, and he correctly points out that under such circumstances, it would be unnecessary to calculate seasonal adjustment factors for the money stock. Most other economists—including most monetarists—do not advocate a monetary control procedure *that* rigid. See Milton Friedman, "Monetary Policy: Theory and Practice," *Journal of Money, Credit and Banking,* February 1982, pp. 98–118.

6

TARGETS AND TARGETING

The immediate results of October 6, 1979—gyrating interest rates *and* volatile money growth rates—left almost everyone dissatisfied with at least some aspect of the Fed's new monetary control procedures. Naturally, the critics' many complaints mirrored their fundamental disagreements over the proper role of targets in monetary policy. Ultimate policy objectives—such as full employment, stable prices, and so forth—are widely shared and thus are seldom a point of contention, though their relative importance may be. Instead, controversy revolved, and still revolves, around the use of monetary targets as guideposts along the way to achieving those ultimate targets.

In general terms, the issue is the extent to which policy should focus on an indicator variable—i.e., an intermediate target, which is not itself related to the national welfare—in order to further the ultimate objectives of policy. Or, to be more specific, is M1 in practice the best guide to achieving "the things that matter"? The answer to that question is decisive for a subsidiary issue: the degree of precision the Fed should attempt to achieve over an intermediate target for M1 or any other variable.

Total reserves targeting

For several reasons, monetarists almost uniformly favor fairly rigid control of M1. For one thing, a rather well developed part of economic theory relates the long-run growth of transaction-money to the long-run growth of spending, a relation that seems to find reasonably consistent empirical support in many countries over a variety of different time periods. Of course, a long-run relation does not necessarily justify close control in the short run. But three considerations have impelled most monetarists to advocate tight short-run control.

First, though the short-run money-demand relationship is quite loose, many monetarists feel there is still enough stability so that it can serve as a useful link between the Fed's policy instruments, e.g., the Fed funds rate or some reserves aggregate, and resultant spending growth. Indeed, some have argued that even the short-run predictability of money demand compares favorably with the reliability of other economic relationships that might be used as policy guideposts instead. Second, while some monetarists might, in principle, concede that precise short-run control is neither necessary nor particularly desirable for long-run stable growth, in practice, they view such control as essential to get from the short-run here to the long-run there. In their opinion, the Fed's institutional attachment to stabilization of interest rates is so complete that only a rule providing for rigid short-run control of money growth, enforced by short-run accountability of policy makers, can overcome what otherwise would be a bias toward a pro-cyclical policy. The implied short-run shocks are considered regrettable, but an acceptable price to pay for long-run economic stability.

Finally, monetarists argue that the Fed could control M1 with precision if it seriously tried to do so. In contrast, control over such a broad aggregate as M2 could never be as effective.[1]

The announcement of the new procedures in 1979 seemed at first to some monetarists the realization of a key part of their agenda. The procedures were, after all, very similar to Meltzer's 1969 proposal. However, as Sternlight had predicted, it did not take long before almost all monetarists agreed that the new procedures, formally described by economists as nonborrowed reserves targeting, were merely a more refined form of interest-rate targeting. This view, as we saw earlier, contains an important element of truth.

Instead, monetarists have long favored a package of measures including (1) uniform reserve requirements, (2) contemporaneous reserve requirements, and (3) a penalty discount rate. Altogether, these measures constitute a total reserves targeting procedure. In addition, many, though not all, monetarists also favor adoption of a relatively rigid rule to govern provision of reserves. But that is a separate issue.

Uniform reserve requirement percentages are highly desirable. If different financial institutions offering similar transactions accounts are subjected to different reserve requirements, then the average reserve requirement on the total of transactions accounts will tend to fluctuate as funds ebb and flow between the various types of institutions. That is a special problem for total reserves targeting, since the tight control of reserve supplies means that any unexpected variation in the reserves multiplier transmits a shock directly to the level of deposits and to interest rates as well.[2]

In any event, a relatively uniform system of reserve requirements is on the way to becoming a reality. Under the terms of the Monetary Control Act of 1980, the reserve requirements applied to nonmember banks and thrift institutions are gradually being phased up, and the reserve requirements of member banks phased down. If all goes as planned, essentially uniform reserve requirements should prevail by the fall of 1987.

From September 1968 to February 1984, reserve requirements were "lagged." Specifically, the amount of reserves a bank was required to keep in its account with the Fed during the current statement week was calculated from the bank's average level of deposits two weeks before. Before then, required reserves in a statement week were calculated on the basis of deposits in the same statement week.[3] The lagged reserve requirement (LRR) system was introduced, with no fanfare and little controversy, solely as a means of reducing some of the perceived inconveniences associated with the contemporaneous reserve requirement (CRR) system as it existed then. A couple of examples will suffice.

For decades, banks have counted cash held in their vaults as reserves. But the practical problem nowadays is that the amount of cash held cannot be tallied until after the tellers' windows have closed. Usually a bank's daily currency inflows and outflows are relatively modest, but almost any bank can cite instances when the movement was highly unpredictable. Under CRR, an unexpected currency flow could throw a bank's reserve account out of balance; the problem would not be discovered, and funds bought or sold as appropriate, until late in the day. The author knows of one large bank which, during the 1960s, dealt with this problem by having someone go down to the banking floor to watch the traffic at the tellers' windows. Long lines were taken to mean that the bank would probably lose cash that day. Both the banks and the Fed thought that sort of thing was a waste of time and resources. More important, if monitoring vault cash was a chore for banks, it posed great difficulties for the Fed, which had little current, accurate data on the quantity of reserves available to banks in their vaults. Accordingly, starting in 1968, member banks counted vault cash as reserves two weeks after the week in which it was held. Result: accurate data for the Fed, and no more monitoring the tellers' lines.

The operational problems of calculating the amount of reserves required against deposits were also considered to justify a simplification. Recall that in the 1960s, bank automation was nowhere near so advanced as it is now. Balancing a bank's accounts required a good

deal of time, and the funds trader often could not receive timely information concerning the total of his required reserves before the funds
market closed on Wednesday night. More important, the Fed could
not receive timely data either, and thus it relied on estimates of required
reserves.

At the time LRR was introduced, the Fed had no formal monetary targets. Consequently, required reserves were simply a fulcrum
on which to apply more or less pressure on banks (and thus on interest
rates) by altering reserves availability. Strictly speaking, it did not much
matter how required reserves were calculated, so long as the calculation
was accurate and not merely an estimate. From the viewpoint of the
Desk manager, knowing required reserves with near certainty meant
that the only remaining source of error in estimating reserves availability were the so-called "market factors" (about which more in the next
chapter).

Thus, almost everyone directly involved was happy with LRR.
However, monetarists were dismayed. Their chief criticism was that
because LRR destroyed the contemporaneous link between reserves
and the money supply, it materially altered banks' behavior in creating
deposits and seriously weakened the Fed's ability to control deposit
expansion, since it made a total reserves targeting procedure a logical
impossibility. And on a more fundamental level, those who wanted
to reduce the scope of discretion available to the Fed recognized that
LRR made it more difficult to prescribe a rule governing provision of
reserves and expansion of the money supply.

From the banks' point of view, CRR—for all its operational
inconveniences—has at least one advantage: it slightly reduces the impact on their reserve accounts of sudden deposit shifts. For example,
if a bank sustains an outflow of deposits (and thus a drain of balances
from its reserve account), its required reserves in the same reserves
maintenance period are reduced commensurately with the reduction
of deposits. Similarly, a bank with increasing deposits would simultaneously increase its required reserves. Thus, by making required reserves
move in tandem with deposit flows, CRR buffers shocks to reserve
accounts resulting from sudden changes in deposits and, in that way,
actually reduces somewhat the burden of managing bank reserve positions.

From the standpoint of monetary policy, the main potential advantage of CRR is that by restoring the simultaneity of required reserves
and deposits, it makes feasible the kind of strict control of reserves
that is a centerpiece of monetarist policy prescriptions. It does not
necessitate such an operating procedure. Indeed, the Fed could perfectly
well frame reserves growth paths in terms of nonborrowed reserves
or target "money market conditions" as it did in the old days of CRR.
But under LRR, the Fed did not even have the option of using a total

reserves targeting procedure. Because required reserves in the current statement week were determined on the basis of deposit levels two weeks earlier, the Fed had no choice but to provide the reserves needed to cover reserve requirements plus a small, "frictional" amount of excess reserves. The only scope for choice was how the reserves would be provided.

The staff of the Board of Governors, as well as many economists outside the system, viewed the greater policy options permitted by CRR as a strong argument in its favor. In addition, the staff maintained that the precision of monetary control would probably be improved somewhat by CRR, irrespective of whether nonborrowed or total reserves were targeted. However, there is considerable dispute among economists concerning the empirical significance of any such improvement. Results to date render no clear verdict. All parties seem to agree, however, that the key question in practice is the nature of the reserves targeting procedures. CRR itself is at best a side issue.

CRR obviously increases the pressure on banks to compile deposit data quickly and accurately. To give banks adequate time to monitor their deposit data, the Board staff devised a CRR system in which the two-week computation period for transactions deposits—i.e., checkable deposits such as demand and NOW accounts—ends two days before the two-week reserve maintenance period. Thus reserve requirements on transactions deposits are contemporaneous $\frac{12}{14}$ ($= \frac{6}{7}$) of the time, while the two-day lag allows reasonably ample time for errors to be located and corrected before the end of the maintenance period.

The CRR system is designed to enhance the Fed's control over M1, but not other monetary aggregates. For that reason, reserve requirements are contemporaneous only for transactions deposits. Reserve requirements on savings and time deposits are lagged four weeks. Vault cash is also counted toward banks' reserves on a four-week lagged basis. That gives the Fed near certainty concerning their reserves impact.

However, CRR may well have reduced the value of the federal funds rate as a source of information about reserves supplies. As noted earlier, a variety of market factors affects the availability of reserves to banks. Not only are these factors not subject to direct control by the Fed, their movements are often quite unpredictable over the course of a reserves maintenance period. Because required reserves under LRR were constant during a statement week, the Fed could validate its projections of reserve supplies somewhat by monitoring the movement of the federal funds rate. For example, a large, unintended miss in supplying reserves will probably prompt a sharp change in the funds rate, which can serve as a warning signal that the reserves projections are in error.

If the Fed aims for tight control of M1, CRR makes such information largely unavailable. The Fed probably would not want to respond, or at least not to the same degree, to movements in the funds rate that might reflect changes in required reserves produced by changes in transactions deposits. Ironically, the tighter the control over money the Fed seeks to achieve, the greater is the impact on both money and interest rates of errors in reserve availability, and the greater is the value of such information as the funds rate might provide.

To monetarists, concerns about short-run interest-rate volatility are much ado about nothing. They argue that it is a small price to pay for enhanced control (through total reserves targeting) of the growth of the money supply, which they in turn expect to lead to a qualitatively more stable price level, lower average levels of interest rates, and so forth. But in considering how likely it is that these desirable objectives will be realized, it is useful to try to ascertain just how large some of those rate movements might be, and how long they might last.

Unfortunately, statistical studies are fundamentally limited by the difficulties of drawing inferences about the banking system's behavior in the present system of two-week maintenance periods under CRR on the basis of historical data for one-week maintenance periods under LRR.

The Fed's research suggested that under the nonuniform and lagged structure of reserve requirements prevailing in the early 1980s, total reserves targeting might have increased significantly monthly deviations of money growth from target compared to what they would be under a nonborrowed reserves targeting procedure. To compound the agony, the monthly average funds rate might have been roughly 10 times more volatile.

However, such estimates almost certainly overstate the difference between the two alternative procedures under the CRR system in place since February 1984. For one thing, as noted earlier, reserve requirements are being made more uniform, and that should improve the relative performance of a total reserves target. Moreover, the CRR system allows banks to carry over from one reserves maintenance period to the next a substantial amount of excesses and deficits in their reserve accounts. That "slippage" tends to make banks' demand for reserves more responsive to interest rates and thus works to buffer somewhat the impacts of unintended shocks on the funds rate and the money supply.

Nevertheless, a total reserves target would probably still create substantially more short-run interest rate volatility than would the nonborrowed reserves target, and the gain in precision of monetary control is unclear. Similarly, it is possible—but not certain—that cyclical swings of interest rates might be reduced through total reserves targeting despite the increase of short-run rate volatility created by greater precision of monetary control. Even if total reserves targeting were to improve monetary control somewhat, many—especially those who do not believe that precise short-run money control is important anyway—would view a qualitative increase in short-run rate volatility as a rather high price to pay for the improvement. Empirical resolution of this issue must await more experience with the present CRR system.

The best way to trace the relationship between CRR and alternative reserves targeting procedures is to employ the graphical analysis of the reserves market developed in Chapter 4. An essential element of the analysis is banks' demand schedule for reserves. Under LRR, that schedule was close to vertical, since required reserves are predetermined, and demand for excess reserves is quite insensitive to interest rates. As illustrated in Chart 6–1, CRR makes the demand schedule somewhat less steeply sloped, since required reserves are no longer predetermined, and the demand for deposits is at least somewhat responsive to interest rates.

As described earlier, a nonborrowed reserves targeting procedure creates a reserves supply schedule that is vertical at the targeted quantity of nonborrowed reserves, and takes a positive slope as the quantity

CHART 6–1
Demand for Reserves: LRR and CRR

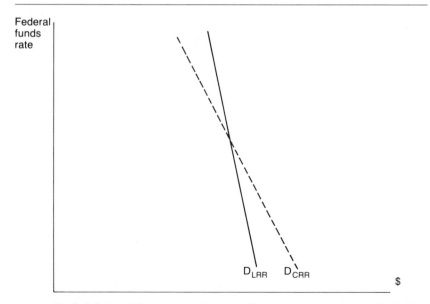

Banks' demand for reserves is somewhat more responsive to the federal funds rate under contemporaneous reserves requirements than it is under lagged reserve requirements.

of borrowed reserves increases. In contrast, a total reserves target maintains discount-window borrowing at zero or minimal amounts by setting the discount rate at a "penalty" level well above the funds rate. As a result, the reserves supply schedule is vertical for all practical purposes and quite unresponsive to interest rates. Chart 6–2 contrasts the two targeting procedures.

When some kind of shock causes the demand for money to increase (decrease), banks' reserves demand schedule shifts to the right (left). In the presence of such a disturbance, interest rates and the actual observed money stock react very differently under the two control procedures. A total reserves target maintains total reserves and the money stock essentially unchanged from their originally targeted levels. That is, of course, the object of precise control of the money stock. All of the impact of the shock is transmitted into interest rates, which rise (fall) sharply, if money demand has increased (decreased).

CHART 6–2
Total Reserves Target

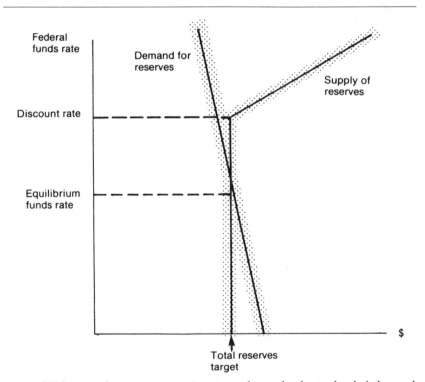

With a total reserves targeting procedure, shocks to banks' demand for reserves are primarily rejected in changes in the funds rate; total reserves usually are maintained equal to nonborrowed reserves.

CHART 6–2 *(concluded)*
Nonborrowed Reserves Target

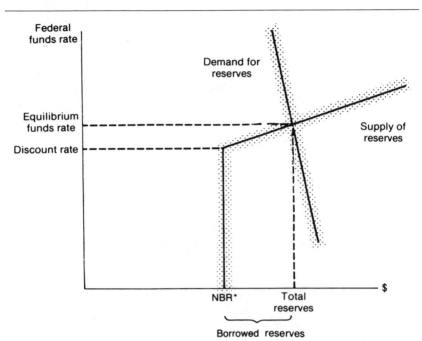

* Path target for nonborrowed reserves (actually path target plus a small, frictional amount of borrowed reserves).

In contrast, with a nonborrowed reserves targeting procedure, shocks to banks' demand for reserves are generally reflected both in changes in the funds rate and in changes in borrowed reserves (and thus total reserves).

In contrast, the nonborrowed reserves procedure divides the shock between the money stock and interest rates. The impact on rates is less than it would be with a total reserves target, while precision of short-run monetary control is reduced.

The relative merits of these two procedures depend entirely on the kind of money demand shocks encountered. For example, if money demand is rising in tandem with an undesirable surge of spending, then the total reserves target assuredly will restrict the expansion more promptly than the nonborrowed reserves target. But if the shocks arise from noise in the money demand relationship itself, from defective seasonal adjustments of the money data, or from some other source essentially unrelated to the strength of spending, then the best policy will completely prevent such shocks from affecting spending. A nonborrowed reserves target does not damp out such shocks completely, but it comes closer to it than a total reserves target does.

However, if instead it is the borrowed reserves relationship that is behaving unpredictably, then conceivably the nonborrowed reserves target might be worse than either a total reserves target or a federal funds rate target. As Chart 6–2 indicates, that is because the borrowing relationship is the main link from reserves to the funds rate in the nonborrowed reserves procedure, while it plays no significant role in the others.

Finally, in the event of an extreme shock to the linkage between money and income, neither approach would be appropriate. Instead, the proper course would be to alter reserve supplies to nullify the shock—precisely what the Fed attempted to do, for example, in 1982 and again in 1983.

The things that matter

Amid all the clamor over operating procedures, some economists, notably James Tobin of Yale University, continued to insist that they were beside the point. In Tobin's view, the money stock is at best an indicator of economic activity, utterly unworthy of all of the fuss. Instead, as Tobin put the point on one occasion, "you should target the things that matter," which in Tobin's view include income, employment, price stability, and so forth. Putting it another way, you should not let a noisy indicator keep you from hearing (and responding to) the call of the ultimate target.[4]

The point is a good one. In general, focusing policy on intermediate targets of whatever stripe can be shown to be inferior to collecting all information available concerning the many determinants of the ultimate target and using all of that information, not just an indicator or two, to guide policy. Only then can policy be said to use information efficiently.

It is clear that the Fed's monetary aggregates targets, and the ancillary nonborrowed reserves targeting procedure, are in themselves woefully inadequate as economic information processors. But judging the issue solely in terms of the utilization of information can be deceptive.

In the first place, the Fed has always insisted on utilizing all possible information. Indeed, the relatively wide range of the targets— 4–8 percent for M1 in 1984, for example—is designed to permit a substantial judgmental input into short-run policy decisions. Moreover, on several occasions the Fed adjusted the targets themselves when doing so seemed appropriate. To a considerable degree, the targets are simply a device for communicating to the public in a general way the Fed's intentions. Though others in the Federal Reserve have often made this point, the central idea was never expressed better than by Volcker himself:

I'm not a disbeliever in all symbolism; in fact, the older I get the more importance I think there is in just conveying a message to the public. You've got to keep things simple in order to affect behavior, without getting caught by the simplicity of what you're saying, and having the real world jump up and bite you.[5]

Thus the aggregates targets communicate to the public the Fed's commitment to a long-term policy of disinflation. They are not now, nor have they ever been, the sole guidepost for policy.

On the other hand, if communication is so important, it is still questionable whether monetary aggregates targets are the best way to go about it. Many in Congress and in the public find it quite difficult to determine with confidence what the implications of a given M1 target are for inflation, for example, and they are far from alone.[6] One possible remedy advanced by Stanford University economist Robert E. Hall, among others, is to set an explicit target for the growth rate of nominal GNP. As Hall puts it:

We need a simple criterion for deciding if monetary policy is too contractionary or too expansionary. The criterion needs to be formulated carefully to take account of everything we know about likely structural changes in the economy. It should be simple. It should be related in an obvious way to the goal of long-run price stability. It should make monetary policy roll with the punch in the short run, so that monetary contraction does not amplify other contractionary or expansionary influences on the economy.[7]

By setting an explicit GNP target, Hall would sidestep completely the vexatious and confusing problems of volatile movements in monetary velocity. Indeed, as Tobin has remarked on more than one occasion, the growth rate of GNP is simply the growth rate of M1 adjusted for changing velocity! A GNP target would be difficult to hit, especially in the short run, but an unambiguous statement of the Fed's disinflation objective would probably help labor, business, and others to plan for the future with more confidence about the price level.

Whatever the merits of such a statement, trying to achieve close control over short-run GNP growth might well make monetary policy a highly destabilizing force in the economy. The reason is that spending decisions are relatively insensitive to interest rates and money growth in the short-run, while their long-run responsiveness is much greater. Consequently, monetary policy would have to swing wildly between short-run stimulus and restraint in the (surely futile) effort to hit short-run GNP targets. Whatever success was achieved would probably be at the cost of long-run economic performance.

Nevertheless, some members of Congress have gone further to suggest additional explicit targets for GNP growth, employment, and so forth on the grounds that formulation of fiscal policy is impeded if the Fed's targets are not consistent with the assumptions of the congressional budget resolution. At face value, this argument has some appeal, since inconsistent assumptions seem certain to produce less than optimal results. However, the real problem with fiscal policy is that over time it has tended to become locked into a stimulative posture, while budget resolutions have been circumvented or ignored completely. Inconsistent monetary policy assumptions are at most only a minor factor contributing to an inappropriate mix of fiscal and monetary policy (more about this in Chapter 9).

There is, however, another dimension to the problem: the perceived need to make the Fed's policy process accountable to Congress. Strictly speaking, accountability has nothing to do with economics. It is a political concept. While the Fed is semi-independent, it is ultimately responsible to Congress for its decisions. And Congress has felt in the past that monetary aggregates targets were a useful way to exercise oversight.

Obviously, it is impossible to hold the Fed accountable for something which it does not control, such as GNP. That is one reason why monetary aggregates are useful. (And the same is true of reserves aggregates, some monetarists might add.) In considering the various possible policy reference points that might serve to facilitate accountability, the aggregates seem altogether superior to the most likely alternative, interest rates. With accountability defined in terms of interest rates, as was by and large the case before the advent of formal, congressionally mandated targets in the 1970s, and to some extent afterwards as well, it did not seem to matter much that the Fed actually did try to look at everything. Policymakers tended to freeze, and typically allowed rates to respond too slowly to emerging economic strains.

Targeting real interest rates

While professional economic opinion is essentially unanimous on the undesirability of targeting nominal interest rates, from time to time a proposal is made to target a real interest rate—i.e., some nominal rate minus a measure of the inflation rate. Usually proponents of such an approach are dismayed with the perceived instability of the linkage between money and spending and seek a way to circumvent both the conceptual and practical problems of monetary targeting. Moreover, they typically profess concern about inflation and want the Fed to maintain real rates at what they take to be distinctly restrictive levels.

The proposal is not altogether far-fetched. For example, had monetary policy focused on maintaining real rates at reasonable levels during 1975–76, instead of allowing them to plunge when M1 growth was sluggish, the ensuing inflation might have been avoided, or in any event would surely have been less troublesome. Nevertheless, while real rates occasionally may serve as a useful indicator of the economic thrust of monetary policy, they are unsuitable as policy targets.

The most obvious problem is that an economically meaningful real interest rate should be computed using the expected rate of inflation. Unfortunately, neither economists nor anyone else seem capable of measuring such expectations reliably. For short-term rates, the problem is not terribly serious, since expectations presumably are close to the observed current rate of inflation. But for real rates on long-term securities—which unfortunately happen to be the rates that are economically most significant—the measurement problem is largely intractable.

Not only that, but it is real, after-tax rates that matter most, and gauging them adds yet another layer of more or less arbitrary assumptions to whatever measure is computed.

Fundamentally, an unobservable variable that is difficult to estimate is peculiarly unsuitable to serve as a monetary policy target. Far from providing a useful policy guidepost or making policy accountable, it would likely have the opposite effect.

Nevertheless, such a measure can be useful in providing a rough test of the consistency of policy with price stability. Sharply negative real rates or real after-tax rates should be, and should have been in the mid-1970s, a warning of an excessively stimulative monetary policy.

Sophisticated credit targets

Credit is, and always has been, an important focus of attention in financial markets and in the Fed. It was only natural, then, that the pronounced difficulties of targeting monetary aggregates should prompt renewed interest in credit as an intermediate target. However, the new advocates of credit targeting have little in common with the availability theorists, who emphasized the special role of bank credit. Nor, for that matter, do they share the mentality of the credit controls program of 1980, which embodied quantitative constraints and guidelines for credit expansion. Almost nobody wants to rerun *that* experiment.

Within the ranks of the Federal Open Market Committee, Boston Fed President Frank E. Morris has been most outspoken in support of a credit target.[8] But easily the most active advocate is Harvard University economist Benjamin M. Friedman. At first blush, that may seem surprising, as Friedman has written extensively in academic journals on the inefficiency, in general, of policy choices that do not utilize all sources of information concerning economic performance. In his view, any intermediate target is inferior to looking at everything, so he logically has little use for monetary aggregates targets, or credit targets, either.

Nevertheless, Friedman has almost singlehandedly inspired discussion of a possible credit target.[9] Two factors seem to lie behind his superficially contradictory position. One is that Friedman's empirical investigations have revealed a previously unsuspected long-run stability in the relationship between credit, defined as the outstanding debt of the nonfinancial sectors, and GNP. For example, the ratio of the net indebtedness of the nonfinancial sectors of the economy to GNP today is just about what it was 60 years ago. While World War II caused a large rise in the ratio, the gradual contraction of federal debt relative to GNP in the ensuing years brought the ratio back to approximately its present level by the early 1960s. Of course, as Chart 6–3 indicates, the ratio has been far from constant in recent years. But the same is also true of monetary velocity. Moreover, Friedman has marshalled extensive empirical support for the proposition that movements in credit have been as closely linked to movements of income as have movements of the monetary and reserves aggregates. Since credit data are readily available, Friedman concludes that the case for using net nonfinancial debt as an intermediate target is as strong as the case for targeting money.[10]

A second consideration that may underlie Friedman's view is a desire to be practical. If looking at everything is impossible in practice, even though desirable in theory, then the sensible second-best approach may be to relax somewhat the rigidity with which policy is implemented through any one intermediate target (or category of targets).

Thus the credit target, as proposed by Friedman, is a supplement to the monetary aggregate target. Together they would constitute the Fed's menu of intermediate targets. That might not be as good as looking at everything, but it would come much closer to it than placing sole reliance on a monetary aggregate. Adding to the practical aspect of the proposal is the fact that the Humphrey-Hawkins Act already enjoins the Fed to set a credit target. In the past, however, the credit target, a proxy measure of total credit extended by banks, was for all practical purposes ignored. Friedman's proposal thus requires no new legislation or regulations.

In early 1983, the Fed went some way toward accepting Friedman's views. Along with the monetary aggregates targets the Fed began to specify a "range of expectation" for Friedman's measure of net debt and indicated that it would monitor its performance.

Some skeptics derided the credit "target" as being akin to a barrage balloon—not a target at all, but a defensive device designed to entangle the enemy. The principal sticking point for many was the fact, which Friedman readily admits, that there is no well-developed

CHART 6–3
Ratio of Net Nonfinancial Debt to GNP

Percent

The ratio of net nonfinancial debt to GNP moved sharply higher in the early 1980s.

theory explaining why credit should be a suitable indicator for policy. In contrast, the theory of money demand, which underlies monetary aggregates targeting, has been years in the making. Friedman counters that if the test of monetary theory is its ability to guide and inform monetary policy, then the instability of monetary velocity in the recent past suggests that the theory and the practice of monetary aggregates targeting could also stand substantial further improvement! Indeed, there is a certain atmosphere of "the pot calling the kettle black" in the debate over alternative intermediate targets.

At this stage, it is too early to say whether Friedman has succeeded in opening the way for a serious credit target. Despite the Fed's apparent willingness to consider the possibility, the performance of net debt in 1982 was not altogether auspicious. Credit velocity, the inverse of the debt ratio, plunged right along with the monetary velocities, so that all of the intermediate targets would have given misleading signals that year. The primary role for a formal credit target, if one is ever adopted, probably will be to encourage the Fed to grope toward looking at everything, to an even greater extent than it already does, rather than to serve as a policy guide in its own right.

Notes

1. The practical reason is that many deposits contained in M2 are subject to very low reserve requirements or none at all, while deposits in M1 are subject to reserve requirements that are both higher and more uniform. Higher and more uniform reserve requirements can contribute to the precision of money stock control, especially when the Fed targets total reserves as monetarists advocate. On a more fundamental level, controlling M2 probably would not be as effective in attaining policy objectives because M2 has displayed relatively little sensitivity to spending growth in recent years. That is not a desirable property in an intermediate target.

2. The reserves multiplier is an identity calculated from reserve requirements that indicates the amount of deposits supported by a given amount of reserves. All other things equal, a smaller (larger) average reserve requirement implies a larger (smaller) multiplier.

3. More precisely, reserves required to be maintained during a week beginning Thursday and ending on Wednesday were calculated on the basis of average end-of-day deposits during a week beginning Wednesday and ending on Tuesday. Hence reserve requirements were only approximately contemporaneous.

4. James Tobin, "Monetary Policy: Rules, Targets, and Shocks," *Journal of Money, Credit and Banking* November 1983, pp. 506–518.

5. Andrew Tobias, "A Talk with Paul Volcker," *New York Times Magazine,* September 19, 1982, p.74.

6. The St. Louis Fed's equation for the implicit GNP deflator, which relates that measure of inflation to past M1 growth plus changes in food and energy prices, began to overforecast the actual inflation rate by progressively larger amounts during 1982–83. By the end of the period, the overprediction was about 5 percent, while actual inflation was under 4 percent.

7. Robert E. Hall, "Macroeconomic Policy Under Structural Change," in *Industrial Change and Public Policy* (Kansas City: Federal Reserve Bank of Kansas City, 1983), p. 102.

8. More precisely, Morris has argued that both credit and total liquid assets would be superior to any of the Ms as targets. See Frank E. Morris, "Do the Monetary Aggregates Have a Future as Targets of Federal Reserve Policy?," Federal Reserve Bank of Boston *New England Economic Review,* March–April 1982, pp. 5–14, and "Defining the Issues," in *Interest Rate Deregulation and Monetary Policy* (San Francisco: Federal Reserve Bank of San Francisco, 1982), pp. 13–19.

9. See Benjamin M. Friedman, "Debt and Economic Activity in the United States," in *The Changing Roles of Debt and Equity in Financing U.S. Capital Formation,* ed. Benjamin

M. Friedman (Chicago: University of Chicago Press, 1982), pp. 91–110, and other works cited therein.

10. Recent research has raised some doubts about this conclusion, however. See Richard D. Porter and Edward K. Offenbacher "Empirical Comparisons of Credit and Monetary Aggregates Using Vector Autoregression Methods," (Richmond: Federal Reserve Bank of Richmond *Economic Review,* November–December, 1983), pp. 16–29.

7

THE RESERVES
MARKET

To most people, the reserves market is nothing specific and concrete. It is a market with no easily recognizable marketplace. And reserves are not the kind of commodity most of us are familiar with. Properly speaking, they are not even securities. To make matters worse, when most economists speak of the reserves market, it is only a theoretical abstraction, a device that allocates reserves among the banks in the banking system, but which has no life of its own and no independent influence on events.

The discussion in earlier chapters was in a similar spirit. There, graphs were used to show where the equilibrium interest rate in the reserves market ought to be. But those were just diagrams, with no people in them. There is nothing really wrong with such a view of the reserves market. Indeed, it is a very convenient way to highlight the main features that might otherwise be obscured by detail.

But there is another way to think about the reserves market, the way Bagehot and many others of kindred spirit would prefer. That is to consider the functioning of the market in its own right, as the daily activity of hundreds (perhaps even thousands) of people. They do their work at the Fed, in the banks, and in the dealer and broker firms that collectively make up the "Street." For them, the reserves market is concrete and real. It can be boring, exciting, and treacherous, sometimes all in one day!

To understand the market, we must first meet the participants and understand who they are, what they are trying to do, and what their problems are. The participants fall into four categories: the Fed, the banks, the securities dealers, and the funds brokers.

The Desk

The Fed, in this context, is most immediately the Open Market Desk at the Federal Reserve Bank of New York.[1] The Desk staff perform several functions. First, staff members prepare estimates of the amount of reserves being provided to the market through channels other than open market operations, in order to gauge the extent to which such supplies meet the market's needs. Informally termed *market factors*, these items are chiefly Federal Reserve float, currency in circulation outside of Federal Reserve Banks, and the Treasury's account at the Federal Reserve banks.[2] The needs consist of reserves required by banks to meet their reserve requirements, as well as a small amount of reserves typically held above and beyond reserve requirements (excess reserves). Though the calculation of supplies and needs is conceptually rather simple, in practice it is quite complex and prone to error.

Other staff members maintain telephone contact with the securities dealer firms with whom the Fed has trading relationships. They collect information concerning fixed-income securities markets—particularly the market for U.S. Government securities—advise the dealers whenever the Fed wants to buy or sell securities, and process the trades.

In this electronic age, the Fed still posts price and yield quotations for securities on one of the few remaining chalk boards on the Street. Offers and bids collected from the dealers in the course of open market operations are sorted and ranked by hand. It is a rather primitive and time-consuming process, but it can be tolerated. After all, though the Fed's trading volume dwarfs that of almost any dealer firm, the Fed rarely trades more than once a day, and often does no trades at all.

The main responsibility of the senior Desk staff is to determine—in consultation with senior staff at the Board, as well as Federal Open Market Committee members, should they become involved—the size and form of any open market operations conducted. However, they perform other functions as well. For example, the Desk is the main contact between the Federal Reserve Board and the Treasury and the securities markets, and the staff monitors developments and relays information to the Board and the Treasury.

One way of collecting information is through brief morning meetings with representatives of the dealer firms. On such occasions, the dealers pass along their interpretations of recent events in the securities markets and their assessments of what will be happening that day and in the near future. In return, the dealers get almost nothing.

Desk officials are very well practiced in keeping their mouths shut concerning recent and near-term Fed policy moves. Such information could be very valuable to a securities dealer, and the staff member who let it out could expect to be relieved of employment as soon as the fact was discovered.

Two other facts about the senior staff members are worth noting. First, almost without exception, they have served at the New York Fed for all of their professional careers, progressing from entry-level jobs to positions of greater and greater authority. Consequently, they have very long memories for past policy decisions, market events, and similar matters. Such a perspective obviously can provide useful guidance for current policy decisions. Second, the environment of the Desk necessarily provides little encouragement to those who thrive on risk taking and who seek the individual visibility and financial rewards that a successful career in the financial markets can offer. The Desk is, after all, the Desk, and it has other priorities. Individuals on the staff whose psychological and intellectual, not to mention financial, needs run in those channels tend to leave the Fed to work at a bank or securities firm after a relatively few years. Thus the Desk has served as the incubator for a rather substantial coterie of financial market professionals.

The banks

While the Desk focuses on the adequacy of reserves supplies for the banking system as a whole, individual banks are concerned only about their own reserve accounts. Because the banks are the center of the payments system, they make and receive transfers of funds every day. Depending on how the inflows and outflows balance out, a bank may end the day with a substantial increase or decrease of funds in its deposit accounts and a corresponding change in its reserve account at the Fed. If the bank is short of funds, it tries to buy what it needs to make up the shortfall. The obvious seller is a bank with an excess of funds. Thus one function of the reserves market—in fact, its original purpose—is to provide a means for banks to adjust their reserve positions to compensate for unexpected inflows and outflows.

That is not, however, the only function. For many banks, especially smaller ones, sales of funds are their primary liquid asset. When they lose deposit balances, they sell fewer funds. When their deposits rise faster than loans and investments, they sell more funds. The opposite side of this behavior are the large, money-center banks that are always net buyers of funds. By standing ready to buy (though not necessarily all the time), they provide a means for smaller banks to hold a highly liquid asset. The result is that the greatest part of net daily transactions in the reserves market—which average about $35 billion—are unrelated to fine-tuning of reserve positions.

Banks operate under a number of constraints in managing their reserve accounts by making purchases or sales of funds. An obvious one is that they must meet their reserve requirements. At present, reserve requirements must be met on a two-week average basis, that is, the average level of a bank's deposits in its reserve account at the Federal Reserve Bank during the two-week reserves maintenance period must at least equal its reserve requirement for that period (subject to a minor exception explained below).

In theory, a bank could meet the reserve requirement by having nothing in its account for 13 days of the period and keeping a balance equal to 14 times the average daily reserve requirement on the last day. By doing so, the bank's average balance would be exactly equal to its average reserve requirement. In practice, however, no bank would ever intentionally manipulate its account in such a fashion. The reason is that if it miscalculated and ended one of the days with a negative balance (or overdraft), the Fed in essence would be lending funds to the bank, a practice that the Fed strongly discourages.[3] Furthermore, if the bank were to run a large excess position early in the period, it might be arithmetically impossible to avoid finishing the period holding average excess reserves without running an overdraft on at least one of the remaining days.

Excess reserves, in themselves, are of no harm to a bank. However, since the Fed allows an excess or deficiency equal to only a small portion of the bank's reserve requirement in the current period to be applied to the next period's reserve requirement, the excess funds may well be useless unless the amount involved is relatively small.[4] And since the Fed pays no interest on reserves, any excess that cannot be applied to the next period deprives the bank of interest income. Consequently, large banks work very hard to keep the balances in their reserve accounts practically identical to their required reserves. The bank's funds trader is primarily responsible for achieving that goal.

Finally, if a bank is short of reserves in its account, it can borrow reserves from the Fed. Funds advanced in this way are simply credited by the Fed to the bank's reserve account. Such borrowings must be backed up with collateral, but that is hardly the major problem from the bank's viewpoint. Much more important is the fact that if a bank is forced to borrow from the Fed for some period of time, other banks and potential depositors will naturally question whether the bank will be able to meet its obligations in the future, and public confidence is absolutely essential to a bank's viability.

If that risk is not sufficiently intimidating, there is always the possibility that, once the bank is beholden to the Fed, the Fed will simply assume effective management of the bank. Such an eventuality, if it occurs, is likely to shorten significantly the tenure in office of the current management, and the stockholders are also likely to find themselves markedly less well off.

Deliberate discount-window borrowing is another matter altogether. For reasons discussed earlier, the discount rate is typically below, sometimes considerably below, the federal funds rate, and therein lies a temptation for banks to lower their average cost of funds by borrowing from the Fed. As long as it does not borrow too often, and as long as its alibi is at least reasonably plausible, a bank has little to fear from the Fed or from the public. When the funds trader undertakes such a maneuver deliberately, he is "arbitraging the Fed."

The dealers

Strictly speaking, securities dealers are not direct participants in the reserves market, since they do not maintain reserve accounts at the Fed as banks do. But in fact, they perform a crucial function in the market. The dealers make money by selling liquidity—i.e., they make it possible for a customer to buy or sell substantial amounts of securities without greatly affecting the price in the market. Obviously, dealers may also make (or lose!) money by speculating that securities prices will rise or fall, but providing liquidity is their key role. And it is liquidity that the Fed needs above all else if it is to be able to conduct its open market operations efficiently. After all, the average size of a Fed transaction is several billion dollars. It takes a highly liquid market to absorb sudden purchases and sales of that magnitude without substantial repercussions.

The link from dealers to the reserves market runs, naturally, through the banks. When the Fed buys securities from a dealer, it transfers funds to the dealer's bank (via the bank's reserve account) to be credited to the dealer's account at the bank. That injects reserves into the banking system, because the bank's reserve account now has a larger balance. Similarly, if the Fed sells securities to a dealer, funds are transferred from the dealer's account at the bank, and the bank's account at the Fed is charged by an equal amount. That drains reserves from the banking system.

Needless to say, dealers do not provide liquidity out of altruism, or if they do, it plays a distinctly minor role. They make money by selling securities for a higher price than they paid for them. Providing liquidity is merely a way to attract customers whose flow of transactions will allow the dealers to profit from the spread of their offer (or selling) price over their bid (or buying) price. Because there are many dealers competing in the government securities market, spreads tend to be very narrow. And when the Fed buys or sells securities, it in effect auctions them. By making the dealers submit secret bids and offers, it assures itself of a competitive price. For dealers, such competition is merely part of the game.

The brokers

A large portion of transactions in the federal funds market are arranged through brokers. The reason is that a purchase or sale of funds is not like buying or selling a commodity; it is actually a loan. And as with any other kind of loan, the lenders are (or try to be) careful with regard to the creditworthiness of borrowers.

In the case of a small bank selling a modest amount of funds to a large money-center bank, the quality of the large bank's credit may be nearly self-evident, and almost any reasonable amount of funds may be borrowed. Similarly, large banks are often willing to lend each other huge sums. (A bank where the author previously was employed once borrowed $600 million overnight from another large bank, but most funds purchases are for much smaller amounts.) In general, however, banks face limitations on the amounts that other banks will lend them. The limit may be zero in some cases.

The broker's job is to match up sellers (or lenders) of funds with buyers (or borrowers) whose creditworthiness is acceptable to them. That allows banks to trade quickly and efficiently. In addition, the brokers provide a central clearinghouse for information concerning who needs money, who has it to lend, and the rates being offered and paid. While a broker will provide interested banks a great deal of information about the market—for example, whether the bid side is stronger than the offer side (suggesting the rate may go up)—he will not reveal the identity of the banks doing the bidding or offering until a trade is completed. That allows the banks a measure of anonymity in conducting their trading.

However, once a trade has been arranged, identities must be revealed so that funds may be transferred between the proper reserve accounts. Consequently, a bank that needs a large amount of funds cannot remain anonymous for long, especially if the market is thin, as it often is in the afternoon, and there are few buyers and sellers.

For bank funds traders, then, funds brokers play a key role. For participants in other financial markets—stocks, bonds, and currencies—the brokers also play a key role, but at some distance. The only contact that most participants in financial markets ever have with a funds broker is the broker's quotation for the funds rate, which is disseminated to a far wider audience than the banks active in the market. The reason, of course, is that for many the funds rate is the most sensitive (if occasionally volatile and treacherous) indicator of monetary policy.

A week in the reserves market

Until February 2, 1984, the reserves market's calendar was divided into "statement weeks" running from Thursday to the following Wednesday. Statement weeks were the units of time during which banks balanced their reserve accounts. In connection with the implementation of contemporaneous reserve requirements, the reserves maintenance period was lengthened to two weeks, running from Thursday through the second Wednesday following. Rather than trying to provide a chronicle of 14 consecutive days in the reserves market, the following account includes only 7. Those 7 days can be thought of as an old statement week or as the second half of the current two-week maintenance period.

Beginning on Thursday, we will follow the market through a fairly typical, though fictional, week. The best way to follow the action is to try to see events through the eyes of the participants in the market. We will do that mainly by looking over the shoulders of an actual funds trader, at an actual money-center bank in New York City. Since it would not be proper to identify him in what is necessarily a stylized account, we will simply call him Larry. While we watch Larry, we will simultaneously observe what other participants in the market are thinking and doing. As will soon become apparent, that gives us a major advantage over Larry in following what is really happening.

Thursday.   At about 8:45 A.M., Larry punches the buttons on the console in front of him that connects him to various funds brokers via direct telephone lines. They tell him that funds will probably open by trading at 9 percent. The market seems to be well bid at that level and well offered at $9\frac{1}{16}$.[5]

Larry swaps a few jokes and some gossip with the brokers as he looks over the sheet of paper that contains various important pieces of information: a very rough projection of his deposits and required reserves, the size of any excess or deficiency he is carrying into the maintenance period, and the amount of funds the Treasury is withdrawing that day from its Tax and Loan Account at Larry's bank. He also notes the amount of reserve need that he wants to cover that day with deposits in his reserve account.

Like other large banks, he wants to run a deficit over the weekend so as to minimize any chance that he might be unable to work off an excess reserve position on a day after the weekend. Most of the sheet contains blank lines at this point. In much of the space he will write in the names of institutions from which he has bought funds and the amounts bought, the names of banks to which he has sold funds, and the names and amounts of any loans to securities dealers.

Working with Larry is the bank's repurchase agreement (RP) trader, who is responsible for securing funds for the bank by borrowing against collateral in the form of securities owned by the bank. Since the amount of securities collateral available usually does not change much from one day to the next, Larry also has a good idea of the amount of funds that will come in through this channel. If the bank is issuing (or "writing") certificates of deposit or raising funds in the Eurodollar market, Larry will take account of those sources as well. Looking over the sheet, Larry calculates that purchases of about $400 million of funds in the broker market ought to put him where he wants to be. It is not a large amount for a money-center bank, so what's the hurry?

It is now 9:00 A.M., and very few trades have been arranged by the brokers. They are bored.

(One broker firm of the author's acquaintance has two means, at least, for dealing with such periods of inactivity. One is an exotic pet tarantula kept in a terrarium. Tarantulas only eat about once a week, so on slow Thursday mornings, the brokers feed the tarantula crickets, especially purchased for this purpose at a pet store. Surely, by the time the last cricket has met his fate, the market will be up and flying. No? Then there is another form of entertainment. The brokers have an aquarium with a removable partition in the middle. On either side are two types of fish that hate each other. When the bored broker pulls out the partition, they immediately attack each other and fight with a frenzy. When the market starts to pick up, the partition is replaced, and the fish are distributed to their proper sides with a small net. Some might regard that aquarium as an allegory on the funds market!)

By this time, Larry has had a brief conversation with his bank's "Fedwatcher," an economist who specializes in predicting and analyzing Fed policy moves as well as routine open market operations. The Fed-watcher reminded Larry that the Fed has a moderate size reserve adding job, about $2–3 billion, to do during the next several days, suggesting that the Fed will do RPs before the weekend, possibly as early as today. Until the job is done, funds are likely to be firmly bid. Larry is also told by the brokers that just about everybody else they have talked to is also looking for the RPs, though there is disagreement as to whether they will come on Thursday or Friday.

It is now time to get started on the day's activity, and Larry puts in his bid at 9 percent. At this stage, he is satisfied to try to wait until the offer side comes to him. After a half hour, he has not done much. Some smaller correspondent banks have called in to sell him modest amounts of funds, which because of the small sizes, he stands ready to buy at a rate ⅛ percent under the market bid rate. He has not gotten much in the broker market, as the offer side is in no hurry either. At last, at about 9:30 A.M., the trades begin to flow— at 9 percent. On the video screens diligently monitored by thousands of financial market participants, the funds broker's quotation reads:

BID	9	OPEN	9
ASK	9 1/16	LOW	9
LAST	9	HIGH	9

Larry shouts to other securities traders in the room with him, "Nine to the sixteenth, trading at nine!"

As the morning progresses, Larry is well on the way to rounding out what he *thinks* is his need for funds. He believes the market is short of money—that it needs the RPs—but that it is not terribly short. He sees little reason to insure against higher rates by covering his position aggressively now or to wait and cover it later in the day when rates might be lower. As the clock approaches 11:40 A.M., activity in the securities markets slackens, as traders wait to see whether the Fed will enter the market as expected. By noon, the Fed still has not come in, and that's it: no RPs. The market reaction is almost nil; after all, the RPs will probably come in tomorrow. Larry and his Fedwatcher are not concerned.

Meanwhile, projections prepared independently by the staffs of the New York Fed and the Board both suggest a modest need to add reserves. Since the amount is not large, there will probably be no harm in deferring the operation until Friday, and there could be a benefit. By Friday morning, the projections will have been revised, so that it should be possible to fix the size of the RPs with more precision than if they were arranged on Thursday. The only harm that could be done by this approach would be to put upward pressure on the funds rate, but the funds market seems to be trading solidly at 9 percent. Thus the market appears to confirm the qualitative character of the staff projections. In the daily 11:15 A.M. telephone conference call between senior Desk staff, senior staff at the Board, and one of the bank presidents currently serving on the FOMC, the decision is made to stay out of the market.

At 4:30 P.M., the Fed releases data on M1 and various reserves measures. The numbers are about as expected, so interest rates are little changed.

Later in the evening, a couple of New York City banks get caught short of reserves and bid up the funds rate to 9⅜ percent as they seek to cover themselves. Larry, amazingly enough, ends up just about where he wanted to be and parts with only small amounts. He would like to sell more, so as to profit from the funds he bought at 9 percent, but his first responsibility is to square up his position. After all, a gain of ⅜ percent overnight means that he would make only a bit more than 10 dollars per million dollars sold. From Larry's perspective, that is not much incentive, particularly when his trading instincts are making him wonder whether there might just be a reason for the firmness of the funds rate

Friday. The funds market opens shortly before 9:00 A.M., trading actively. There is good reason. On this one day, funds traders are covering their positions for $\frac{3}{14}$ of the maintenance period. There is no time to lose. The broker screen shows:

BID	9	OPEN	9
ASK	9 1/16	HIGH	9
LAST	9	LOW	9

It looks like a carbon copy of yesterday morning's market. Market participants are still looking for RPs from the Fed.

Early in the morning, the reserves forecasters at the Board and the New York Fed were informed of several operational difficulties encountered the previous evening by the Fed's check-clearing division. It seems fairly clear that the problems are going to increase the level of Federal Reserve float, thus adding reserves to the banking system. Unfortunately, it is impossible to know precisely, at this point, how large the injection is going to be. The forecasters make what seems like a good guess.

It now appears that the market's need for reserves is either zero or negligible. Once the senior staff of the Desk are informed of the changed outlook for reserves supplies, a consensus quickly forms in favor of staying out of the market today, and the decision is ratified in the conference call. To provide reserves through RPs, as seemed necessary only yesterday, might create an excess, forcing the funds rate sharply down and perhaps creating misleading impressions of a change in the Fed's policy stance. In view of the new situation, it seems clear that refraining from entering the market on Thursday was prudent. It is hoped that doing the same thing on Friday will be equally prudent. In any event, the funds market is giving no indication of a serious shortage of reserves.

Funds continue to trade at 9 percent through the morning, but as "Fed time" draws nearer, the funds traders grow increasingly nervous. Where are the RPs? What's going on? At 11:48 A.M., with no sign of the Fed, Larry does not like the looks of it. He shouts to the other traders around him, "Going higher!" He should know, since he and his assistant are in process of taking money currently being offered at $9\frac{1}{16}$ percent. An instant later the video screens are showing:

BID	9 1/8	OPEN	9
ASK	9 1/4	HIGH	9 1/8
LAST	9 1/8	LOW	9

Larry's problem is that he needs to buy another $200 million for Friday, while he expects to need to buy about $1.2 billion on Monday. He tries to get a forward market going for Monday, i.e., to arrange trades today for actual execution on Monday. If he can get money that way, he will have a leg up on his Monday job. And not so incidentally, he will lock in what now seems to him to be an attractive funds rate. The brokers contact sources that might be interested: no dice. The offer side lacks conviction. Maybe the funds rate really is moving higher, in which case they might stand to lose by selling funds forward for Monday.

Nervousness is not confined to the funds market. In the Treasury securities market, rates increase slightly. Dealers, once confident that the Fed was holding its policy stance unchanged, now are unsure. Traders in that market as well as other markets rapidly check the screens displaying prices in the futures markets for Treasury bills and bonds. Because futures contracts are traded on exchanges, price reactions are much more visible and easily quantified than in the cash markets. Sure enough, the futures markets are reacting to the new situation, and traders in the cash markets rapidly get their quotations into line. By early afternoon, funds have traded up a quarter of a percent from their opening level; reaction in other markets has been limited to a few basis points.

Monday. On Monday morning, it is clear to the Fed's reserves forecasters that Friday's guess was wrong: float provided much less reserves than projected. Moreover, that miss has been compounded by the fact that borrowing by banks from the discount window was less than had been expected, despite the firmness of the funds rate. Since these errors occurred on a Friday, their impact on average reserves availability for the maintenance period was magnified, and the banking system is now seriously short of reserves.

The senior staff of the Desk and the Board take the news of this situation in stride. The same kind of problem has occurred hundreds of times before, and it is obvious that the reserves can be provided by doing overnight RPs today. Unless something happens to throw the reserves forecast farther off the mark, that should be all that is needed to put the market in balance for the rest of the maintenance period.

his position is. By about noon he is done. Now begins the wait for the close.

Larry cannot say with precision what his funds needs are because late transfers in and out of his reserve account may push him into a surplus or deficit at the end of the day. That can happen any day, of course, but today is special. It is the last day of the maintenance period, and (beyond his modest allowable carry-in, equal to about $100 million) any deficiencies must be covered, while any excesses must be sold immediately or lost forever.

At about 4:00 in the afternoon, Larry begins to get information concerning the flow of transfers. So far, so good: the account is about in balance. Other banks are having worse luck. A couple of large New York banks are bidding aggressively for funds, probably to cover large deficiencies that might force them into the window.

Larry hits no bids, because he does not want to force himself out of balance. Then at about 5:45 P.M.—miracle of miracles!—because of several large payments just received in his account, he's got $400 million to go (i.e., available to sell)! Funds are bid at 10 percent, offered at 10½. Larry quickly hits a couple of bids for a total of $150 million. He now knows—or thinks he knows—who needs money tonight. Unfortunately, the banks on the bid side also know who has money—Larry. They accordingly drop their bids to 9 percent almost immediately. Thus begins a colossal poker game. "I'm all out," Larry tells the brokers.

The reality, of course, is that his reserve account is not even: he is still $250 million long. But they don't know that. After about 30 nervous minutes, the bid is back at 10 percent. Larry unloads $200 million to one bank at that rate, then quickly hits another bid at 9½ for the remaining $50 million. This time, he *is* out. In the few minutes remaining before the close at 6:30, the rate sinks to 8 percent.

The markets routinely ignore this kind of Wednesday rate volatility. But was there a message this time? Fedwatchers will glean some of the answers the following day when they sort through the data on reserves availability in the Fed's afternoon data release. But by then the next maintenance period will already be underway. All Larry can be sure about at this point is that the average rate on his net funds purchases—that is, his purchases less his sales—was 15 basis points below the weekly average in the funds market. The way funds traders keep score, he came out ahead.

What's going on here?

Before leaving our tour of the reserves market, let's reflect for a moment on what we saw. We witnessed a superefficient market capable of handling billions of dollars of transactions per day, with relatively few glitches. Sometimes it is easy to lose sight of that fact amid the volatility and confusion. Nevertheless, the market has some problems, of which two stand out.

One is the pronounced nervousness in financial markets concerning the funds rate. To many, the funds rate is quite simply the cutting edge of monetary policy. But with the Fed controlling the rate less tightly than it did prior to October 6, 1979, it is easy to become confused about the direction of policy. That is a problem for the securities dealers most of all, since their high leverage makes them quite vulnerable to being left behind in the race to anticipate near-term interest-rate movements. But more generally, it is a problem for anyone for whom near-term interest-rate trends are a significant part of the economic environment.

Another striking feature of the funds market is the way the Fed systematically withholds information that might potentially reduce the day-to-day volatility of the funds rate and make other money market rates less erratic. Of course, under the Fed's current operating procedures, there will always be some ineradicable uncertainty concerning just where the funds rate should be trading. For one thing, as we saw in Chapter 6, the relationship between borrowing by banks from the discount window and the spread of the funds rate over the discount rate is variable and imprecise. Short of changing the operating procedures, the Fed cannot do much about that.

Nevertheless, much could be done to improve the situation. The funds market labors under significant uncertainty concerning reserves supplies and the degree to which they are being affected by factors only the Fed has (sometimes incomplete) knowledge about. When policy is changing, it is obviously appropriate for interest rates to respond. It is unfortunate when they react because of a lack of information about float or some similar influence on the availability of reserves.

The author, who has pondered these things for some time, has at length come to the conclusion that withholding information serves only three purposes. One is that it allows the Fed to distance itself from the hurly-burly of the reserves market, and to maintain the fiction that the market, not the Fed, is primarily responsible for the level of the funds rate. It is easy to see that keeping a low profile in the funds market has political advantages for the Fed, and perhaps also for anyone who values an independent monetary policy.

Second, it contributes mightily to the self-esteem of the Desk personnel, for they—and only they—are the vessels of knowledge in the reserves market. Third, it ensures reasonably secure employment and comfortable remuneration for quite a few Fedwatchers, much of whose imperfect information and analysis would be promptly displaced by free, high-quality information. It remains for the reader to form an opinion as to the merit of these considerations.

Notes

1. Space limitations do not permit a detailed description of the hour-by-hour routine of Desk operations. For such a description, the reader is referred to Paul Meek, *U.S. Monetary Policy and Financial Markets* (New York: Federal Reserve Bank of New York, 1982).

2. Federal Reserve float can be created when the Fed, in the process of collecting checks presented to it by one bank for collection from another, credits the reserve account of the first bank before it can post an offsetting charge to the other bank's reserve account. This often occurs when bad weather conditions disrupt the air couriers that serve the Fed's check transit system. Float can also be created—or actually made negative!—by breakdowns in the Fed's wire transfer system; the precise impact depends on whether credits or debits are most affected. In general, anything that causes the posting of credits and debits to be *asynchronous* causes a change in Federal Reserve float.

Currency in circulation affects banks' reserve accounts because the Fed charges the reserve accounts of banks to whom it supplies currency and credits the accounts of banks turning it in to the Fed. Banks' holdings of currency in their vaults may be counted toward meeting their reserve requirements, but only in a period subsequent to the period in which it is held. Consequently, an increase in currency in circulation reduces the availability of reserves to banks.

The effect of payments to and from the Treasury's account at the Federal Reserve Banks is similar. Payments to the Treasury's account cause debits to be charged against banks' reserve accounts, thus reducing the availability of reserves.

3. Recently the Fed has gone even further and has discouraged banks from allowing overdrafts to develop in their reserves accounts *during* a business day.

4. To facilitate the introduction of contemporaneous reserve requirements, the Fed provided that for six months following the start-up in February 1984, the "carryover" percentage would be 3 percent; for six months after that $2\frac{1}{2}$ percent; and afterward 2 percent.

5. Federal funds were routinely quoted in sixteenths through Friday, October 5, 1979. After that, the turmoil in the funds market caused spreads to widen to eighths or larger fractions. Finally, late in 1983, the market resumed quoting in sixteenths most of the time.

6. If the reader should be in a similar condition, kindly consult the appendix.

8

WATCHING THE FED

The extraordinary attention that investors accord the Federal Reserve reflects the key role the Fed plays in determination of economic policy. More than anything else, what sets the Fed apart from other agencies charged with formulating the nation's economic policy is *suspense*.

Though fiscal policy is ultimately just as important to economic performance as monetary policy, it is the product of a long process of congressional deliberation and administrative implementation. Investors and others have plenty of time to form an appraisal of fiscal policy, which thus holds little mystery and almost no suspense, even if its ultimate economic consequences may be uncertain.

In contrast, monetary policy has a large discretionary element. It can change significantly almost overnight, as it did in the Saturday Night Special. Under these circumstances, it is hardly remarkable that a disproportionate sense of mystery and suspense surrounds the Fed.

The financial markets' absorption in the details and nuances of Fed behavior is never so much in evidence as when the chairman testifies at the monetary policy oversight hearings held twice a year, as required by the Humphrey-Hawkins Act. Testimony usually begins at about 9:00 A.M., but two or three hours earlier, professional Fed-watchers and all manner of other interested persons will have lined up outside the hearing room in order to assure themselves an opportunity to listen to the nuances of the testimony itself, together with the repartee of the question-and-answer session, a performance that easily can last several hours. It is not at all uncommon for 100 to

200 spectators, in addition to a couple of dozen members of the press, to be jammed into the hearing room. No other hearings on Capitol Hill come anywhere close to that attendance.[1] While some have compared the occasion unfavorably to a circus—no doubt in part because most circuses provide better seating arrangements for their spectators— the spectacle and clamor are merely a pale reflection of the intensity with which many investors and others are watching the Fed.

And many have a very difficult time indeed trying to form a judgment concerning the Fed's policy stance. The difficulty was well illustrated by the following exchange between Chairman Volcker and a questioner at a meeting of the National Council of Savings Institutions on December 5, 1983:

> Q: Mr. Chairman, you mentioned turbulence in the financial markets. I think some of the turbulence may be due to market perceptions of Fed policy. In recent weeks in the newspapers I've read that many experts have concluded the Fed has increased the degree of restraint based on the reserves numbers published by your institution. However, during the same weeks the federal funds rate has actually been softer than in preceding weeks. As market observers, should we focus more on the funds rate, bank reserves positions, or kind of a combination of both in assessing the degree of restraint? [laughter]
>
> A: Well, we look at a variety of things. [laughter] Perhaps the intelligent observer is forced to as well. I would like to think that it's reasonably apparent that there have not been any major changes in posture. But when I—you know, part of the difficulty here, if I may just amplify a bit, is there are so many measures of what is ease or tightness, and different people of different analytic or theoretical persuasions will use different measures. The money supply has been relatively calm in recent months. It hasn't been growing very rapidly. Some people think that's the equivalent of tightness. As you note, some interest rates may have come down a little bit. And that's the immediate measure for some people. That's the be-all and end-all: which way are interest rates going? And then there's a measure, which has some operational significance, of how much pressure is being put on bank reserves positions. So I think you have to look at all these things, and you have to make your semantics pretty clear, if you're reporting something, as to which measure you're talking about and what the significance of that is. [silence, then laughter][2]

While almost everyone who has anything to do with financial markets is necessarily interested in Federal Reserve policy, relatively few have any need for the kind of analysis provided by professional Fedwatchers. Despite enormous differences in the quality of analysis they provide, Fedwatchers in general are sensitive monitors of the nuances of monetary policy, and they routinely forecast such minutiae as the Fed's daily open market operations and changes in the monetary aggregates.

Actual open market operations, for example, are compared to projections in order to divine whether a policy change is in process. Such information is quite valuable to highly leveraged securities trading firms, which stand to gain or lose substantial sums on modest changes in interest rates. In contrast, most individuals can well afford to follow events at a more relaxed pace.

The biggest part of the job, after all, is not the minutiae of open market operations. Rather it is understanding what economists term the Fed's *reaction function*—the way monetary policy responds to various economic events. Behavior of the monetary aggregates is obviously a major determinant of policy responses, but the aggregates are far from the whole story. On numerous occasions in the past, the Fed has temporarily disregarded the aggregates when their behavior seemed inconsistent with the economy's real growth and price performance. Hence one wants to obtain a sense of the Fed's priorities among economic objectives, as well as its appraisal of current economic developments. That is the main reason why so many people crowd into the hearing room when the chairman testifies. Few, if any, would express it this way, but they are refining their estimates of the Fed's reaction function.

Occasionally even the best Fedwatchers will fail to anticipate the next policy move. When that happens, it is important to be able to recognize the error and to learn as quickly as possible just what is under way. Analysis of reserves positions and open market operations can sometimes be helpful in doing this. But quite a bit can be learned by monitoring several relatively straightforward indicators.

Following the reserves market

Since the immediate locus of Federal Reserve policy is the reserves market, that is a logical starting place for anyone seeking to do his or her own Fedwatching. Unfortunately, as the preceding chapter presumably has made clear, the reserves market is a strange place, and the federal funds rate in particular is subject to all manner of distortions that may be wholly unrelated to the stance of monetary policy. A disruption of the payments system, such as figured in the previous chapter's narrative, is one illustration.

Another is the significant upward pressure on the funds rate that often occurs around quarter-end statement dates, as banks for various reasons attempt to hold larger than normal amounts of excess reserves, thus lifting overall reserves demands. In the past, the Fed typically accommodated such demands by providing extra reserves, but recently the Fed has refrained from doing so, for the most part, and has been willing to tolerate the resulting temporary upward pressure on the funds rate. For example, on the last business days of 1982 and 1983, the funds rate was about 1–2 percent higher than it was a week earlier and a week later. Similar, though generally less extreme, pressure occurred on other quarter-end dates during those two years. Notwithstanding the predictability of these events, a number of market participants sometimes jump to the mistaken conclusion that the Fed is beginning to tighten the monetary policy screws. Such errors are all the more unfortunate for being avoidable.

As noted in Chapter 4, under the operating procedures in effect, with modifications, since late 1979, the key link between the Fed and the federal funds rate is the amount of reserves that the banks must borrow from the Fed's discount window. Consequently, the best single indicator of the degree of pressure the Fed is putting on the reserves market is the amount of borrowed reserves—i.e., "adjustment" borrowings.

Many analysts are divided on the merits of focusing attention on borrowed reserves or net borrowed reserves. The latter is simply borrowed reserves minus excess reserves. Since the level of excess reserves is typically relatively modest, looking at one is often just as good as looking at the other.

However, borrowed reserves does have the advantage of being released to the public on a weekly basis, whereas excess reserves and net borrowed reserves are released only every other week following the end of a two-week reserves maintenance period. Unfortunately, that advantage may be more apparent than real, as early experience with the system of two-week maintenance periods suggests that the distribution of discount-window borrowings during the two weeks is rather erratic. The average for the period as a whole may be more meaningful.

Conceptually, the level of net borrowed reserves is simply the arithmetic difference between the amount of reserves which banks must have (in the form of required reserves) and the amount which the Fed is willing to supply (in the form of nonborrowed reserves). Many find that relationship easy to keep in mind.

Moreover, some kinds of distortions affect net borrowed reserves less than they do the borrowed reserves figure. For example, an interruption of the payments system that prevents banks from controlling their reserves positions accurately will produce a larger than normal amount of excess reserves that are effectively unavailable for sale in the funds market. The funds are unavailable simply because banks are not aware of their true reserves positions. Otherwise, they would sell any excess funds so as not to lose interest income.

As a result of the reduced effective supply to the funds market, some banks will be forced to cover their positions by borrowing from the discount window. The result will be increased levels of both borrowed reserves and excess reserves. But since the increases in those two items will tend to offset each other, net borrowed reserves will be little affected. Consequently, in such a situation—termed a "poor distribution of reserves" by funds market professionals—net borrowed reserves is less likely to produce a misleading signal of a policy change than is borrowed reserves alone.

Nevertheless, it is possible to rely too much on net borrowed reserves. For example, early in 1983, excess reserves positions were temporarily enlarged as a result of the difficulties that many banks experienced in coping with the reduced levels of reserve requirements provided by the Garn-St. Germain Act. The same thing happened following the introduction of contemporaneous reserve requirements in February 1984. In both cases, the Fed was well aware of the distortions and accommodated the increased demand for reserves. The result was that borrowed reserves remained at nominal levels while excess reserves ballooned, thus creating a substantial net free reserves (i.e., negative net borrowed reserves) position. In the former instance, quite a few analysts mistakenly interpreted that development as an indication that the Fed was "pumping" the reserves market in advance of a contemplated discount rate cut (more on pumping below). Money market rates declined sharply, only to rebound in a few weeks as the error became apparent.

The moral in all this is that a change in borrowing pressure is not a perfectly reliable signal of a shift in policy. In general, a policy shift is indicated when a substantial change in borrowed reserves is unaccompanied by distortions in the reserves market. Even then, however, it is possible to go awry, as the author can attest from personal experience. Nevertheless, (net) borrowed reserves is usually the best indicator of the degree of pressure that the Fed is putting on the reserves market.

Once a change in borrowing pressure sets in, the new level tends to persist for a while. The Fed typically does not change course quickly, despite the more or less automatic adjustments produced in principle—though not always in practice—by the nonborrowed reserves targeting procedures.[3] Even so, divining the funds rate likely to be associated with any given level of borrowing is a tricky matter. There are basically two reasons for that. One is that borrowed reserves really are not uniform; the other is that the relation between borrowing (however defined) and the funds rate is itself rather hard to pin down.

Who does the borrowing matters a great deal. Small banks, which for all practical purposes do not have access to the funds market, borrow, if at all, for days at a time, and the impact of such borrowing on the funds market is likely to be quite modest. In contrast, large money-market banks typically will bid aggressively for funds before they are forced into the window. This problem of interpretation primarily affects low levels of borrowing—e.g., a weekly average of \$300 to 500 million or less—when borrowing by smaller institutions is generally large relative to the total.

Similarly, there is always some residual, "frictional" borrowing. For example, in recent years, borrowing has never dropped to zero during a statement week even when the Fed was aggressively injecting reserves, as in the spring of 1980. Such irreducible, frictional borrowing has no implications for the funds rate. In terms of the graphical description of the reserves market employed in Chapters 4 and 6, an irreducible minimum level of frictional borrowing simply shifts the interest-sensitive portion of the reserves supply schedule to the right.[4]

Most investigators have concluded that borrowed reserves must rise to a weekly average level of \$300–500 million before any very significant impact on the funds rate occurs. Levels below that amount are of little relevance. Consequently, a movement of borrowing above that frictional level takes on special significance for money-market interest rates.

As mentioned earlier, a tightening of reserves availability can proceed almost automatically (provided, of course, that the Fed so wills) under the nonborrowed reserves targeting procedures, as banks' deposit expansion causes their required reserves to outpace the growth of nonborrowed reserves, thus forcing borrowing to rise.[5]

An easing of reserves pressure can operate in much the same way, as a slowing growth of required reserves closes the gap between it and nonborrowed reserves. But in that case, there obviously is a limit to the automaticity of the procedures. When borrowing pressure is essentially nil, any further expansion of nonborrowed reserves relative to required reserves would primarily enlarge excess reserves. At some point, the discount rate would lose all influence on the funds rate, thus setting the stage (as described in Chapter 4) for a pell-mell plunge of the funds rate. Since the Fed—despite its affinity for the nonborrowed reserves targeting procedures—is not going to allow *that* to happen, some borrowing pressure will be maintained in order to preserve the relevance of the discount rate, while further moves to ease policy will take the form of discount rate reductions.

As a result, once borrowing pressure is essentially nil, as it was, for instance, during early 1983, tracking reserves positions is almost superfluous; the discount rate occupies center stage.

Well, then, how does one know when the discount rate is about to be changed? Obviously, one doesn't. But if, for example, repeated increases in borrowing pressure have not produced a slowdown in growth of the monetary aggregates, it is a better than fair bet that the Fed will move to reinforce the impact of borrowing pressure with one or more discount rate hikes. Similarly, slow monetary growth, or perhaps more accurately, poor economic performance, relative to target prepares the ground for discount rate cuts, especially when borrowing pressure has declined so far already as to leave no other alternative.

In addition, one of the Fed's more peculiar behavioral traits may also help to signal an imminent discount rate cut. Frequently, discount rate cuts have been preceded by a sharp decline in the funds rate caused by an extra-hearty injection of reserves. Fedwatchers and quite a few other financial market professionals call that process pumping the funds rate. The buildup of excess reserves is merely temporary, typically being mopped up by the end of the reserves maintenance period. Its only purpose is to allow the Fed to state, in a press release announcing the cut, that the action was taken "in order to bring the discount rate more into line with other market rates"—or some such boilerplate. Doing this allows the Fed to maintain the fiction that it actually exercises little control over interest rates, even in the short run. From the political standpoint, that may well be a highly convenient ruse. Nevertheless, in the words of one thoughtful observer of the process, it does constitute something of a "shortfall of candor."

Actually, there was a time when the boilerplate in the press release was literally true. When the Fed was targeting the funds rate, any change in the discount rate, unless undertaken for some more or less inscrutable symbolic purpose, served merely to allocate reserves provision between the discount window and open market operations, with no significant impact on the level of money market interest rates. But just as funds rate targeting in the old days was substantially different from the current operating procedures, discount rate policy (press releases to the contrary notwithstanding!) now proceeds in an altogether different fashion.

The shortfall of candor would not matter much were it not for the fact that some persons, even financial market professionals, do become confused. An excellent example occurred in December 1982. The Fed apparently intended to pump the funds rate as it had prior to previous discount rate cuts that year, but for some reason the rate remained firm. Nevertheless, the Fed went ahead with the cut, merely changing the wording of the press release slightly.[6] The result? Some Fedwatchers thought the Fed's policy stance was becoming palpably more aggressive, so much so, in fact, that they began to be concerned about a 1970s-style reflation. Yields on Treasury bonds rose by about 10–15 basis points, and several days passed before the markets regained their composure.

Other ways of watching

While many people are interested in monetary policy, few would find themselves capable of sustained interest in the reserves market. Probably the proper analogy is with B-grade movies. Almost everyone has seen them from time to time, and quite likely enjoyed some of them, but no one (except possibly someone so obsessed as a Fedwatcher or a securities trader) would watch such fare all the time. Fortunately, other means of gauging monetary policy exist that are appropriate for a more long-run (and more sedate) focus. Unfortunately, to antici- pate the story a bit, they are not always simple to apply.

Perhaps the most obvious approach is to track the monetary aggregates, especially M1, the transactions aggregate to which the Fed typically, but by no means always, has accorded most weight in formu- lating policy. But there are major pitfalls in making comparisons be- tween the actual weekly M1 data and the Fed's announced target range for the aggregate. On the narrowly technical level, as Chapter 5 pointed out, the weekly data are subject to substantial distortions due to inade- quate seasonal adjustment procedures. The Fed is often well aware of these problems, as are most Fedwatchers, but it is difficult for anyone not familiar with the pattern of seasonal distortions in the monetary data to filter the weekly numbers reliably.

Consequently, the layman's best recourse is to follow M1, if at all, only as an average over some period of time, for example, six months to a year. That long a span significantly reduces the "noise" component in the numbers. Unfortunately, it also diminishes whatever value the M1 data might have as an early-warning indicator of emerging economic developments.

On a more fundamental level, tracking money growth can give a misleading indication of the degree of restrictiveness of Fed policy if conventional monetary relationships are undergoing a significant change. For example, during the mid-1970s, the Fed pursued an ex- tremely expansionary policy, even though M1 growth was quite slug- gish. At the time, velocity was growing far faster than its trend rate. No one knows for sure the reasons for that event—Chapter 5 provided some suggestions—but whatever its source, the result was to make M1 a temporarily unreliable guide to the economic consequences of monetary policy.

More recently, the same thing happened again, in reverse. Begin- ning in late 1981, M1 velocity plunged at a rate wholly unprecedented in the postwar period, and as of this writing (spring 1984), there is no solid indication that it will return to its trend growth rate anytime soon. The result of the velocity plunge was that relatively rapid M1 growth appeared considerably more stimulative than it actually was.

Faced with such a formidable set of problems, some analysts recommend tracking the growth rate of some reserves aggregate such as nonborrowed reserves or the monetary base (defined as bank reserves plus currency in the hands of the public). But that is only a superficial solution to the problem. If aberrant velocity movements are occurring, and the Fed attempts to adjust its policy instruments to take those movements into account, then the growth of reserves—which are linked to deposits via reserve requirements—will be just as misleading an indicator of the restrictiveness of policy as that of M1 itself. Moreover, seasonal adjustment of reserves data is even more difficult, and thus less reliable, than adjustment of deposit data, though that fact is not generally recognized. Finally, a reserves aggregate such as the monetary base (approximately three-fourths of which consists of currency) has no central role in the Fed's operating procedures. If one must track a reserves aggregate at all, borrowed reserves is probably superior.

However, the day may come when that last statement will not be true. For example, if the Fed were to adopt a total reserves targeting procedure, as many monetarists advocate, growth of reserves would be much more tightly linked to the targeted growth of M1, while discount-window borrowing would be minuscule and of little significance. Even so, erratic velocity behavior would then pose just as much a problem for interpretation of policy as it does now.

It appears that our efforts to uncover a reasonably reliable aggregate measure of the thrust of monetary policy have produced a rather meager result. Wherever one turns, it seems, problems of interpretation crop up. While ignoring those problems (as some analysts do from time to time) has the attraction of simplicity, analytical techniques that are both simple and wrong leave a great deal to be desired.

Fortunately, there is another, relatively straightforward measure which, though not without its own pitfalls, can provide some indication of long-run implications of monetary policy—levels of real, after-tax interest rates.

As explained in Chapter 6, there are significant theoretical and practical obstacles to using real rates as a policy target, but that does not mean that they cannot provide a useful reference point in assessing the restrictiveness of monetary policy. Intuitively, if real rates are high relative to historical experience, then there exists a premium in favor of saving rather than spending, and economic activity will tend to be retarded. If real rates are very low, the opposite will tend to be true.

Now for the pitfalls. Obviously, the real, after-tax interest rate consistent with noninflationary economic growth is not constant, but depends on the degree of strength of those portions of aggregate demand that are relatively insensitive to interest rates. Included are government expenditures, many kinds of consumption spending, and (in the short run), business investment in inventories. For example, government spending provided relatively little stimulus to the economy during the decade following the Korean War, allowing quite small (by the standards of recent years) changes of interest rates to have large impacts on the pace of economic activity. Beyond a doubt, much higher real rates are required today to achieve similar impacts. (This issue is explored further in the next chapter.)

In addition, there is a large selection of interest rates to choose from. Most economists feel that long-term interest rates have a greater impact on spending decisions than do short-term rates. However, there is no very reliable technique available for independently estimating the inflation rate expected to prevail during the next several decades. The problem is vastly simpler for short-term interest rates. For them, a relatively short-run inflation estimate is sufficient to gauge their real returns. As a practical matter, no great harm is done by comparing rates on money-market instruments with current inflation rates.[7] Ironically, then, the interest rates that matter most—expected real long-term rates—are the most difficult to estimate, while those that matter least—expected real short-term rates—are the most easily quantified.

The next problem is to adjust for taxes. The adjustment is necessary because expected *after-tax* interest rates are what actually affect spending decisions. Unfortunately, determining the proper tax rate to use is even more difficult than estimating the inflation rate. For example, a business firm earning little or no profits may be paying no taxes and thus may not benefit from the tax-deductibility of interest payments. For such a firm, the full real rate is what matters. In contrast, other individuals or businesses may be paying marginal rates on the order of 30–50 percent. Since there is no simple way to determine the relevant tax rate precisely, it is probably best to use a range of rates in the expectation that "the" proper rate will fall within the range.

The results of such a computation, similar to that in Chapter 4, but using the interest rate on three-month certificates of deposit, and a range of tax rates, are presented in Chart 8–1. It is immediately apparent that while the real after-tax rates that prevailed during 1981–82 were distinctly on the high side of the previous two decades' experience, the differences are much smaller than simple comparisons of nominal rates suggest.

But what is even more striking about the data is the massive negative rates observed in 1975–76, even when calculated on an after-tax basis. The record of real short-term rates suggests strongly that despite Chairman Burns' vaunted reputation as an "inflation hawk," monetary policy at that time was extraordinarily stimulative. The contrast with policy in the aftermath of 1979 could scarcely be greater.

Chart 8-1
Real After-Tax Yields On 3-Month CDs

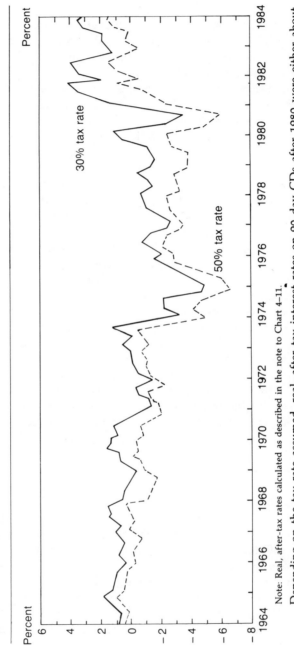

Note: Real, after-tax rates calculated as described in the note to Chart 4-11.

Depending on the tax rate assumed, real, after-tax interest rates on 90-day CDs after 1980 were either about the same or slightly higher than they were in the mid-1960s.

Notes

1. Recently, the electronic age has come to the hearings, in the form of a cable television network that routinely broadcasts them. Those with access to the broadcast can follow the testimony and questioning much better than almost any of the people physically present in the hearing room, and in vastly greater comfort.

2. The author is indebted to Mr. Tom Herman of *The Wall Street Journal* for making available the transcript of this exchange.

3. The most dramatic illustration of the Fed's willingness to override the policy adjustments called for by its operating procedures occurred, of course, during late 1982, when policy was eased in the face of strong M1 growth. Almost as dramatic was the period from the end of 1982 to early 1984, when borrowed reserves were maintained about unchanged, except for a few minor, short-lived policy adjustments and variations due to errors in providing reserves.

4. Similarly, the "extended credit" provided by the Fed to certain troubled financial institutions is properly regarded as part of nonborrowed reserves and not as a part of "adjustment" borrowings, or borrowed reserves. The reason is that institutions requiring such assistance almost certainly have no access to the funds market, and thus their reserves needs can have no influence on the funds rate.

5. However, because of a technicality, the tightening could probably not be fully automatic, even if the Fed wished to allow the procedures to operate unhindered. The reason is that, as described in Chapter 4, the shape of the borrowed reserves function is relatively uncertain at high levels of borrowing, so that increased pressure on banks to borrow may or may does not translate into a commensurate increase in the funds rate. That problem can be overcome by increasing the discount rate, which should induce an approximately equal increase in the funds rate.

6. The operative portion of the December announcement read as follows:

> The further half-point reduction in the discount rate was taken in the light of current business conditions, strong competitive pressures on prices and further moderation of cost increases, a slowing of private credit demands, and present indications of some tapering off in growth of the broader monetary aggregates.

In contrast, the November announcement was in the traditional mold:

> The further half-point reduction in the discount rate, *which is broadly consistent with the prevailing pattern of market rates,* was taken against the background of continued progress toward greater price stability and indications of continued sluggishness in business activity and relatively strong demands for liquidity. [Emphasis supplied.]

7Of course, there is another problem in choosing among several alternative measures of inflation. In general, a variable-weight price index is to be preferred, such as the implicit deflator for GNP or for consumption expenditures. Analysis of the relative merits of the various alternatives is unfortunately beyond the scope of this chapter.

9

RUBBING SHOULDERS WITH THE TREASURY: THE FISCAL/ MONETARY POLICY MIX

During the last several years, when interest rates have been at or close to record-high levels, there has been a general consensus that fiscal and monetary policies were at fault, either singly or in combination. Concerning specific policy flaws, however, agreement has been far more limited.

Economic effects of budget deficits

Do budget deficits matter? The stormy political debate over the federal budget suggests that many people think they matter quite a great deal. And yet, a number of economists have argued exactly the opposite: that government expenditures financed by borrowing—i.e., financed by a deficit—are the equivalent of spending financed by taxes, and have little or no effect on the total of spending in the economy. Given certain assumptions, that conclusion follows logically. In particular, individuals must believe that taxes will be increased in the future to pay off the borrowing, and they must treat the capitalized value of the *future* taxes required to pay the interest and principal on government debt just as they would an identical amount of taxes on *current* income.

Most economists regard such an assumption as quite extreme and unrealistic, maintaining that individuals are likely to respond much more to spending in the here-and-now than they do to the prospect of an unknown, and probably unknowable, burden of taxes in the indefinite future.[1]

For one thing, quite a range of beliefs is possible regarding the consequences of deficit-financed government expenditures for future budget policy. One possibility, mentioned above, is that taxes will rise in the future. Another is that expenditure growth will be reduced. In addition, the debt might be paid off, in effect, by printing money. And, of course, the debt might simply be replaced at maturity with additional debt issues.

Depending on which alternative, or combination of alternatives, is believed most likely, the impact of a current government deficit on consumption and investment spending should vary considerably. But, unless they are strongly and confidently held, such beliefs might not matter very much after all. Indeed, if individuals are highly uncertain about the possible future development of budget policy, they may simply react to the current budget, leaving future budgets for another day. If so, then fiscal policy (i.e., government tax and spending decisions) can have major impacts on the current pace of economic activity, relatively unhobbled by offsetting expectational effects.

Even so, those economists who do believe in the potency of fiscal policy to stimulate or retard the economy—probably a majority of the profession—generally assign a much more critical role to expectations in determining the impact of taxes and government spending on total aggregate demand than they did some years ago. In particular, expectations with respect to the permanence or temporary character of taxes and deficits are widely thought to affect significantly the extent to which individuals and business firms will make corresponding alterations to their own production and spending plans.

Though it is important to keep in mind possibly significant qualifications from such expectational factors, the following important propositions would enjoy support from most professional economists.

1. If the economy is operating significantly *below full employment*, a budget deficit can provide short-run economic stimulus without necessarily causing inflation or reducing, i.e., "crowding out," business investment. The reason is that the stimulus to investment from growth in current spending outweighs the negative impact of higher interest rates due to the government borrowing finance the deficit. Moreover, the interest-rate impact can be reduced, at least temporarily, by financing the deficit in part through accelerated monetary growth. In fact, under these circumstances, the stimulus may actually lead to an improved utilization of resources which, through enlarging the economic pie, permits investment to have a bigger slice; that result has been termed "crowding in."

2. However, if the economy is already operating *at or very close to full employment*, crowding out is essentially absolute. Any resources claimed by increased government expenditures are obviously unavailable for use by the private sector, irrespective of whether the government decides to finance those expenditures via additional taxes, borrowing, monetary growth, or some combination. Naturally the means chosen to finance the government expenditures determine the incidence of crowding out of private-sector spending. For example, personal income taxation affects primarily consumption, while government borrowing probably affects mainly housing, consumer durables purchases, and business investment.

3. Even if the economy initially is operating at significantly less than full employment, continued fiscal stimulus must lead, at some point, to much fuller resource utilization. Consequently, crowding in (or at least noncrowding out) is at best a temporary, short-term phenomenon, while crowding out holds in the long run.

To some extent, these propositions are embodied in the terminology used to describe the budget deficit. Because of the income tax and corporate profits tax, weakness in wage and salary incomes and profits produces a significant reduction in government receipts, while strength in those areas augments the government's tax take. On the other side of the ledger, expenditures, such as those for unemployment benefits, are also sensitive to the pace of economic activity. In combination, these effects add to budget deficits during recessions and contribute to surpluses during expansions, thus offsetting somewhat the cyclical swings in aggregate demand. It is only natural to term that portion of a budget deficit produced directly by cyclical weakness the *cyclical deficit,* while the remainder, the cyclically invariant portion, is the *structural deficit.*

At this point, it might be tempting to conclude that cyclical deficits do not crowd out other spending (since, by definition, aggregate demand is weak anyway) while structural deficits do. Unfortunately, it's not that simple.

No matter what the stage of the business cycle, increased government spending, financed by increased Treasury borrowing, in general implies interest rates higher than they otherwise would be. Higher interest rates pare back interest-sensitive private-sector spending. However, if economic slack exists, such crowding out is more than offset by the increase in government spending. Hence total production increases, despite the higher interest rates. Division of the deficit into cyclical and structural components is helpful in clarifying the immediate determinants of government spending and financing needs, though the concepts are considerably fuzzier than is generally supposed. But such a division is largely irrelevant to crowding out.

A budget deficit must be financed, of course, and the means chosen determine the incidence of whatever crowding out occurs. There are two basic financing alternatives: monetization (purchase of Treasury debt by the Fed) and borrowing from the public. The choice between them is integral to the mix of fiscal and monetary policy. In addition, borrowing from the public can take the form of short-term debt or longer-term debt. Determination of the mix of debt maturities is usually referred to as debt-management policy.

In recent years, economists generally have given increased attention to the financing choices implied by a government deficit. Monetarists stimulated the trend by initiating a reassessment of the simple Keynesian models, much in vogue during the early 1960s, which largely assumed, implicitly or explicitly, that the deficit was financed by borrowing.

In the monetarist view, the most economically potent financing technique is for the Fed to monetize the Treasury's debt by purchasing it. That adds to bank reserves and, all other things being equal, permits a more rapid expansion of the money supply. Indeed, some monetarists have claimed—despite the preponderance of statistical evidence to the contrary—that money demand is tightly linked to income and insensitive to interest rates and similar factors, so that the *only* way fiscal policy can have any economically expansive effect is through monetization. On that view, an increase of the deficit provides no net stimulus to aggregate demand, not even initially. It merely changes the composition of spending. However, as noted earlier, most economists would reject such a view as unfounded.

If substantial economic slack exists, monetary expansion will primarily lift the level of real activity, with little impact on inflation. However, continuation of a monetization policy when reasonably full utilization of resources has been attained would mainly exacerbate inflation. In such a case, inflation acts as a tax, reducing the real purchasing power of most financial assets and thereby making real resources available for government expenditures. Whether such crowding out mainly affects private consumption or investment spending in principle depends on a large number of factors, but in practice, there are strong grounds for thinking that it is detrimental to investment.

The problem is not simply that nominal interest rates rise to reflect the higher expected inflation. Rather, if profits are taxed on a current-dollar basis, with no indexation of depreciation and capital gains for inflation, then inflation transforms a tax on profits into a tax on wealth. Such a levy obviously constitutes a major disincentive to saving and investment.

The deductability of interest from taxable income means that an increase in inflation may actually lower real, after-tax interest rates. Lower rates favor debt-financed investment, but they discourage saving. Moreover, higher nominal rates imply that a larger portion of the real cash flow generated by an investment will be preempted by interest charges in its early years. That makes the owner's solvency more of a concern. On balance, inflation is almost certainly detrimental to investment.

If instead the deficit is financed by borrowing, economic theory suggests quite clearly that the principal impact would be to increase real interest rates, both pretax and aftertax. That is unqualifiedly detrimental to investment, except insofar as the initial existence of economic slack allows the favorable (but temporary) impact of fuller resource utilization to overcome the negative impact of higher interest rates.

Debt-management policy also is potentially an important determinant of the incidence of interest-rate pressure and thus of the incidence of crowding out. The reason is that the debt instruments the Treasury sells to the public to finance its deficit must compete with private debt securities for a place in the portfolios of investors. If investors prefer to invest in primarily short-term securities, an attempt by the Treasury to finance its deficit in substantial degree through issuing long-term bonds may result in a significantly smaller amount of long-term financing being made available for—or, to say the same thing another way, higher rates being charged on—bonds issued by business firms to finance their investment projects. Thus, by artificially raising long-term interest rates, Treasury finance could conceivably crowd out some investment. But by the same token, the Treasury might actually crowd *in* some investment if, for example, its debt were issued primarily in the short-term markets, while reserving the long-term debt markets for business firms. However, though it seems certain that effects like these do exist, most economists believe them to be relatively small.

In principle, a number of different mixes of fiscal and monetary policies could be devised to produce a given level of spending. However, the alternatives may produce very different proportions of consumption and investment. In general, the policy mix most favorable to investment combines a restrictive fiscal policy with an accommodative monetary policy.

Who got crowded out?

In broad outline, the events of 1979–82 read like a textbook case of crowding out. There is no doubt whatever that crowding out occurred, and it was overwhelmingly the product of a severely restrictive monetary policy. Real GNP in 1982 ($1,485.4 billion) was almost unchanged from its level in 1979 ($1,479.4 billion). Similarly, real M1 (deflated by the implicit GNP price deflator) was actually slightly *lower* in 1982 ($231.2 billion) than in 1979 ($238.0 billion), despite the boost provided by the influx of balances in NOW accounts.

The picture was even more dramatic in credit markets. In real terms, total net credit market funds raised by nonfinancial sectors (nonfinancial businesses, households, and government on the federal, state, and local levels) in 1982 were $191.2 billion, fully 19 percent lower than in 1979. In contrast, during the three years from 1976 through 1979, real funds raised had expanded at an average compounded rate of almost 9 percent per year. Only in 1983, the first year of sustained economic recovery since 1979, would real funds raised regain their level of five years earlier.

In sum, not only was crowding out present during 1979–82, but the forced compression of real credit demands, and the associated, almost unprecedentedly high real interest rates, were easily the most prominent features of the economy during the period.

Within the declining total of real funds raised by domestic nonfinancial sectors, households were the big losers, with the federal government the big gainer.

Reflecting the impact of high interest rates as well as the 1980 credit controls program, funds raised by households—chiefly in the form of residential mortgages and consumer credit—plunged, so that the household share of total funds raised was only about half as large in 1982 as it was in 1978. Of course 1978 is hardly an ideal standard of comparison, since it represented just about the high-water mark of the rising tide of inflation-anticipation behavior by consumers.

As the 1970s drew to a close, credit to finance housing and other consumer durables purchases was bloated by the accelerating shift of consumer preferences away from financial assets in favor of tangibles, which appeared to have more promise of maintaining their value. Nevertheless, as Chart 9–1 indicates, if any one sector could be said to have been crowded out during 1979–82, it clearly was the household sector.

In contrast, the business sector maintained essentially intact its portion of credit market funds until late in 1982. Moreover, business capital spending, for inventories as well as fixed investment, remained relatively robust in the face of enormous interest-rate pressures. There is no question that business investment projects were canceled due to high rates, but overall, the decline was hardly a rout. The same is true of the state and local government sector, which accounted for about the same portion of funds raised in 1982 as it did in 1978.

The federal share of funds raised soared from about 15 percent in 1978 to over 40 percent in 1982. In large part, the expansion was cyclical in nature, reflecting weakness in other sectors. In 1975, for example, as the economy began to recover from what had been, up to that time, the deepest postwar recession, the federal share of funds raised also reached more than 40 percent. Strictly speaking, then, the magnitude of the Federal claim on credit during a period of cyclical weakness was not unprecedented. In any event, its expansion was inadequate to prevent a decline in the real total of funds raised.[2]

CHART 9–1

Funds Raised by Domestic Nonfinancial Sectors
Percent of Total

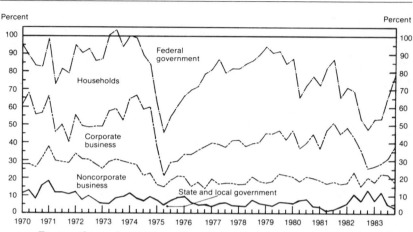

During the early 1980s, net credit market funds raised by the Federal government expanded relative to total funds raised.

Nor does the Treasury's debt-management policy appear to have had a major impact on the credit markets. Since the end of 1975, the average maturity of privately held Treasury debt has increased by approximately one and one-half years, reaching an average about equal to that at the end of the 1960s (Chart 9–2). But only a relatively small portion of that change occurred during 1979–83. On the whole, changes in the maturity composition of the Treasury's debt since the end of the 1960s appear rather modest, at least when viewed from the perspective of the postwar pattern of steadily declining average maturities. However, it is possible that even less reliance on long-term financing by the Treasury would have created a marginally more favorable setting for business long-term finance. A number of studies have suggested that such may be the case.

Two general conclusions emerge from this brief review of crowding out during 1979–82. One is that, although total real credit demands were compressed significantly, the sector most drastically affected was households. Though economists and other participants in the debate over the fiscal/monetary policy mix habitually speak of the crowding out of business investment, that sector's share of funds raised was not greatly altered. A significant decline in the business share did not occur until late 1982 and 1983, when a strong rebound of cash flow made the nonfinancial corporate business sector temporarily self-financing.

CHART 9–2
Average Maturity of Privately Held Treasury Debt

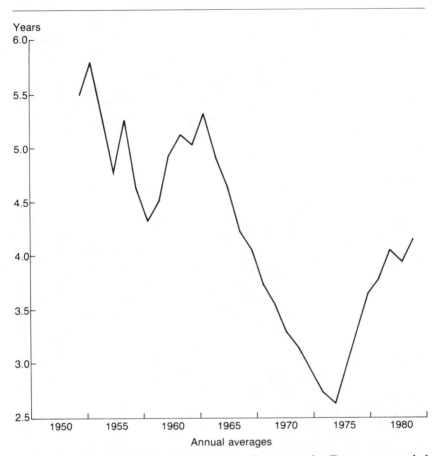

Years

From the mid-1970s through the early 1980s, the Treasury extended the average maturity of its debt, to its approximate average in the late 1960s.

Within the business sector, of course, some industries were far more sharply affected than others. Prominent among them were industries exposed to foreign competition—about which more in Chapter 11. Nevertheless, households still accounted for the largest reduction of credit demands.

A second conclusion is that, however dramatic the expansion of Treasury credit demands may have been, it was not terribly out of line with earlier cyclical behavior and, in any event, was inadequate to prevent the total of real credit demands from declining sharply to a low level that it maintained for three years.

Consequently, if one must oversimplify an admittedly complex issue, it is probably more accurate to say that a highly restrictive monetary policy produced record-high interest rates that devastated the credit demands of sectors other than the Treasury, rather than that strong credit demands were themselves the primary factor behind high interest rates.

But one must be careful not to give casual approval to a "normal" fiscal policy when the economy's behavior was anything but normal. The fact was that in 1979 the inflation spiral was still accelerating. Fiscal policy should have swung sharply toward restraint, rather than leaving monetary policy to go it alone. Had it done so, interest rates almost certainly would have been far lower than they were.

Monetization

The Fed's extraordinary policy of monetary restraint decisively broke the accelerating inflation trend, and yet there were many who doubted whether such a spectacular achievement could endure. The most important reason for skepticism was the enormous scale of federal deficits anticipated for the duration of the 1980s. For the first time in U.S. peacetime history, reasonable projections suggested that even as the cyclical portion of the deficit declined, the structural portion would continue to increase, so that mega-deficits might be a fact of life for years to come.

A survey of financial decision makers taken in December 1983 found that out of over 600 respondents, almost two thirds agreed with the following statement:

> One can have no confidence in the staying power of disinflationary monetary policy as long as federal deficits remain in the triple digits.[3]

What was at issue was the willingness of the Fed to avoid monetizing Treasury debt or, if pushed to extremes, its ability to do so.

A widely remarked 1981 study by two prominent monetarist economists, Michael J. Hamburger and Burton Zwick, concluded:

> The execution of monetary policy may be determined by the Federal Reserve, but the overall formulation of policy is heavily dependent on the fiscal policy decisions made by the executive and legislative branches of the Government. During the 1950s and 1960s this interconnection of economic policy tools was not particularly inflationary as fiscal policy tended to be rather conservative. However, since the mid-sixties the combination of expansionary fiscal policy and the Federal Reserve's focus on moderating interest rate movements has been a principal cause of the persistent drift toward higher U.S. inflation rates.[4]

The argument, in essence, was that in the past the Fed had tended to be unwilling to offset completely the intended stimulative impact of fiscal policy by allowing interest rates to rise to sufficiently high levels. To forestall (temporarily) such rate increases, the Fed had monetized a substantial portion of the Treasury's debt, thus fueling a rate of monetary expansion that proved inconsistent with stable prices.

These conclusions have not gone unchallenged. For example, an investigation by Princeton University economist Alan S. Blinder not only found no evidence to support the view that federal deficits caused a significant degree of monetization, but actually concluded that the Fed tended to engage in "reverse monetization," i.e., deliberate restriction of bank reserves, when inflation was high and when government purchases were expanding rapidly.[5] As of this writing, there is no professional consensus on the issue.

In any event, as explained in Chapter 3, most financial market participants were, by 1983, fairly impressed by the Volcker Fed's determination to avoid monetization of deficits. However, they were simultaneously skeptical about the staying power of that policy.

The principal reason behind their attitude apparently had little to do with determination and a great deal to do with feasibility. In a clash between a Fed determined to pursue a disinflationary monetary policy and a Treasury financing stepped-up expenditures through burgeoning deficits, who wins in the end? For two very different reasons, quite a few thought the Fed was unlikely to come out on top in such a confrontation.

The first was practical politics: since the president has the power to appoint the chairman and other members of the Board, the Fed can never stray too far from the broad policy goals of the party in office. Moreover, as a practical matter, confrontations are unlikely to require resolution through new appointments. In a democracy, the elected government necessarily carries a mandate that an appointive agency cannot possibly match, and the Fed would ignore that fact at its peril. To say the same thing another way, in the end, the political accountability of the Fed would probably subordinate monetary policy to fiscal policy.

A pessimistic appraisal of the ability of the financial system to withstand a clash of fiscal and monetary policy pointed to the same conclusion. Many feared that swelling Treasury financing demands, if not accommodated by monetization, would force real interest rates sharply higher—so high, it was feared, that some sort of financial crisis would result, in which the Fed, true to its role as lender of last resort, would be forced to become more accommodative, if only to shore up the financial system.

Skepticism was not universal, however. The Treasury—predictably, perhaps—had an opposing view. The logical structure of that view appeared to rest on two key assumptions:

1. Nominal interest rates consist of an essentially constant real return plus an added premium for the expected future rate of inflation.

2. The inflation rate is exclusively determined by the rate of monetary growth.

Given these assumptions, it followed that fiscal and monetary policy could be compartmentalized. The Fed's job was to maintain a tight rein on monetary growth, preferably in such a credible fashion that expectations of future growth, and thus of future inflation, would decline. That happy result would, in turn, lead to lower interest rates, especially in the longer maturities, where the impact of improved expectations presumably would be greatest.

The Treasury harbored no affection for deficits, but it was unwilling to compromise its tax-reduction program significantly in order to reduce them. It instead favored cuts in various government spending programs. If these could not be obtained from Congress, then the deficit would have to take care of itself. In the Treasury's view, there was no discernible correlation between changes in government borrowing and changes in interest or exchange rates.[6] Consequently, if problems occurred in those areas, then almost by definition they were attributable to defective execution of monetary policy.

Most economists, and the vast majority of financial market participants, instinctively and intellectually rejected this compartmentalization of fiscal and monetary policy. They did not dispute the proposition that, in the long run, inflation is a monetary phenomenon (though many naturally questioned whether the relation was so simple as the Treasury seemed to assume). Rather, they took issue with the view that expected inflation alone determined nominal interest rates. Instead, the burden of financing the large deficits anticipated for much of the 1980s seemed certain to result in upward pressure on real interest rates, quite apart from their impact on expected future inflation.

Predictably, Volcker was one of the most outspoken proponents of that view:

> the actual and prospective size of the budget deficit inevitably complicates the environment within which we work. By feeding consumer purchasing power, by heightening skepticism about our ability to control the money supply and contain inflation, by claiming a disproportionate share of available funds, and by increasing our dependence on foreign capital, monetary policy must carry more of the burden of maintaining stability and its flexibility, to some degree, is constrained.[7]

Volcker appeared only too well aware of the irony in this contention: by arguing that the enormous prospective budget deficits constrained monetary policy, he lent support to those who, though they were impressed with the Fed's determination, nevertheless questioned its staying power under such circumstances.

Why interest rates were—and are—so high

The bottom line for any practicing economist or for any financial market participant is to be able to explain why interest rates soared during 1980–81 and remain, in real terms, at historically high levels as of this writing (spring 1984). One factor appears to have been of overwhelming importance—what Blinder characterized as the Fed's "reverse monetization" of Treasury deficits. Not only did the Fed resist and, indeed, overwhelm the stimulative impact of fiscal policy during 1979– 82, but it kept policy distinctly restrictive even after the recovery got under way in late 1982. Its policy looked beyond the recovery and sought to postpone the day when the burgeoning structural deficit would overstimulate an economy nearing a traditionally inflationary degree of capacity utilization. The Fed, in a sense, was reverse-monetizing *future deficits.*

The result was that during 1983, the first year of recovery, real short-term interest rates were high and on a gradual rising trend.

But if the Fed held short-term rates at high levels, it was in principle only one of many influences on long-term interest rates. Because long-term securities are claims on payments to be made far into the future, expectations concerning future events play a commensurately large role in determining their yields. Though economists universally recognize the critical role of expectations in theoretical and empirical models of interest rate determination, they unfortunately know relatively little about how expectations are formed.

What is known with reasonable certainty is that many conventional measures of expectations—whether garnered directly from surveys or indirectly through analysis of yield curves and other relationships—often show persistently biased forecasts that respond rather sluggishly to incoming economic information. Sluggishness does not prevail at all times, however. In particular, it appears that certain rather symbolic events, such as a currency reform, introduction of a dramatically stimulative government budget, or disarray among the members of the OPEC cartel, may have impacts on expectations seemingly quite disproportionate to their direct economic impacts.

What kind of expectational process could have caused long-term rates to remain at elevated levels while inflation plunged to its lowest rate in a decade and a half? For one thing, few were prepared to rule out the possibility of a rebound of inflation in the future. For example, the poll of financial market participants and analysts referred to earlier showed inflation expectations for the next five years lodged slightly above 6 percent in March 1983 (down from over 9 percent in 1980), despite the sharp declines in oil prices then in progress.

Subsequent surveys during the year reported increases in the five-year expected inflation rate totaling about one-half percent, although almost all measures of inflation were establishing new cyclical low readings during that time. It is hard to avoid the conclusion that many investors viewed inflation as only temporarily in remission. For them, years might be required before lower inflation could be viewed as an established fact.

If investors were cautiously optimistic about the inflation outlook (arguably more cautious than optimistic), that optimism was overshadowed by their concern that the extraordinarily large federal deficits forecast for the years ahead might produce high real interest rates, as crowding out resumed in earnest. Indeed, growing pessimism on this score was, if anything, more dramatic than the reduction of expected inflation. In the survey cited earlier, the percentage of respondents envisaging a balanced budget sometime within the next five years rose from a bit more than 20 percent in 1980 to almost 50 percent in early 1981 (the high-water mark of supply-side euphoria following Reagan's election victory) and then plunged back to about its 1980 level by 1983.

Amid such gloom, there were some who argued, as did the Treasury, that federal deficits had nothing to do with either inflation or interest rates. That view does, indeed, receive some superficial empirical support from a cyclical comparison of deficits and interest rates. In the past, rates have usually been lowest precisely when deficits have been peaking. The reason, of course, is that business credit demands are typically quite slack in the early stages of a recovery, while monetary policy has often swung toward stimulus at such times. In any event, very few financial market participants were persuaded. On the contrary, they tended to view past relationships between deficits and interest rates as almost irrelevant, because of the qualitatively new feature of the situation. Not only was the cyclical portion of the deficit of record proportions, but the long-term, structural portion of the deficit promised to bloat credit demands throughout the business recovery. In peacetime, that was an altogether unprecedented event. While federal debt relative to GNP had been trending down during almost all of the postwar period, reasonable projections now portended a reversal of the trend. That alone seemed to many to be adequate cause to view with skepticism claims that deficits would have little impact on interest rates.

Moreover, if investors had learned nothing else during the years following the Saturday Night Special, they perceived that the juxtaposition of a restrictive monetary policy and an expansive fiscal policy was a prescription for high and almost certainly volatile real interest rates, and quite possibly also for increased political pressure on the Fed to monetize the Treasury debt. Consequently, high interest rates undoubtedly incorporated an "anxiety premium" to compensate investors for the perceived risk in owning long-term securities paying fixed rates of return.

With such a superabundance of reasons for elevated long-term interest rates, it at first seems altogether shocking that, relative to short-term rates, long-term rates during the first 12 months of recovery (December 1982–November 1983) were actually little different from those during the first year of previous recoveries. The yield curve was not unusually positively sloped. On the contrary, as Table 9–1 indicates, the "pick-up" from rates on short-term securities to rates on long-term issues was only about ½ percent higher than the average during the first year of previous postwar recoveries, and it was actually less than in 1975–76. Considering that the Treasury has been attempting to extend the average maturity of its debt since late 1975—thus putting some upward pressure on long-term rates—the "anxiety premium" does not appear to have been terribly large.[8]

Other interpretations are possible, however. It may have been that the enlarged anxiety premium just about offset the favorable impact of the improved inflation outlook, so that the relation of long-term rates to short-term rates was about unchanged—by a fluke. In addition, the higher level of rates effectively shortened the duration of long-term securities, so that their yields should have behaved more like the yields on shorter-term securities.[9] That effect, to the degree it was present, would have masked the impact of the elevated anxiety premium.

If, instead, the yield curve was simply about as normal, then

TABLE 9–1

Treasury Yield Spreads in the First 12 Months of Recovery: 30-Year Bonds versus Three-Month Bills

Business Cycle Trough	Average Yield Spread (percent)
May 1954	1.71%
April 1958	1.51
February 1961	1.57
November 1970	1.57
March 1975	2.56
November 1982	2.36

Note: The 1980–81 recovery is omitted from the comparison due to the special circumstances of that period. The yield spread is defined as the yield to maturity of 30-year bonds less the yield on three-month bills.
Source: Salomon Brothers, *Analytical Record of Yields and Yield Spreads.*

economists may have overrated the role of expectations—particularly when poorly defined and subject to considerable uncertainty—in the determination of long-term interest rates. On that view, the reason for high long-term rates in the first year of recovery mostly boiled down to the fact that short-term rates were high.

At the very least, expectations clearly made little contribution to lowering long-term interest rates. Investors were insufficiently confident of the durability of the disinflation trend, while they realistically felt threatened by prospective budget deficits. It might have been otherwise. Had fiscal policy been more restrictive, thus allowing monetary policy to be more stimulative, rates would have been lower, both because of the Fed's direct influence as well as more supportive policy expectations among investors. Instead, fiscal and monetary policy took almost the directly opposite configuration, and high rates were the inevitable result.

Notes

1. For a concise statement of the arguments involved, see Martin Feldstein, "Government Deficits and Aggregate Demand," *Journal of Monetary Economics,* January 1982, pp. 1–20.

2. Another indication of the similarity of the behavior of Treasury financing needs during the two periods is the deficit as a percentage of GNP. On a National Income Accounts basis, the deficit rose to 4.5 percent of GNP in 1975. In 1982, it hit 4.8 percent—higher, but not a qualitatively different level.

3. Richard B. Hoey and Helen Hotchkiss, "Decision-Makers Poll" (New York: A. G. Becker Paribas, Inc., December 21, 1983). Previous surveys turned up similar responses to the question.

4. Michael J. Hamburger and Burton Zwick, "Deficits, Money and Inflation," *Journal of Monetary Economics,* January 1981, pp. 141–150.

5. Alan S. Blinder, "On the Monetization of Deficits," in *The Economic Consequences of Government Deficits,* ed. Laurence H. Meyer (Hingham, Mass.: Kluwer-Nijhoff, 1982).

6. For the view of the Treasury's Assistant Secretary for Economic Policy, see Manuel H. Johnson, "The Effect of Deficits on Prices of Financial Assets: Theory and Evidence," processed, Department of the Treasury, January 1984.

7. Paul A. Volcker, testimony before the House Committee on Banking, Finance, and Urban Affairs, February 7, 1984, p. 19.

8. Moreover, spreads computed on a real, after-tax basis probably would have shown even less of a discrepancy, although as noted earlier, measurement of real long-term rates is fraught with uncertainty primarily due to the difficulty of gauging inflation expectations.

9. The duration of a security is the time-weighted average of the present values of its payments of interest and principal. A security's duration is always shorter than its final maturity unless there are no payments before maturity, in which case the two are equal. As a rule, the higher the coupon interest rate, the greater the portion of payments made before maturity, and the shorter is the duration. For example, for a bond with a 30-year maturity, coupon interest rates of 5, 10, and 15 percent create durations of 15.8, 9.9, and 7.1 years, respectively.

10

CRISIS!

A financial crisis is an actual or threatened breakdown of the free and efficient functioning of financial markets. To understand the dynamics of financial crises—and the Federal Reserve's approach to forestalling them—it is necessary to be very clear about what makes financial markets work. In one word, what makes them work is *credit.*

Credit and liquidity

Credit is one of the most venerable notions in financial markets. At present, the most common meaning of the word in financial usage has to do with the act of lending funds, as in extending credit. But in its traditional usage, credit—as suggested by its Latin root, *credere,* to trust—referred to the ability and willingness of an individual to make good on his word. That is the meaning captured in the old saying that a man's most valuable possession is his credit. Credit in this sense is the foundation of financial markets and indeed of all contracts.

At root, many financial crises are characterized by a loss of credit through actual or feared defaults on obligations of various kinds. If the loss is widespread, normal financial relations become either difficult or impossible. The most conspicuous casualty of such a crisis is the liquidity of financial assets.

Most people think of liquidity in context of the balance sheet of an individual or firm. Liquidity then refers to holdings of cash-type assets, or perhaps the proportion they represent to current payment obligations. But liquidity in financial markets has a different, and more specific meaning: it is the ability to trade large amounts of securities quickly without appreciably affecting their price.

For example, the most liquid market in the world is the U.S. Treasury bill market. Trading—conducted almost exclusively over the telephone between securities dealers and other market participants—routinely totals many billions of dollars each day. Even the multibillion-dollar trades executed by the Federal Reserve's Open Market Desk are but a small portion of total trading volume and thus need have little or no impact on interest rates on bills. Were it not for the credit of the participants in the bill market, such performance would be inconceivable. Not only that, but without liquid markets for financial securities, financial intermediaries—banks, thrift institutions, insurance companies, etc.—as currently constituted could not exist. Much of what one takes for granted about the financial superstructure is erected upon the rock of credit.

Even in the best of times, some deterioration of creditworthiness is always taking place among individual firms. For their own peculiar reasons—perhaps involving poor management, fraud, or simply bad luck—some business firms fail, others turn out to need additional time to pay their obligations, and so forth. But because they are relatively few in number and are perceived to be isolated events, such developments have little or no impact on the liquidity of markets.

What lies at the heart of panics, in contrast, is the fear of increasing and widespread unwillingness or inability of financial market participants to meet claims on them. Such concerns are hardly groundless. Because of the high degree of interconnectedness among the many participants in financial markets, a sudden attempt by those participants to insulate themselves from the consequences of a default or failure may in turn precipitate additional, domino-like failures as credit—in both its older and newer meanings—dries up.

Lender of last resort

Nobody ever understood the psychological dynamics of financial panics, the emotional manifestations of collapsing credit, better than Walter Bagehot. He had lived through several panics, including the famous panic of 1857, precipitated by the collapse of Overends, Gurney and Company, a London "bill broker," which very nearly devastated the London money market. As an editor of *The Economist* magazine, Bagehot chronicled these panics and turned his systematic intellect to trying to understand how they developed, and how they might be contained. In doing so, he wrote the classic exposition of the concept of the "lender of last resort," a notion so commonplace these days that most use it without feeling any need for explanation or analysis.

Much of Bagehot's *Lombard Street* is devoted to explaining why the central bank, as the repository of the nation's monetary reserves, should be prepared to advance credit if necessary to forestall financial collapse.[1] In 1873, when the book was first published, the idea that the Bank of England should lend freely during a panic rather than attempting to hoard cash like anyone else was still quite novel. In some quarters, such a view was considered positively seditious. Bagehot summarized concisely the principles involved:

> The end is to stay the panic; and the advances should, if possible, stay the panic. And for this purpose there are two rules.
>
> First. That these loans should only be made at a very high rate of interest. This will operate as a heavy fine on unreasonable timidity, and will prevent the greatest number of applications by persons who do not require it. The rate should be raised early in the panic, so that the fine may be paid early; that no one may borrow out of idle precaution without paying well for it; that the banking reserve may be protected as far as possible.
>
> Secondly. That at this rate these advances should be made on all good banking securities, and as largely as the public ask for them. The reason is plain. The object is to stay alarm, and nothing, therefore, should be done to cause alarm. But the way to cause alarm is to refuse someone who has good security to offer. The news of this will spread in an instant through all the Money Market at a moment of terror; no one can say exactly who carries it, but in half an hour it will be carried on all sides, and will intensify the terror everywhere.[2]

Some of Bagehot's concerns happily do not apply, or at least not with equal force, in this day and time. For example, Bagehot feared that the officers of the Bank of England, still a private corporation at the time, would likely display "unreasonable timidity" toward lending in a crisis situation. Accordingly, they were to be bought off, in effect, by dangling before them a very high rate of interest (in the form of an increase of the Bank's discount rate) as a reward. Such inducements currently are *not* required to incite the Fed to action in a crisis. That is progress.

Similarly, in Bagehot's day, Britain's monetary reserves took the form of gold. This created the possibility that an abrupt shipment of gold abroad—as happened on a few occasions—might precipitate a multiple contraction of the money supply. Raising the discount rate to a high level early in the panic thus served to discourage a potential drain of monetary reserves—what Bagehot called the "banking reserve"—to foreign countries. Fortunately, the Federal Reserve today has no such problem.[3] The reserves of the banking system consist of currency in bank vaults and deposits at the Fed, and the latter are created when the Fed buys securities or makes loans.[4] While the Fed might well be concerned about the impact of a financial crisis on the foreign exchange value of the dollar, that problem need not trigger measures to defend the supply of reserves available to the banking system. Recent proposals for a return to the gold standard notwithstanding, that is also progress.

If we abstract from the institutional details peculiar to Bagehot's time, his rules for dealing with financial panics boil down to two points. The first is to provide liquidity. That is achieved by ensuring that there is always at least one buyer—the central bank—for all good quality securities offered by those under pressure to meet their obligations.

The second is to keep market participants from developing an addiction to using the central bank's credit facilities, i.e., to assure that the central bank is their *last* resort. That can be achieved by charging an above-market rate on advances, so that when a crisis occurs, the central bank will be the last to be asked for assistance and the first to be paid off when the crisis has blown over.

While the Fed serves as a lender of last resort, a function specifically contemplated in the original Federal Reserve Act, its technique is rather different from that which Bagehot recommended. The most striking difference is that the Fed almost always maintains the basic discount rate applied to short-term "adjustment" borrowing somewhat below market interest rates, and a crisis is probably the last situation in which it would increase the rate.[5] In part, this difference is due to the fact that the Fed, unlike the Bank of England in Bagehot's day, need not concern itself with defense of the "banking reserve." Moreover, in keeping with the spirit of the 1913 act, the Fed has encouraged banks suffering temporary reserves shortages to avail themselves of the window's resources, subject to the admonition that such assistance is "a privilege, not a right."

The logic in this approach is that transitory disturbances in reserve supplies are inevitable, and that there is nothing to be gained by amplifying their impact on banks and financial markets. In the Fed's view, the important thing is to prevent banks from becoming habitual borrowers from the window. That is achieved (in principle) by reserving the right to deny assistance, not by setting a high discount rate as Bagehot recommended.

Finally, in Bagehot's day, the concept of monetary policy had hardly entered the vocabulary of political economy. Indeed, the very idea of a central bank having public responsibilities different from those of any private bank was the insight for which Bagehot argued. Consequently, it is no wonder that the central role currently played by the discount rate in the current nonborrowed reserves targeting procedures should not have occurred to Bagehot.[6]

The result, then, is that when the Fed acts to defuse a real or potential crisis, the discount rate is largely on the sidelines. Instead, the liquidity of financial markets is insured primarily by the Fed's ability to provide reserves through open-market operations or discount-window lending. In this key respect, the Fed's technique for dealing with panics is the same as that which Bagehot espoused.

The best way to understand how the Fed copes with financial crises, however, is to contemplate the process in action. The most prominent crises in recent years were precipitated by the bankruptcy of Penn Central in 1970, the failure (in all but the narrowest legal sense) of Franklin National Bank in 1974, the silver bubble in 1980, and the collapse of Drysdale Government Securities in 1982. We will now take a look at how each of these events threatened the viability of the financial system and how prompt, intelligent action by the Fed defused them.

(As this book was about to go to press, the Continental Illinois National Bank and Trust Company, the eighth largest bank in the United States, was unable to stem a mounting outflow from deposits and other funding sources. A multibillion dollar assistance package was assembled by the Federal Reserve, the Federal Deposit Insurance Corporation, and a consortium of banks to cover Continental's funding requirements until either the bank could overcome the loan losses that had eroded investor confidence or else find a suitable merger partner. At present, the ultimate resolution of Continental's problems is still unclear.)

Penn Central

On Sunday, June 21, 1970, following the collapse of efforts to secure a federal bailout two days before, the Penn Central Transportation Company filed for bankruptcy. The railroad's earnings had been deteriorating for months. Many outside the firm, however, had not perceived the true extent of its financial weakness, or had not seriously considered the possibility that the federal government would allow such a large firm to fail. At the time, Penn Central had some $82 million of commercial paper outstanding.

Commercial paper is an unsecured promissory note, in effect, an IOU. Those firms considered to be strong credits often use commercial paper to borrow for very short periods of time ranging from a few days to a few months. As described in Chapter 3, the Fed had attempted for months to severely restrict banks' access to funds by maintaining Regulation Q ceilings on interest rates which they could pay on CDs at levels well below market rates. Consequently, firms resorted more and more to borrowing under their own name in the paper market. Simultaneously, the banks' ability to make good on the credit lines backing those issues became more questionable due to the uncertain ability of the banks themselves to raise the funds that would be needed by a paper issuer unable to roll over maturing paper.

The bankruptcy of Penn Central threw the paper market into a panic, and none but the very strongest credits could obtain funds to roll over maturing issues. Within three weeks, outstanding commercial paper contracted by $3 billion.

Widespread financial insolvency, involving major banks as well as many industrial firms, was a clear and immediate threat. However misguided it may have been in preparing the groundwork for the crisis by disrupting the normal channels through which banks could raise funds, the Fed did not hesitate once the consequences were clear. As described in Chapter 3, banks were immediately given renewed access to the CD market by the summary suspension—effective Tuesday, June 23—of Regulation Q ceilings on short-term CDs. But that move, though essential to a resolution of the crisis, probably would have proved inadequate by itself. Thus, the Fed also announced that it would make available the resources of the discount window to any banks unable to acquire funds to lend to creditworthy firms unable to roll over their maturing paper issues.

As it happened, the volume of loans made for this purpose was never large, amounting to only about $500 million over a span of a few weeks. But the number of dollars involved is quite beside the point. What the Fed did was to provide assurance to the financial markets that the liquidity essential to their operation would be preserved. If panicky investors refused to renew their holdings of commercial paper, preferring Treasury bills, bank deposits—anything!—instead, their extreme preference for safety would not be allowed to contribute to widespread insolvency. Once everyone understood that, there was little reason for panic.

Of course, Penn Central's lenders faced the dreary prospect of years of litigation with an uncertain chance of recovering the full value of their investments. But those not directly involved could now regard Penn Central as a special case. However nervous financial market participants might be over the close call, the confidence underlying the markets was no longer threatened.

Franklin National

As interest rates declined sharply toward the end of 1973, many financial market participants concluded that the "down-cycle" of interest rates was upon them. The Arab oil embargo, begun in October 1973, seemed certain to deepen a recession that many viewed as the inevitable result of the record-high interest rates reached only a few weeks earlier. Thus, the consensus view was that interest rates would continue to decline. That outlook, if correct, had major investment implications, not least for commercial banks.

The typical pattern in a recession is for business demands for credit, particularly for the short-term loans that are banks' staple product, to decline substantially. At the same time, the weakening economy, in tandem with a generally more accommodative monetary policy posture, produces significantly lower interest rates. That hits bank earnings with a double-whammy. Not only is demand for commercial loans weak, but the interest received on loans or any other investments also declines. From the standpoint of bank profitability, it is an altogether dismal prospect.

The traditional tactic for dealing with such a cyclical earnings squeeze is for a bank to extend the maturities of securities in its investment portfolio when interest rates are close to their highs for the cycle. The idea is that the investment portfolio will provide capital gains to offset reduced earnings from commercial lending and other sources as interest rates decline.

In late 1973, most banks in the country were probably following this tactic to a greater or lesser extent. But Franklin National Bank, then the twentieth largest bank in the country, went much further than others. It took very large foreign exchange positions and established substantial positions in long-term securities.

As it turned out, interest rates did not decline but started rising in February 1974 and reached new highs by the middle of the summer. The investments that banks had expected to cushion income declines started producing capital losses instead. Franklin was saddled by a poor quality loan portfolio which to a large extent had to be supported by funds purchased at high rates. Its losses in foreign exchange trading compounded the cash hemorrhage.

Finally, on Friday, May 10, Franklin's management announced publicly that the bank had suffered huge losses in foreign exchange trading, that it would recommend suspension of dividends, and that it had requested that trading in the shares of Franklin New York Corporation (the parent holding company) be suspended. For months before the announcement, many banks had refused to participate with Franklin in foreign exchange transactions and had tightened the terms on which they would lend funds to the bank. With the confirmation of what earlier had been rumored, Franklin's ability to secure funds in the CD market and the federal funds market vanished completely, leaving no alternative but to borrow from the Fed.[7]

In many respects, the failure of a large bank like Franklin presents a special problem for the monetary and regulatory authorities. A small bank can simply be closed or merged with a stronger institution.

If the bank is closed, the Federal Deposit Insurance Corporation (FDIC) can pay off the insured depositors without drawing appreciably on its reserve fund. Mergers will also minimize the drain on the FDIC's resources, as the acquiring institution takes over responsibility for the deposits, and some or all of the assets of the closed bank. But simple closure of a bank the size of Franklin, with almost $5 billion in assets at the time of the announcement, would have seriously impaired the FDIC's reserves, which then aggregated only about $6 billion.

The virtual depletion of the FDIC's reserve fund quite possibly could have eroded the almost complete, unquestioning confidence that Americans have in FDIC deposit insurance, potentially contributing to a much more widespread financial disturbance. Unfortunately, a prompt merger was impossible—not least because of the deliberate fraud practiced by Franklin's management in a desperate effort to conceal the true extent of the bank's losses. That made it difficult for interested buyers to put a solid valuation on the bank.

The Fed's approach was to lend Franklin whatever was necessary to meet its need for funds to pay off maturing deposits, while the FDIC tried to arrange an acquisition. At the high point, prior to the formal declaration of insolvency on October 8, the Fed had lent Franklin $1.7 billion. In order to make an acquisition feasible for potentially interested banks, the FDIC had to be willing to take over certain assets—aggregating about $2 billion—and to assume the Fed's loan to Franklin. Paying off the loan would have claimed almost one-third of the FDIC's reserve fund, creating precisely the kind of potential threat to public confidence that closure might have entailed. Accordingly, the Fed's loan to Franklin was converted, in essence, to a three-year loan to the FDIC itself.

Public confidence in the FDIC was indeed preserved. However, some argued, quite properly, that investors in Franklin's CDs were allowed to escape intact when they should have been forced to suffer the consequences of their poor investment judgment.

Even so, the Franklin affair had a palpable impact on the money market, as investors began to differentiate much more carefully than they had previously between the riskiness of CDs issued by different banks. Only the largest banks could assume any longer that their access to the CD market was unquestionable, but the markets continued to function with only slightly less liquidity than they had before. A potentially devastating collapse had been contained.

The silver bubble

The origin of the collapse of the price of silver in early 1980— down more than 75 percent in two months following its brief peak

of $47 per ounce in mid-January—lay in the ebbing of the heady specu-
lative fervor that drove it up over 600 percent during the previous
year. Behind that spectacular rise was a growing pessimism about the
prospects for ever bringing inflation under control. The clear corollary
of that view was that wisdom lay in acquiring tangible assets and
financing the purchases with (soon to be depreciated) debt. Though
this attitude permeated almost every corner of the economy, the markets for precious metals were a natural focus. In particular, the action
in the silver market was animated by the activities of the Hunt brothers,
who leveraged their enormous wealth to amass positions controlling
unknown hundreds of millions of ounces of silver.[8]

By early 1980, however, the logic behind such commodity speculation was being seriously undermined. The strategy of borrowing to
finance commodity positions was profitable as long as the rate of appreciation of commodity prices exceeded the average interest rate paid
to finance the positions. That condition had been satisfied during most
of 1979, but the sharp increases in interest rates following October 6
of that year almost doubled the costs of financing speculative commodity positions by early 1980.

That naturally put pressure on the commodities markets, and
price declines in turn prompted margin calls on "longs" whose contracts
for future delivery of silver were worth less than before. The need
to provide additional funds to maintain margins increased still further
the burden of financing costs. Finally, the Fed had gone to some lengths
to discourage banks from lending to finance speculation.

The press release announcing the Saturday Night Special had
included the following statement:

> The Board also stressed that banks should avoid loan activity that
> supports speculative activity in gold, commodity, and foreign exchange
> markets.

Though the request apparently had been widely ignored, at least where
the Hunts were concerned, the proscription against such credit was
given added force through the "voluntary" guidelines contained in
the credit controls program announced on March 14, 1980.

Thus, in a fashion strikingly similar to that in the Penn Central
crisis 10 years earlier, the stage was set for a disruption of financial
markets. The similarity lay in the fact that banks might be prevented
from acting to contain the impact of a default. In 1970, banks had
been unsure of their ability to secure funds to meet lending commitments. This time their access to funds was not threatened (though it
was made somewhat more complicated and expensive by the new reserve requirements on managed liabilities), but their ability to lend
was in doubt.

The first phase of the crisis was triggered by the Hunts' default on margin calls required to support silver futures positions they established on the Comex, the premier silver futures exchange in the United States. That default in turn threatened the viability of a number of large broker-dealer firms that had lent hundreds of millions of dollars to the Hunts. The uncertain financial condition of those firms implied that other members of the Comex clearinghouse might also be threatened, with the threat ultimately extending to the exchange itself.[9]

On Wednesday, March 26, rumors began to circulate that the Hunts had defaulted on margin calls, as in fact they had, and the silver price began to drop sharply. The Hunts had done most of their trading through Bache, Halsey, Stuart Shields, Inc. Under normal circumstances, the brokerage firm would have sold out a customer's futures position, if that were necessary to meet a margin call, and would have made up any shortfall out of its own pocket. But that procedure, intended for coping with small-and medium-sized trading accounts, was difficult to apply to the Hunts' colossal position, especially since Bache was thinly capitalized. Naturally, the threat to Bache would only be exacerbated by a continued decline in the silver price.

Accordingly, Bache promptly requested that Comex close the market and force settlement of all contracts at the closing price of the day before. And, for good measure, Bache called Volcker to request that he urge such a course on the Commodity Futures Trading Commission (CFTC), the regulatory agency with authority over all U.S. futures exchanges. Comex refused to comply, and Volcker gave no commitment. Instead, he arranged a meeting of all of the relevant government regulatory authorities to review the situation. During the day, the silver price dropped $4.40 to $15.80 per ounce at the close of trading, a whopping 23 percent decline.

On Thursday, the Hunts also asked the CFTC to close the market, a request that the Commission denied. By noon that day, the silver price had plunged to about $10.80, chalking up an almost 50 percent drop in a day and a half. Thereafter, the price recovered a bit. Though Bache actively liquidated some of the Hunt silver position on Friday, the price closed at $12.00. That price gain, plus capital infusions into other trading firms involved, ensured that there would be no defaults among members of the Comex clearinghouse. Thus the market stayed open, and there was no rush by lenders to demand immediate payment of all margin loans to silver market participants, an event which, had it occurred, would surely have forced some brokerage firms into insolvency. Thus by Friday, March 28, the first stage of the crisis, centering on the threat of the Hunt default to the Comex and its members, appeared to have been contained.

The second stage of the crisis got underway Friday afternoon when Engelhard Minerals and Chemicals Corporation let it be known that it would be looking for full cash payment of the $665 million that the Hunts had earlier undertaken to pay on the following Monday for 19 million ounces of silver. Obviously, the Hunts did not have the requisite cash. A suit by Engelhard would again raise expectations of massive sales from the Hunts' positions, putting still more downward pressure on the silver price—and thus resurrecting the threat to Comex and the dealers. Engelhard, aware of the problem, floated the idea of arranging a bank loan to the Hunts, who then could use the proceeds to pay off Engelhard. Despite the obvious inconsistency between such a loan and the credit controls program, Volcker indicated on Saturday that he would have no objections to it.

As it happened, the Reserve City Bankers Association, which included in its membership all the large banks that would have to be called on to extend a loan of the necessary size, was meeting that weekend in Boca Raton, Florida. Volcker (accompanied by E. Gerald Corrigan, then his assistant), Comptroller of the Currency Heimann, and Treasury Secretary Miller were scheduled to attend. The Hunts and representatives of Engelhard flew there as well. During the ensuing negotiations, it became clear that the banks were not interested in making a loan directly to the Hunts. Engelhard ultimately was persuaded—in the early hours of Monday morning—to accept, instead of the promised $665 million, the original 19 million ounces of silver on which the Hunts had failed to take delivery, another 8.5 million ounces from the Hunts' horde, and a 20 percent share of a Beaufort Sea oil and gas concession owned by the Hunts.[10] That averted the threat of a Monday morning suit by Engelhard.

The Hunts, however, still owed more than a billion dollars to various banks and brokers. If payment on those loans was forced, the result could be a desperation sale of the Hunts' silver hoard. And such a fire sale might very well renew pressure on the silver price, again threatening Comex and the various dealer firms, to say nothing of the security underlying the loans themselves.

To forestall that chain of events, negotiations during the month of April ultimately produced an arrangement by which the banks made a secured term loan to Placid Oil Company, a Hunt-controlled firm. Placid in turn made a loan to the Hunts, who used the proceeds to pay off the previously existing loans, and who also retained the silver horde with its attendant risks. Thus was risk transferred away from the banks, the dealers, and Comex to the Hunts' "deep pockets."

Neither Volcker nor Corrigan took a direct role in the negotiations that culminated in the $1.1-billion loan to Placid, but their influence was felt. Volcker was kept continually informed of the status of the negotiations, and he did give the crucial assurance that the credit controls program would not be allowed to interfere. Moreover, Volcker insisted that, as a condition of the loan, the Hunts desist from speculating in commodity markets for the term of the loan, i.e., until

1990. Was that, along with their massive losses, adequate punishment for the Hunts? Any answer is inherently subjective. However, it seems quite clear that in Volcker's mind the question was wholly secondary to the task of excising the systemic threat of multiple failures of securities firms and Comex.

Drysdale

The failure of Drysdale Government Securities, Inc. in May 1982 briefly appeared to have the potential to damage seriously, if not actually to destroy, many of the Street's major securities firms. Had that happened, the liquidity of the Treasury securities market, as well as all of the other financial markets in the country, would have been reduced dramatically.

The tale of how Drysdale, a new and undercapitalized dealer firm, managed to amass Treasury securities positions totaling billions of dollars prior to its collapse is highly complex and has been told well elsewhere.[11] In contrast, the threat that Drysdale presented to the markets' viability is relatively simple. Drysdale had borrowed Treasury securities to be able to make delivery of the huge amounts it sold short. Through an accounting quirk, which has since been remedied, this process of selling and simultaneously borrowing securities permitted Drysdale to accumulate a large, interest-free loan. Drysdale used the funds thus acquired to finance its trading positions. Because of trading losses—and, some have alleged, because of ploys devised by other securities firms to upset Drysdale's little game—the firm was unable to pay to the lenders of the borrowed securities interest totaling in excess of $160 million, which was due on Monday, May 17. Almost all of the securities borrowed by Drysdale had been acquired through three New York banks: Chase Manhattan Bank, Manufacturers Hanover Trust Company, and United States Trust Company. Of the three, Chase's role was by far the largest.

Most of the Street firms knew that Drysdale had failed to make the payment, or suspected as much, but they did not regard it as *their* problem. Their attitude changed quickly, however. On Monday afternoon, Chase described the situation to officers of the Federal Reserve Bank of New York and suggested that the Fed convene a meeting of major market participants that Chase had identified as being owed interest payments by Drysdale. At the meeting, Chase intended to propose a plan of joint action to resolve the problem. Volcker agreed to the meeting being held at the New York Fed, but explicitly dissociated the Fed from endorsing any specific solution to the problem, the true dimensions of which were obviously still unclear.

The meeting was held at 6:00 P.M. Chase argued that it had served merely as an *agent* for the securities dealer firms that had lent the securities that Chase, in turn, passed on to Drysdale. The bank accordingly maintained it had no legal responsibility for either the defaulted payments or the ultimate return of the securities. The dealers claimed, however, that they had never dealt with Drysdale, but only with Chase itself. The Merrill Lynch representative reportedly added a threat to that relatively dry and unemotional argument: If Chase were to remain obstinate, the Merrill Lynch money funds would liquidate every Chase CD and banker's acceptance in their portfolios, and they held hundreds of millions of dollars' worth. Because of the fundamental dispute over legal responsibility, given emotional force by the potential multimillion dollar losses involved, the meeting ended without any agreement having been reached on the disposition of the problem.

And the problem was not going to go away by itself. Many of the Street's largest securities firms were now faced with the prospect of immediate insolvency. Because litigation of the Drysdale affair could take years, the securities and payments due could well be frozen indefinitely. In the meantime, the firms most directly involved would probably fail to perform their obligations to make payments and deliver securities, causing still other firms to experience similar difficulties.

In this highly charged and uncertain situation, the banks reacted like anyone else, giving first priority to their own interests. Most, if not all, banks restricted their financing of securities firms. One large New York bank, about which the author has extensive knowledge, flatly refused to lend either cash or securities to any securities firms, including such heavyweights as Merrill Lynch, Salomon Brothers, and Goldman Sachs. Such behavior, of course, made it even more likely that a large number of dealers would be insolvent before long. The Treasury securities market was rapidly approaching a condition which (by that time Minneapolis Fed President) Corrigan aptly described as "gridlock." To put the same idea another way, panic was not far off.

As it happened, Tuesday, May 18, was the date of a Federal Open Market Committee meeting. Corrigan and Volcker had had dinner the night before with only a very incomplete notion of what was going on. Early Tuesday morning, Volcker began to receive reports, many of them vague, unsubstantiated, and conflicting. The New York Fed was then examining Drysdale's records, but found them haphazard, incomplete, and incapable of clearly defining Drysdale's financial situation.

Sternlight, the Desk manager, was of course in Washington to participate in the FOMC meeting. He attempted, without much success, to pin down the facts over the telephone. Anthony Solomon, the New York Fed president, was ill and thus not present. As the meeting was getting under way, the true dimensions of the situation were still far from clear. Finally, Volcker pulled Corrigan aside and told him to take the air shuttle to New York immediately, find out what was going on, and report back.

Why Corrigan? One reason probably was that Corrigan has a well-developed "underground" of personal acquaintances in the New York financial community developed during his years as an officer of the New York Fed, an asset essential for eliciting information quickly. Another surely was Corrigan's experience in dealing with other crises, notably the silver bubble. Finally, stature was obviously important. Everyone who mattered in the financial markets knew that, because of his official position and especially his close working relationship with Volcker, Corrigan would effectively represent the chairman in discussions and negotiations. That's important, since the chairmen of large banks and securities firms are not accustomed to dealing with minor officials.

Once on the scene, Corrigan began making telephone calls. He fairly quickly confirmed who was most directly involved and began to understand the rough dimensions of the problem. The banks were caught on the horns of a legal dilemma. If, on the one hand, they contributed to insolvencies among dealer firms by refusing to make the interest payments, a possibly adverse legal ruling later on might expose them to a large and incalculable liability for the damage done. On the other hand, if they made the payments for Drysdale, they might merely join the ranks of Drysdale's many creditors, with no control over the liquidation of Drysdale's securities positions.

The timing of the liquidation, in particular, the prices at which the securities were sold, obviously would be crucial to determining the ultimate size of the loss. The dilemma was clearly greatest for Chase, because it had by far the largest exposure. Naturally, only the banks could make a decision as to their course of action. The Fed's role essentially was to emphasize the urgency of "getting the money on the table," as well as the relative legal risks in the alternative courses of action open to the banks.

Meanwhile, the unwillingness of banks to lend in such an uncertain environment made financing dealer positions quite difficult. Accordingly, the Desk informed the dealers on Tuesday morning that it stood ready to execute RPs with them. Instead of simply collecting proposals and executing a desired amount within a few minutes as is normal practice, the Desk remained ready to accept proposals for several hours in order to allow dealers uncertain of their true financing needs to submit them. That day, about $3.5 billion in RPs were arranged, not a terribly large job by Desk standards. But no chances were taken. A Desk staff member later recalled that the week was the first time in memory that Desk traders were allowed to send out for lunch rather than leave their posts.

The injection of reserves into the banking system, if not offset in part, would have added materially to the banks' excess reserves. In such a situation, money market rates might well have plummeted as banks tried to disencumber themselves of their excess reserves. To counter the glut, the Desk asked the Treasury to initiate withdrawals from its Tax and Loan accounts at the banks. As the banks remitted funds from those accounts to the Treasury's account at the Fed, the excess of reserves was drained from the banking system, thus restoring a rough balance to reserves supplies. The tactic, in essence, funded the dealers while simultaneously draining reserves from the hoarding banks.

At 8:45 A.M. on Wednesday, Manufacturers Hanover announced that it would pay the $29.3 million of interest due its customers on securities lent to Drysdale and would complete the securities transactions it had executed for Drysdale. United States Trust followed at 10:15 A.M. and added in its statement that its minor exposure would have no material impact on its financial condition. Finally, at 11:45 A.M., Chase announced that it would make payments of approximately $178 million to cover interest due on securities borrowed by Drysdale including the $160-million payment missed on Monday. It also announced an agreement with Drysdale by which the title, rights, and interests of virtually all of Drysdale's property were assigned to Chase. That gave Chase control over the liquidation of Drysdale's securities positions, control that was crucial to determining the size of the bank's ultimate loss. Chase reserved the right to sue other parties involved for later recovery of damages.

The assumption of responsibility by the banks was an essential step in resolving the crisis, but much of the blockage in the markets still remained to be unraveled. The Desk arranged over $4 billion of RPs on Wednesday. That helped with the dealers' financing. The Fed also addressed the problem of the inability of firms to deliver borrowed securities by temporarily liberalizing its conditions for lending Treasury securities from the Fed's own portfolio. Such borrowings—which amounted to some $2 billion at the high point—were, of course, fully collateralized by other securities, so there was no net increment to the amount of securities controlled by the dealers. The only result, precisely as had been intended, was to break the gridlock threatening the market.

These extraordinary measures lasted only a few days, but were so effective that the Drysdale crisis never reached anything close to its potential destructiveness. Probably the most remarkable aspect of the whole affair was that, except for some market professionals, few were aware that the Fed had done anything at all other than host a meeting between Chase and the dealers.

The next crisis

No one knows when or under what circumstances the next crisis might occur, and that is the essence of the problem. Among the crises reviewed in this chapter, Penn Central and Franklin National were clearly the most tractable, simply because the basic problems emerged slowly enough so that the Fed could stay on top of the unfolding situation. Penn Central's problems had been known for months. The only important unknown was whether a last-minute federal bailout might possibly forestall the crisis. Similarly, the Fed was alerted early to the deteriorating situation at Franklin and accordingly began to prepare contingency plans about six months before the collapse in May. In the Hunt and Drysdale crises, the Fed's lead time, if it existed at all, was measured in hours.[12]

The Fed has no black books filled with contingency plans, for the details of each event are inherently unique and beyond the ability of anyone to anticipate. To the extent that there is a common strategy for dealing with crises, it is first to identify all of the problems involved as quickly as possible and then to determine whether they are containable without the Fed's intervention, or whether they constitute a systemic threat requiring such intervention.

This is, of course, the same process that the public follows in appraising the unfolding situation. The problem is that information may be sparse and of doubtful validity. Fearing the worst, individuals and firms may take actions, as some banks did during the Drysdale crisis, that, although perfectly prudent from the private point of view, may compound a nascent threat to the entire financial system.

Unfortunately, the essential first step in dealing with a crisis—collecting all relevant information about the problem—is, if anything, getting more difficult. The greater the number of parties involved, and the less time available to define, analyze, and rectify the problems, the more difficult it is to cope. The progressive internationalization of the financial system increases the number, the interdependence, and the remoteness of major market participants.

At the same time, the greater speed with which most financial transactions are settled makes prompt resolution of problems more urgent than before. Computers and electronic monitoring systems are certainly helpful, but they do not greatly alter the basic difficulty. They certainly did not help much in the Drysdale affair.

Successful resolution of the next crisis will depend—just as in

Bagehot's day, and just as in the crises described in this chapter—on a high degree of human judgment unfettered by preconceptions.

Notes

1. Walter Bagehot, *Lombard Street: A Description of the Money Market* (London: Kegan, Paul & Co., 1873. Reprinted by John Murray, 1922.)

2. Ibid., pp. 187–88.

3. Prior to passage of reform legislation in the 1930s, however, the Fed *did* have this problem, as the allowable issue of Federal Reserve notes was legally limited by holdings of gold. In fact, as Friedman and Schwartz document in detail, it was the Fed's obsession with the potential "external drain" of reserves abroad that led it to raise the discount rate and to ignore both the "internal drain" of bank reserves into individuals' cash hoards and its own deliberate failure to provide for even seasonal needs for currency. Thus the Fed unfortunately had understood Bagehot incompletely. See Milton Friedman and Anna J. Schwartz, *A Monetary History of the United States, 1867–1960* (New York: National Bureau of Economic Research, 1963), pp. 393–96.

4. Since the Fed pays for securities purchases by simply posting a credit to the reserve accounts of appropriate banks, such purchases add to the total of balances in such accounts and thus increase the quantity of reserves available to the banking system.

5. The Federal Reserve also makes a relatively minor amount of loans to smaller banks through a seasonal lending facility. Like adjustment borrowings, such credit is charged the basic discount rate, and most analysts regard seasonal and adjustment borrowings as functionally almost identical.

Adjustment borrowings are expected to be repaid within a few days. For financial institutions experiencing a prolonged reserves deficiency, the discount window may make extended credit available. Depending upon the period of time such loans are outstanding, a rate somewhat higher than the discount rate may be charged.

In addition, the Fed also has the authority to lend directly to individuals, partnerships, and corporations in "unusual and exigent circumstances," provided that there is evidence of their inability to obtain adequate credit from conventional banking sources. However, this authority has not been used for many years.

6. Interestingly, the penalty discount rate that monetarists advocate as part of a total reserves targeting procedure (see Chapter 6) bears much more similarity to Bagehot's concept.

7. The best study of the Franklin collapse is Joan Edelman Spero, *The Failure of the Franklin National Bank* (New York: Columbia University Press, 1980). Another useful source is the 1974 annual report of the Federal Reserve Bank of New York. This chapter has benefited from these accounts.

8. The best description of the events surrounding the Hunts' plunge into silver is Stephen Fay, *Beyond Greed* (New York: Viking Press, 1982). The brief account in this chapter draws heavily on Fay's reportage.

9. Futures exchanges rely on the device of a clearinghouse to permit efficient trading of futures contracts. When one buys a futures contract, the contract is actually between the buyer and the exchange's clearinghouse, which also has an offsetting contract with the seller. By thus standing in between the buyer and seller, the clearinghouse permits trading to proceed unimpeded by expensive and time-consuming mutual investigation of the creditworthiness of all participants. Since positions are "marked to market"

at the close of each trading day, participants may be called upon to provide extra margin if their positions have lost substantial value during the day. If all margin calls are met, the clearinghouse will have no net exposure, since its losses on some contracts will be offset by identical gains on others. But that is not true if the required margin calls are *not* met. In the event of such a default, all members of the clearinghouse are obligated to provide funds to cover the exposure thus created. That is why the failure of a large clearinghouse member potentially could drain the capital of other members and force the clearinghouse—and thus the exchange—into insolvency.

10. It is unclear whether or not Engelhard profited by this transaction. Profits may well have been realized on the silver involved. However, as of this writing, the Beaufort Sea concession is still undeveloped and appears unlikely to be developed for some years to come; that property is probably worth substantially less now than it was in 1980. But any losses on that account must be compared to what might have happened to Engelhard—as well as other firms—had the company remained adamant in its demand for cash.

11. The best popular accounts are in Chris Welles, "Drysdale: What Really Happened," *Institutional Investor*, September 1982, pp. 73–83; Marcia L. Stigum and Rene O. Branch, Jr., *Managing Bank Assets and Liabilities* (Homewood, Ill.: Dow Jones-Irwin, 1982); and Marcia L. Stigum, *The Money Market* (Homewood, Ill.: Dow Jones-Irwin, 1983). The Federal Reserve Bank of New York's official report on the affair is "A Report on Drysdale and Other Recent Problems of Firms Involved in the Government Securities Market," processed, September 15, 1982. The brief account in this chapter relies on the New York Fed's report for many details.

12. In the case of Drysdale, the Desk had been informed several months earlier that the firm was conducting an inordinate amount of trading relative to its capital, and was well aware that a number of dealers refused to do business with it. Moreover, in early 1982, the Fed had alerted other regulators of financial institutions to the growing use of RPs and the potential risks involved, and directed the same warning to banks and securities dealers. Nevertheless, the full scope of the Drysdale problem was unknown when the Monday payment was missed.

THE INTERNATIONAL SPHERE

The Federal Reserve has little formal authority over the international aspects of U.S. economic policy, although in one key area—exchange rate policy—it has an operational role. As mentioned in Chapter 2, when the Fed enters foreign exchange markets to buy or sell dollars and foreign currencies, it does so only under authorization of the Treasury, which by law has responsibility for such matters. Similarly, though the Fed maintains close working contact with foreign central banks and monitors developments in foreign exchange markets through the Foreign Desk at the Federal Reserve Bank of New York, its role is clearly subordinate to the Treasury. At times, Fed officials' expertise may give them influence in the Treasury's deliberations on international economic policy, but they wield little independent authority.

However, as will presently become clear, in recent years, the Fed in fact has played the leading policy role in the major issues of international economic policy, among which the international debt crisis stands out.

Who calls the shots?

The true locus of authority over exchange rate policy was highlighted when the Reagan administration came into office. The administration, in the person of Under Secretary of the Treasury for Monetary Affairs Beryl Sprinkel, the official directly responsible for foreign exchange policy, announced that, as a matter of principle, the United States would not intervene in foreign exchange markets to try to influence foreign exchange rates. Intervention, if it occurred at all, would be confined to extraordinary circumstances. Sprinkel described such an intervention policy as "minimal."

> By "minimal" I mean each day when I come into my office I expect the market will take care of the exchange rate, not the Federal Reserve or the Treasury . But there may well be occasions where, after discussion with the proper Federal Reserve officials, we may say this is an exception.[1]

Sprinkel meant what he said. During the administration's first three years, such operations were undertaken on only a few occasions, one of them being the immediate aftermath of the attempted assassination of President Reagan, and in no case for very sizable amounts. That was quite a break with prior years, when intervention had been frequent and often substantial in scale.

The new policy was far from being universally popular. A number of European governments were especially critical. The domestic price levels of those countries are highly sensitive to movements of foreign exchange rates, due to the large role of foreign trade in their economies. For most Western European countries, exports and imports of merchandise each constitute between one-fifth and one-half (sometimes more) of gross domestic products; for the United States, the corresponding figure is about one-tenth. Moreover, since OPEC oil prices are fixed in dollar terms over the short run, an increase in the dollar's value relative to their own currencies directly increases the cost, in domestic currency, of their oil imports. Under those circumstances, it was perhaps understandable that the Europeans resented the hands-off policy of the United States. Intervention admittedly had a spotty record, but in European eyes, it did at least offer some hope of moderating short-run swings in dollar exchange rates.

However, Sprinkel was adamant about the new policy and appeared to relish the loss of stature that it seemed to imply for the personnel at the New York Fed's Foreign Desk who had earlier been responsible for conducting intervention. And in any case, quite apart from the personalities involved, a decision to engage in intervention or to abstain from doing so did not, in practice, have major implications for prevailing exchange rates.

To see why, consider how intervention works. When the Federal Reserve intervenes in foreign exchange markets, the intervention is always "sterilized," so that it does not affect the quantity of reserves available to the banking system. For example, suppose the Fed is selling dollars and buying German marks for its own account in order to support the value of the mark against the dollar. In order to pay for the mark purchases, the Fed posts credits to the reserve accounts of banks where the dollar buyers have their accounts. All other things equal, that *increases* the volume of reserves available to the banking system.

But all does not remain equal. Simultaneously, the Fed *drains* a like amount of reserves from the banking system through its domestic open market operations.[2] That results in debits to reserve accounts that offset the impact of the credits. Thus the foreign exchange operation is sterilized. It cannot affect (here it is tempting to write "infect") the availability of reserves to banks in the United States, and by extension, the U.S. money supply. In this way the Fed comes to own deposits at the German central bank—the marks that it bought—and, as is standard practice, uses those balances to purchase German government debt or other interest-earning mark assets.

(If instead the Fed's intervention activities were conducted as agent for the Treasury, the mechanics of the transactions are different, but their reserves impact would still be sterilized.)

The end result, then, is that the private sector owns more U.S. Treasury securities (which the Fed sold) and fewer German government securities (which the Fed bought). In principle, neither country's domestic money supply need be affected. Securities markets in the two countries need not be greatly affected either, since the proportional changes in total dollar and mark securities outstanding will certainly be nominal. With relatively limited impacts on the domestic markets involved, it is hardly surprising that intervention on less than a gargantuan scale would produce little fundamental impact on the exchange rate that links them.

Proponents of U.S. intervention had not, for the most part, believed that such operations could have a lasting effect on foreign exchange rates. The conceivable scale of intervention was simply too small relative to the huge trading volumes of the foreign exchange markets and the net exchange positions of private market participants. Rather, their principal concern was to damp out some of the short-run volatility in exchange rates. In part, volatility was viewed as the product of an unstable expectations process in which an initial shock to the market causes a sharp displacement of the exchange rate. In turn, this fuels expectations of further movements in the same direction, cumulating in a much larger change, until something causes the process to reverse itself and swing in the opposite direction. While such a characterization lacks some nuances, it is not completely alien to market realities. Anyone who has ever witnessed the emotional dynamic of a foreign exchange trading desk would be hard put to deny at least some role to cumulative expectations. In any event, if one regards such a snowball effect as a prominent feature of the market, a role for central bank intervention to provide constructive guidance in the formation of expectations makes sense. Accordingly, after the collapse in 1973 of most major countries' efforts to maintain fixed parities against the dollar, intervention operations primarily had the limited objective of "countering disorderly market conditions."

Perhaps the best concise description of the approach was given by a senior official of the Federal Reserve Bank of New York:

> What constitutes disorderly trading is not easy to define precisely. But sharp fluctuations in the exchange rate, a reluctance of bank traders to make two-way markets or a distinct widening of the bid-offer spreads of the two-way prices they do make, and a tendency for rate movements to accumulate in one direction have been among the characteristics of a disorderly market.
>
> In such circumstances, there is a risk that exchange rates will fluctuate in a manner out of keeping with underlying economic trends, and a risk that normal commercial and financial transactions may not be readily accommodated in the market. To reduce those risks, intervention may be appropriate to provide depth to the market and smooth erratic rate fluctuations, but not to direct the exchange rate to any particular level. The size of operations needed to counter disorderly conditions varies according to the situation. Minor disturbances may be calmed with minimal intervention. But periods of severe disorder may call for sizable intervention over a number of days or weeks.[3]

Clearly, there is a difficult problem of judgment in implementing such operations. Disturbances due to changes in fundamental economic factors (which should not be resisted) must be distinguished from changes due to nonfundamental causes (which, from this point of view, should be).

Critics have pointed out, however, that the judgments of Treasury and Fed officials were not particularly likely to outperform the judgments of private-sector professionals. Without systematically superior judgment or exclusive access to relevant information, the Fed's Foreign Desk could not avoid losing money by trying to stabilize exchange rates. Quite often, in fact, central banks have been left holding the bag as they bought (sold) currencies that sooner or later declined (increased) in value anyway. That can be extremely expensive.

The Bank of France provided an outstanding illustration of this point when, during a few weeks in the spring of 1983, it reportedly managed to lose something on the order of several hundred million dollars in a wholly futile effort to check the decline of the franc in the foreign exchange markets. If some high social purpose were being served, incurring such costs might be justifiable, but many felt that the probable tab for slightly reducing the volatility of foreign exchange rates was altogether excessive.

Fundamentally, Volcker agreed with that view. Yet unlike Sprinkel, he was not opposed in principle to intervening in foreign exchange markets, if only because intervention offered the opportunity to make traders in those markets a bit more cautious in their speculation. Considering the prominent role that Volcker tended to assign to psychological factors in economic relationships, such an attitude was quite in character. In a widely remarked speech to the Rome meeting of the Trilateral Commission on April 17, 1983, Volcker described his approach toward foreign exchange intervention as follows:

> The evidence suggests that intervention is a limited tool that cannot, itself, alter major market forces, but there may be times and circumstances in which it can be useful in damping fluctuations, expressing policy intentions, and supporting other measures. . . . if we are not too ambitious, we can constructively do something to help stabilize exchange rates within the general framework of the floating system. As we see inflationary forces receding, and as confidence in our ability to keep inflation under control increases, we should have room for more short-term flexibility in monetary policy. We should be properly modest about our ability to judge the "right" exchange rate, but we can probably reach a consensus from time to time when those rates seem "wrong"—at levels that are unsustainable and mutually damaging to our economic objectives. In such instances, the question of intervention could be approached pragmatically, reinforced if needed by domestic policy.

What Volcker had in mind, of course, was small-scale intervention designed to affect the psychology of the markets but little else. He could see no merit in trying to affect market fundamentals through the feeble device of intervention. In particular, intervention could never substitute for a disinflationary domestic monetary policy.

Volcker's views on intervention naturally received considerable public attention, despite the fact that the Treasury, not the Fed, was the formally responsible authority. The reason for this attention was quite straightforward. Where it counts, in the fundamentals, the Fed has vastly more discretionary influence over foreign exchange rates than does the Treasury. The most important fundamental factors determining foreign exchange rates are relative interest rates, relative inflation rates, current account balances, and political stability.

The Fed might not be able to do much about the latter, but it clearly had enormous power to influence interest rates. In contrast, while the Treasury could influence fiscal policy—in the sense that the president proposes while the Congress disposes—its discretionary authority was virtually nil.

In recent years, U.S. international economic policy has been little more than a reflection of domestic fiscal and monetary policy. International concerns definitely influenced policy formulation, but the policy itself was still basically domestic in its orientation. It lacked a well-defined international reference point. This shows through dramatically in the two greatest international problems that the Fed has faced in recent years: the enormous appreciation of the foreign exchange value of the dollar and the international debt crisis.

The dollar

Before tracing the dynamics behind the massive appreciation in the foreign exchange value of the dollar during 1980–83, it will be helpful to outline the basic elements involved in the joint determination of domestic interest rates and exchange rates. There are several ways in which that might be done, but one of the simplest, and by all odds the most intuitive for many, is to consider the problem from the standpoint of an investor choosing between investments in the United States and some foreign country.

The investor naturally will compare the expected real rates of return available in the United States and abroad by adjusting the prevailing nominal interest rates for his subjective expectation of U.S. and foreign price inflation. In addition, however, the investor estimates the rate at which the U.S. dollar will appreciate or depreciate during the holding period. If the dollar seems likely to rise in value relative to other currencies, dollar investments are obviously more attractive than they otherwise would be. Finally, peace of mind is worth something, and the investor makes a judgment of how much of a premium he is willing to pay to enjoy the greater security of investments in the United States compared to other locales.

Assuming that a large number of investors go through this process, the following relationship will hold approximately:

$$R_{US} + P_{US} + A_{US} = R_F$$

where R_{US} is the expected U.S. real interest rate in percentage points, R_F is the expected foreign real interest rate, P_{US} is the premium which U.S. investments can command due to their greater security (expressed as an annual percentage rate), and A_{US} is the expected annual rate of appreciation of the dollar relative to other currencies. In so many words, what the equation says is that, on a risk-adjusted basis, the total return expected from U.S. investments must equal that expected from investments abroad. That is because if one or the other yields were out of line, investors would have an incentive to shift their investments between countries until yields had been forced back into proper alignment.

In general, if one of the variables in the relationship changes, offsetting changes will occur in the other three. But since the equation merely describes an equilibrium relationship that exists after all adjustments have been made, it says nothing about which variables will respond.

For example, suppose that R_{US} declines. Then, when all adjustments have been completed in capital markets, R_F may have declined (with P_{US} and A_{US} unchanged), A_{US} may have risen (with P_{US} and R_F unchanged), or some other combination of changes may have occurred. The key point is that *something* must make a compensating adjustment when one of the variables changes. Moreover, if circumstances permit adjustments to occur in all three variables, those adjustments in general will be smaller in magnitude than they would be if one or other of the variables were constrained in some way. To say the same thing another way, the less responsiveness allowed in some of the variables, the greater the responsiveness of the remaining variables must be.

Much of the massive rise in the dollar during 1980–83 is explained by the fact that although both U.S. real rates (R_{US}) and the "safe-haven" quality of U.S. investments (P_{US}) increased during the period, foreign rates were prevented from compensating fully for the changes, forcing the brunt of the adjustment into an expected depreciation of the dollar, i.e., A_{US} became significantly negative.

How did that happen? Capital inflows into dollar assets lifted the current (or spot) dollar exchange value far above any level that would allow the United States to remain reasonably competitive in world markets. The flip side to the dollar's massive appreciation was the creation of a strong expectation that, sooner or later, a decline to a lower, and more economically sustainable, value would occur. Had upward pressure on U.S. rates been less severe, had foreign rates been allowed to rise further, and had the dollar's role as safe haven dissipated more quickly, then the upward pressure on the current, or "spot," dollar exchange rate would have been considerably less. As it was, however, the dollar's trade-weighted value soared over 30 percent from late 1980 to the end of 1983 (Chart 11–1).[4]

It is impossible to identify precisely the unfolding sequence of events that produced that result since the safe-haven premium is unobservable and unquantifiable, even though everyone acknowledges that it exists. Similarly, as discussed in earlier chapters, economists' measures of expectations are at best rather crude, so that quantification of expected returns and expected dollar depreciation are also subject to a fairly substantial margin of error. Nevertheless, a reasonable description would proceed as follows.

In late 1979, nominal U.S. interest rates rose sharply, but inflation was rising, if anything, even more sharply, so that the expected real U.S. rate probably did not change greatly, and may have declined somewhat, especially during the plunge of interest rates that followed the credit controls program in 1980. At the same time, the Iranian hostage crisis, the invasion of Afghanistan, the second OPEC oil price shock, and other international tensions probably contributed to some increased attractiveness of dollar assets. The net result was about a wash, and

CHART 11–1

Trade-Weighted Foreign Exchange Value of the Dollar

1980 – 82 = 100

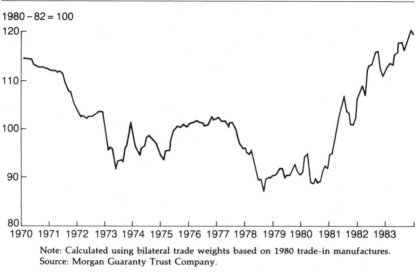

Note: Calculated using bilateral trade weights based on 1980 trade-in manufactures.
Source: Morgan Guaranty Trust Company.

From late 1980 through early 1984, the foreign exchange value of the dollar soared.

there was little adjustment in the dollar exchange rate, though it did strengthen somewhat in late 1980.

That balance was soon disrupted, however, as U.S. nominal rates soared to new highs in late 1980 and remained there during most of 1981. High nominal rates and a crumbling inflation rate produced postwar record high real interest rates. Even the sharp rate decline in the second half of 1982 provided only temporary respite. Rates were little changed during 1983, while inflation slowed still further to a new cyclical low; real rates accordingly rose almost to their 1982 levels.

International tensions also worsened during the period, with widespread fighting in the Mideast, conflicts in Latin America, and an emerging international debt crisis. The premium on dollar assets surely went still higher.

Under those circumstances, foreign real interest rates should have risen to levels considerably in excess of U.S. rates, if previously existing currency relationships were to be preserved. But that did not happen. Instead, since foreign governments were, by and large, unwilling to wreak still further punishment on their weak economies, foreign rates were not even allowed to rise to match the lofty U.S. rates. Consequently, the full burden of adjustment was forced onto the exchange rate, which soared as foreign capital sought outlets in the United States.

By the end of 1983, then, there existed a U.S. interest rate level substantially higher than that abroad, a sizable premium favoring dollar assets, and necessarily, an expectation of massive dollar depreciation to come. As noted earlier, precise quantification is impossible, but the 1984 *Annual Report of the Council of Economic Advisers,* written under the direction of Chairman Martin Feldstein, did attempt a "ballpark" quantification of the size of the expected decline in the dollar's exchange value in a calculation that implicitly assumed that the safe haven premium on dollar assets was zero. The result: a 32 percent overvaluation![5] Moreover, due to the clearly too cautious assumption regarding the dollar premium, that figure may well have been a serious underestimate of the actual expected dollar depreciation.

The two most dramatic consequences of the soaring dollar were the devastation of the U.S. balance of trade with foreign countries and its financial counterpart, and swelling imports of capital from abroad. The plunge in U.S. real net exports, i.e., real exports less real imports, did not seriously get under way until 1981, although dollar strength had been building since late 1980.

The availability of cheaper imports gradually caused U.S. consumers and firms to substitute foreign goods for U.S. products, thereby boosting the real volume of imports. At the same time, foreigners reduced their purchases of U.S. goods in favor of lower-cost sources of supply. In addition, financial difficulties in a number of developing countries that were major markets for U.S. exports also contributed to the shrinkage, but that factor, as will be seen presently, was also related to dollar strength.

The result was a delayed, but protracted, erosion of U.S. net exports. The process shows up clearly in Chart 11-2, which displays U.S. net exports together with the dollar exchange rate lagged 4 quarters. From the end of 1980 to the end of 1983, declining net exports reduced real GNP by almost $50 billion dollars, or more than 3 percent. Production losses were concentrated in the economic sectors most sensitive to foreign competition. Autos, steel, capital machinery, and chemicals were among the industries most severely affected.

As noted earlier, the flip side to a current account deficit produced by deteriorating international competitiveness is a capital account surplus. The two go together. It is, by definition, impossible to have one without the other. The reason is that if foreigners in the aggregate wish to buy less from the United States than they sell to the United States, they necessarily must be willing to hold some form of dollar asset. That investment might be in bank deposits, real estate, Treasury securities, shares of corporate stock, or some other financial or real asset. Whatever the form such investments actually take, they are simply the financial counterpart to the deterioration in U.S. net exports.

Similarly, it is incorrect to speak as though the deterioration

CHART 11-2

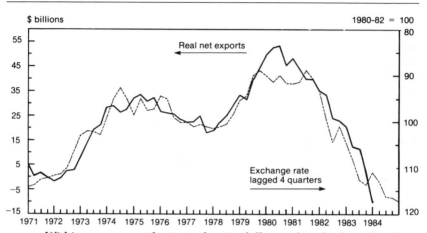

Within a year or so, the strengthening dollar produced a sharp deterioration in U.S. real net exports of goods and services.

of the trade balance caused the capital imports, or vice versa. They were the joint products of a common phenomenon. Specifically, the high level of real U.S. interest rates relative to those abroad, the increased attractiveness of the United States as a safe haven in a troubled world, and the soaring dollar—that constellation of factors created the conditions in which U.S. net exports declined and U.S. capital imports increased.

Consequently, it is seriously incomplete to say, as quite a few found it convenient to do, that U.S. capital imports served to mitigate the effects of crowding out created by large federal deficits. Capital imports did no more to reduce crowding out than declining net exports did. They were both part and parcel of the same phenomenon. Moreover, the actual influence of the capital imports was not so much to offset domestic crowding out (as was often alleged) as it was to transfer its incidence away from such interest-sensitive sectors as housing and business investment and toward exchange-rate sensitive sectors—i.e., export-and import-competing industries. Thanks to the influx of foreign capital, housing and investment spending were larger, and net exports smaller, than they otherwise would have been.

Foreign economies, in the aggregate, realized significant benefits from the deterioration of U.S. competitiveness. However, the distribution of these benefits from one country to the next was highly uneven. Among the prime beneficiaries were such countries as Canada, Mexico, and several Asian nations that for years have enjoyed substantial trading relationships with the United States and for whom exports to the United States constituted a substantial portion of their production.

In contrast, those countries—in Western Europe, for example—for whom exports to the United States were not very significant relative to their total production did not benefit so directly from the U.S. recovery's pull on foreign export industries. Nevertheless, the plunge of European imports from the United States, together with the relatively modest increase in exports to the United States, promptly erased the earlier European deficit in merchandise trade with the United States. However, the appreciating dollar partly offset that benefit by making the effective cost of some of their imports, notably petroleum, more expensive. For quite a few, the net result was that dollar strength actually resulted in more inflation and little, if any, recovery in real economic activity. As we shall see in a moment, much the same was true of many of the less developed countries whose financial difficulties constituted the core of the international debt crisis.

Thus, it was hardly surprising that foreign criticism of U.S. economic policy should have been so intense. Because of the size of the U.S. economy and the central role of the dollar in the world payments system, U.S. policy decisions to a considerable degree were imposed on the world.

The debt crisis

The international debt crisis originated in the same inflation psychology that gripped the United States during the late 1970s. During the 1970s, prices of the commodities that constitute most developing countries' major source of export earnings rose rapidly. The explosion of oil prices benefited some countries while hurting others, but even excluding oil, commodity prices rose at an average compound rate of 11–12 percent per annum during 1971–80, so that at the end of the decade, prices were about three times as high as in 1970. That rate of gain vastly exceeded the interest rates at which most countries borrowed. Three-month Eurodollar rates averaged about 8.5 percent in those years, and spreads between lending rates and deposit rates were under steady downward pressure during most of the period.

Finally, roughly 90 percent of the countries' borrowings were denominated in dollars, and the dollar's foreign exchange value was declining during virtually the whole period. Small wonder, then, that borrowing to finance all manner of domestic expenditures appeared to many countries to be as sensible as taking out multiple mortgages did to some California homeowners.[6]

The period of greatest expansion in the borrowers' debt was 1976–81. World trade was surging. Moreover, international banks were avidly seeking profitable new lending outlets for the burgeoning deposits accumulated by OPEC members. Developing countries conveniently provided the demand for what the banks had to supply.

In retrospect, it is easy to see that what was being created was, from the historical vantage point, quite peculiar. First, most foreign-country lending was now being done by syndicates of banks. Previously, these countries had relied primarily on bond issues and loans from various governmental and international agencies. The difference was of crucial significance. Had the OPEC countries lent directly to the developing countries through bond purchases, they would have been forced to bear the risk that their own actions, such as the 1979 oil-price shock, might threaten the issuers' ability to pay.

Instead, the banks intermediated between the depositors and the lenders and took that risk on themselves. From the mid-1970s to 1980, a large and growing portion of international banking activity revolved around the recycling of the swelling OPEC current account surplus to less developed countries lacking domestic petroleum resources (nonoil LDCs). In this task the banks were far more than passive intermediaries. They not only recycled the OPEC surplus; they lent large amounts of funds raised in the industrialized countries to the LDCs. In short order, the recycling problem ceased to exist during the early 1980s. After peaking at a $111 billion surplus in 1980, the OPEC current account balance plunged to a $16 billion deficit by 1982 as worldwide recession and softening oil prices took their toll.

The banks' motive for lending to the LDCs was purely economic. Highly competitive (and relatively unprofitable) domestic lending markets made banks more willing to step up their foreign lending. Naturally, individual banks sought to diversify their risk exposure to individual borrowers, some admittedly with more determination than others. But no lending bank could diversify away the risk that the inflationary assumptions underlying many of the calculations of debt coverage ratios and other lending guidelines might be overturned in the near future. And very few seemed interested in doing so, for the second great peculiarity of the emerging system was that it was predicated on a continuation of the inflation spiral.

As long as commodity price inflation continued at rates generally higher than interest rates, the borrowers were solvent. Their export earnings were sufficient to cover interest and principal payments on their loans.

Beginning in 1981, however, insolvency loomed as a real prospect for many borrowers. From 1980 to 1982, as inflation rates in the industrialized countries began to slow, non-oil commodity prices plunged 25 percent. Disinflation in the industrialized world meant *deflation* in the developing world. That alone would have been a disaster for the borrowers. But the impact was compounded by the fact that the widespread recession sharply reduced the borrowers' export volumes as well. Furthermore, since most international debt is indexed to short-term interest rates (typically LIBOR, the London Interbank Offered Rate), the rapid increase in rates to levels almost twice the 1970s average directly raised the burden of foreign countries' debt service. Thus did the assumptions underlying the new international financial system crumble.

Banks had become increasingly concerned about international lending during 1981 as East European debt problems surfaced, but Mexico's request for a moratorium on its debt in August 1982 assumed special significance. Mexico was one of the two largest international borrowers, with roughly $90 billion of chiefly dollar-denominated private and governmental debt outstanding. Mexico was also a country with substantial oil resources, and not even earnings from that source had sufficed to avert the crisis. Instead, by 1982, interest payments on Mexico's debt were about half as large as its total export earnings.

The other big Latin American borrowers—Argentina, Brazil, Chile, and Venezuela—were in a similar condition, as was the Philippines.

The remaining half of export earnings was obviously inadequate to cover necessary imports, let alone principal payments due on the debt. Consequently, it required no great stretch of the imagination for lenders to surmise that other sovereign borrowers likely would soon follow Mexico into either a moratorium or perhaps even an outright default.

Widespread defaults, had they occurred, could have precipitated a collapse, not only of the economies of the borrowing countries, but of a substantial portion of international trade as well. The situation had special significance for U.S. banks, which were easily the largest lenders to Mexico and Latin America. Defaults could have erased the capital base of some of the largest banks in the country and thereby could have threatened major domestic financial dislocations.

As was the case during the crises sketched in the preceding chapter, as soon as creditworthiness began to be called into question, liquidity—in the form of the borrowers' continuing access to essential commercial credit—vanished. Many banks wanted out, especially smaller banks with minor exposures which in all likelihood never would have entered international lending in the first place had they not assumed that their larger brethren in the loan syndicates knew what they were doing. But as Bagehot, had he been alive, would surely have observed, a crisis is precisely the time when, if the "terror" is not to spread and feed on itself, lending must *increase*. Even such fundamentally solvent countries as Mexico could not hope to avoid default if they were abruptly shut off from access to the credit required to keep their debt payments current.

And that was precisely the direction in which the banks' newly aroused prudential instincts were taking the international financial system. According to the Federal Reserve's Flow of Funds accounts, the year 1982 was the first year in well over a decade in which U.S. banks reduced their net foreign credit extension, and the largest reductions in exposures were made during the second half of that year, following the Mexican moratorium.

Volcker and the Fed had been monitoring the situation for some time before that. In fact, Volcker maintains that he first became seriously concerned at the course of developments in the international debt markets in the early 1970s, following the first OPEC oil price shock. As difficulties began building to a crisis, the Fed perceived that righting the situation required two essential initiatives.

The most immediate need was to provide stop-gap financing packages so that the borrowers could pay for essential imports and debt service. That, it was hoped, would forestall defaults and the unknown, but surely dangerous, systemic threats that they implied. In essence, the task was to prevent the contraction of liquidity in the international credit markets from pulling the system down with it.

The second initiative involved devising long-term adjustment plans between the borrowers and lenders. That was hard for banks to do on their own. There were simply too many lending banks involved—several hundred in most cases—to expect that they would be able to agree on a proper plan if left to themselves. Each would be faced with a major incentive to cut a deal, get out, and leave the others holding the bag.

Second, the borrowers, sovereign nations all, also would have faced major political incentives to play the banks off against one another, while delaying the economic reforms necessary to achieve long-term economic viability. Indeed, probably nothing is so humiliating to a national political leader in a developing country as being seen kowtowing to private banks.

In essence, then, what was needed was to roll back, at least in part, the newly enlarged role of banks in providing and administering international credit. Only the International Monetary Fund (IMF) possessed the expertise, buttressed by international political clout, to design economic adjustment programs, negotiate their implementation with the borrowing governments, and then see that they were adhered to. The usual procedure is for the IMF to put up a portion of the funds in a financial package, with private banks anteing up the rest.

Unfortunately, the IMF's reserve fund did not appear adequate to the task.[7] Despite periodic increases over the years, its resources had lagged behind the growth of world trade. Negotiations in late 1982 and early 1983 eventually resulted in the Fund's Board of Governors authorizing, on March 31, 1983, an increase of its basic resources in the form of quota subscriptions by $32 billion—a 47.5 percent increase—of which the U.S. share was $5.7 billion. In addition, the United States and 10 other industrialized countries agreed to expand from about $7 billion to more than $18 billion their credit lines to the Fund under the General Agreements to Borrow (GAB), with the United States providing $2.6 billion of the total increase.

Volcker reportedly had drafted a plan for dealing with the situation in early 1982, well before the Mexican debt moratorium underscored its seriousness. For the plan to work, an expansion of the GAB was essential. Volcker was then rebuffed by Reagan administration policymakers, who had relatively little background in international finance, as well as an ideological predilection for letting private markets sort out their own problems without government involvement. In late 1982, as the full implications of possible defaults were becoming manifest, the administration found it expedient to ditch its ideological principles, at least temporarily, and to support the plan, essentially as it had been proposed originally.

However, legislation was required to authorize the increased U.S. commitment to the IMF, and many in Congress were opposed. The reasons varied. Some called attention to the need to reduce federal spending and argued that not putting up $8.3 billion for the IMF would be a good place to start.[8] Others were opposed on more narrowly ideological grounds. Their free-market philosophy told them that imprudent borrowers and lenders should be made to suffer the consequences of their poor judgment. Some suspected the plan was a camouflaged bailout of the banks. Their political philosophy could not countenance expenditures for such a purpose, especially when cuts were simultaneously being made in a variety of domestic social welfare programs. Finally, many Democrats in Congress were suspicious that if they voted to support the appropriation, Republicans would use it against them as a campaign issue.

The most cohesive and organized support for the IMF appropriation came from the Fed and the banks. Volcker testified numerous times in support of the legislation and privately urged the administration and congressional leaders to push for it as well. And they did so. Finally, late in the year, after months of debate and following an intense lobbying effort, the legislation passed and was signed into law.[9] The debt crisis was obviously far from over, but the prospects for containing it had been greatly improved.

Regard for the Fed also improved as a result of its early perception of the emerging crisis and skillful efforts to defuse it—so much so, in fact, that demonstrated expertise in such matters was widely understood to have been one of the principal factors behind President Reagan's decision in May 1983 to reappoint Volcker to a second term as chairman.

International lenders of last resort

The debt crisis raised in stark relief the issue of the international lender of last resort. Where sovereign borrowers are involved, the IMF is the only agency with sufficient authority to play that role—but the IMF is not a lender of last resort. The problem is that the IMF, unlike central banks serving as lenders of last resort for their domestic banks, cannot create monetary reserves. Instead, it must borrow them from member countries. That fact very nearly became an insuperable obstacle to ameliorating the debt crisis.

Another aspect of the issue concerns "offshore" banking institutions, many of which are little more than corporate shells owned by foreign banking firms. Typically they are subject to only loose regulation by the monetary authorities of the mostly obscure, low-tax locales where they officially conduct their business.

The problem was highlighted in July 1982, when Banco Ambrosiano Holdings, a Luxembourg-based financial holding company owned by Banco Ambrosiano, then Italy's largest private bank, was declared in default on unpaid interest and principal owed to a consortium of 120 lending banks. Both the holding company subsidiary and its bank parent had sustained massive losses as a result of apparently fraudulent transactions involving a number of dummy Panamanian companies.

Since 1975, the major monetary authorities have had a mutual understanding, called the Basel Concordat, that makes each authority responsible for the supervision of bank branches established abroad by its country's banks. Responsibility for supervision does not, of course, imply responsibility for bailing out the depositors of a failed bank—though many participants in the interbank lending market relied on the comfortable assumption that, in practice, it did. Moreover, supervisory responsibility extended only to banks and bank branches, not to nonbank subsidiaries.

In early August, when the Bank of Italy placed Banco Ambrosiano in liquidation, it declared that it had no responsibility to pay off the obligations of the subsidiaries. Similarly, the Luxembourg authorities also rejected responsibility, since Banco Ambrosiano Holdings was not a bank. That left the lending consortium holding the bag for over $590 million in unpaid claims. Under the terms of a settlement reached almost two years later, it appeared that most of the consortium participants would receive compensation for about 70 percent of their claims.

The Ambrosiano incident shocked banks that had lent freely to one another in the Euromarkets on the tacit assumption that when needed, central bank assistance would, in practice, be forthcoming—even if the failure fell short of posing a systematic threat. Volcker's reaction? As far as the author has been able to determine, he never made a public statement on the subject. But had he done so, it probably would have been something along the line of not losing sleep worrying about the unregulated and untaxed offshore institutions, as long as their misadventures posed no threat to the system. Indeed, from Volcker's point of view, the Ambrosiano incident—for all its bizarre and, in one instance, lethal, aspects—was probably an invigorating tonic for the Euromarkets, where in his opinion, banks had paid far too little attention to risk exposures created by their lending activities.

The international dimension of domestic policy

Despite the protracted drama of the debt crisis, in recent years, public discussion of monetary policy overwhelmingly has focused on narrow, domestic objectives. Most conspicuously, the Fed's proximate objectives have been framed in terms of growth rates of various monetary aggregates. To much of the public those targets *are* the Fed's objectives.

Not surprisingly, such a view greatly misrepresents the Fed's actual policy approach. For example, Mexico's debt moratorium request in August 1982, especially its potentially systemic implications, was almost certainly one of the concerns that impelled the Fed to temporarily set aside its M1 target and proceed to ease its policy stance. Yet the fact remains that there is no formal incorporation of foreign policy considerations in the public representation of policy objectives. In the United States, such considerations typically receive little or no public discussion, unless some especially acute development with an immediate and visible domestic impact—such as the plunge of the U.S. balance of trade, with its attendant severe impacts on U.S. regional economies—thrusts them to the forefront.

Recently, a number of proposals have been made to improve this situation. One of the most provocative stems from a hypothesis aptly dubbed "world monetarism." The basic argument—which has been advanced chiefly by Stanford University economist Ronald I. McKinnon—is as follows.[10]

Investors are assumed to substitute freely between different national currencies as they react to shifting expectations of future movements of exchange rates. Their underlying demand for money is stable, but the money in question is not any one national currency, but rather the stock of "world money," the sum of the major, freely convertible currencies.

Investors' efforts to substitute between currencies create pressures for exchange-rate adjustments. These pressures need not affect the size of the world money stock if all exchange rates are allowed to float freely or if all are maintained at fixed parities, as in the old Bretton Woods system. In the former case, the national money stocks could expand independently of one another; in the latter case, excessive growth of one would be offset by slower growth of another.

However, McKinnon argues that in practice, a pattern of "asymmetric sterilization" prevails in which the United States sterilizes the impact of all central bank foreign exchange transactions on domestic monetary reserves, while the major foreign countries do not. In other words, unlike the United States, foreign central banks attempt to stabilize their exchange rates even at the cost of forcing an expansion or contraction of their domestic money stocks.

This process would make the rate of growth of world money expansion, and thus the world inflation rate, subject to the vagaries of investors' volatile currency preferences. The result is a chronic tendency toward bouts of either inflation (due to an expected depreciation of the dollar) or deflation (appreciating dollar). In McKinnon's view, the remedy for this state of affairs is for the United States to adjust its domestic monetary policy so as to offset overshoots or undershoots in the non-U.S. portion of the world money supply. On an operational level, that means that the Federal Reserve should use *un*sterilized intervention to maintain a foreign exchange rate that seems consistent with the desired growth of world money.

As it happens, several key features of this story have been rather soundly rejected by students of international finance.[11] Probably the most critical is McKinnon's contention that growth of world money is more important in determining any country's domestic inflation rate than is the growth of its domestic money stock. Statistical tests suggest strongly that the opposite is the case. Such a pattern is consistent with the existence of a substantial amount of domestic policy independence, such as one would expect in a system of floating exchange rates.

Other critics of current policy argue from a different perspective than McKinnon. They emphasize that large, persistent swings of exchange rates away from their equilibrium levels involve substantial social costs in the form of depressed output and employment, and that a policy of unsterilized exchange-market intervention could avoid many of those costs. Most advocates of this approach favor specification of a wide band—for example, plus or minus 10 percent—around the estimated fundamental equilibrium exchange rate. Intervention policy would be oriented only toward the limited objective of keeping the actual exchange rate within the band. Proponents do not necessarily support intervention to stabilize exchange rates as in the pre-1971 period. Instead their major objective is to limit the scale of possible misalignments.[12]

Under current conditions, the overvaluation of the dollar could be addressed through unsterilized intervention and a considerably more expansive U.S. monetary policy, with a commensurately increased risk of resurgent U.S. inflation. To reduce that risk, adherents to this view often favor a more restrictive fiscal policy that would allow scope for the stepped-up monetary accommodation.

That caveat calls attention to the fact that the exchange rate reflects, among other things, the mix of fiscal and monetary policy. Some have argued that the strong dollar is not necessarily bad, given the highly expansive U.S. fiscal policy. Were the dollar to be held down artificially, for example, through some form of capital controls or possibly sterilized intervention on a massive scale, then the higher implied level of aggregate demand would, in turn, force inflation and interest rates higher. And that would shift the burden of crowding out from sectors sensitive to foreign competition to others, such as residential housing construction and business investment, which are most sensitive to interest rates. That might, or might not, be a smart political move, but such intervention definitely would not produce any macroeconomic miracles.[13]

Indeed, the dollar problem is political to a marked degree. Without some device for modifying fiscal policy appropriately, mandating the Fed to modify its monetary policy in whatever way might be required to achieve the desired exchange rate, simply amounts to one more way to assure the subordination of monetary policy to fiscal policy. For example, an overly expansive fiscal policy would, on this line of reasoning, require an expansive monetary policy in order to avoid disrupting foreign exchange rates. Such a monetization policy conceivably might achieve some exchange-rate objectives temporarily. But, as the Fed's experience with funds-rate targeting suggests, it could be disastrous for domestic monetary policy.

Notes

1. Testimony before the Joint Economic Committee, *International Economic Policy*, May 4, 1981, pp. 17–18.

2. In practice, the reserves impact from such a foreign exchange intervention would be lumped with all other so-called "operating factors" affecting the availability of reserves to the banking system; the total thus calculated might or might not require an offsetting open market operation. For details, see the appendix.

3. Roger M. Kubarych, *Foreign Exchange Markets in the United States* (New York: Federal Reserve Bank of New York, 1978), p. 42.

4. This statement is based on the bilateral trade-weighted foreign exchange value of the dollar calculated by the Morgan Guaranty Trust Company. Other measures, using other weights, generally show an even larger appreciation during the 1981–83 period.

5. *Economic Report of the President* (Washington: U.S. Government Printing Office, 1984), p. 53.

6. The July 6, 1981, issue of *Barron's* reported on a foreclosure of a house in Los Angeles worth about $250,000 that was encumbered by no fewer than *nine* mortgages

totaling $273,800. Foreign inflation psychology apparently did not differ generically from the domestic variety.

7. In the nature of the case, no precise calculation of adequacy was possible, since the scale, timing, and duration of necessary assistance could not be foretold.

8. $8.3 billion was vastly more than the Treasury's actual expenditure in meeting such a request. The true cost was the interest expense the Treasury would incur to borrow the sum, *less* the interest received from the IMF, *less* the cost of whatever financial disruption might be avoided.

9. The final legislation made the IMF appropriation more politically palatable by attaching a series of provisions toughening large banks' capital requirements and financial disclosure standards.

10. Ronald I. McKinnon, "Currency Substitution and Instability in the World Dollar Market," *American Economic Review,* June 1982, pp. 320–33.

11. See Henry N. Goldstein and Stephen E. Haynes, "A Critical Appraisal of McKinnon's World Money Supply Hypothesis," *American Economic Review,* March 1984, pp. 217–24.

12. John Williamson, *The Exchange Rate System* (Washington, D.C.: Institute for International Economics, 1983).

13. This view is argued at length in Paul Krugman, "International Aspects of U.S. Monetary and Fiscal Policy," *The Economics of Large Government Deficits* (Boston: Federal Reserve Bank of Boston, 1983), pp. 112–33.

12
THE YEARS AHEAD

Before looking ahead to the challenges confronting monetary policy in the future, one must ask of monetary policy during the years since 1979, was it worth the price?

The Volcker Fed's great achievement was to arrest decisively the inflation spiral that by 1979 had been accelerating for well over a decade. From its peak rate (on a year-over-year basis) of almost 15 percent in early 1980, the consumer price index decelerated to a mere 3 percent rate by the end of 1983. Most economists would have thought so massive a slowdown impossible to achieve in such a short span of time, and almost none had sufficient foresight to predict it. But if the scale of the disinflation was monumental, so were the costs of achieving that success.

Inflation slowed in large part because of massive economic slack. From the end of 1979 to the end of 1982, the civilian unemployment rate rose from 5.9 percent to a postwar record high of 10.8 percent. Capacity utilization in the manufacturing sector plunged to levels only rarely approached in the postwar period. And three years after the Saturday Night Special, real output in the economy as a whole was at about the same level as in late 1979, marking a period of protracted stagnation without parallel in recent decades.

The dollar's soaring foreign exchange value also played a major role. Due in no small part to the extraordinarily high levels to which real interest rates were pushed, the dollar soared more than 30 percent between late 1980 and the end of 1983, creating a severe competitive compression for those industries most dependent on world markets.

By some estimates, the appreciation of the dollar alone may have accounted for almost half of the plunge in the inflation rate.

The staggering economy, combined with a fiscal policy that paired tax cutting zeal with a manifest unwillingness to rein in spending, pushed the federal deficit to previously undreamed-of levels. Lofty interest rates assured that one of the fastest-growing components of federal spending were the interest payments required to service the federal debt—up from $40.6 billion in fiscal year 1979 to $90.6 billion during fiscal 1983, when they made up almost half of the $185.7 billion deficit. Moreover, projections suggested that interest might be well over half of the deficit in succeeding years.

A similar result ensued in the international economy, when the upward lurch of interest rates added billions of dollars annually to the debt servicing burdens of less developed countries by the end of 1983.

It is more than a little misleading, however, to attempt precise comparison of the benefits from ending the inflation spiral versus the costs of foregone employment and production. Volcker and many others argued repeatedly during those years, and still do, that there really was little choice in the matter. Accelerating inflation must eventually produce economic chaos. The bitter pill was better swallowed sooner than later. This line of thought was probably best articulated by Henry C. Wallich, the Board member with perhaps the longest and most consistent record of support for a restrictive monetary policy stance in the Federal Open Market Committee:

> Critics of monetary policy frequently measure the cost of disinflation in terms of the shortfall of output and growth from some potential, and in terms of unemployment in excess of some frictional or inflation-neutral level. The cost thus computed is very high, but the premises of the computation are illusory. We do not have a realistic option of ignoring inflation. We cannot measure the cost of disinflation by comparing it with an economy operating satisfactorily and as if inflation did not exist. Neither can we measure the cost on the assumption that inflation, ignored, would stabilize or otherwise become predictable. . . . inflation, at any level, imposes costs because reliable expectations cannot be formed, because the tax system is not adjusted for inflation, and because existing contracts and the consequences of past decisions cannot quickly be adjusted if at all. Inflation ignored by the policy maker, moreover, as a practical matter is bound to accelerate. There is no satisfactory way of living with inflation. Business cannot do it, nor can other institutions. The cost of disinflation must, therefore, be measured against the realistic option that inflation, uncombatted, would impose high costs of its own and, moreover, would almost certainly accelerate. I feel confident that the cost—in present-value terms—of letting inflation run is far higher than the temporary pain of bringing it down.

Again as a practical matter, I doubt that private enterprise and the market system, at least in our country, can permanently survive with high and unpredictable inflation. The role of government is bound to increase as more enterprises come in need of public assistance, price controls are tried from time to time, profits erode, and individual saving becomes an unreliable means of providing for the future. The ultimate cost of inflation, in other words, is the loss of the system. Whoever regards this as, indeed, a loss, rather than as an extra dividend on inflationary policies, will have to factor it into his estimates of the probable cost of inflation.[1]

While other FOMC members might have expressed themselves with a somewhat different emphasis, most were clearly in substantial agreement with Wallich's views. Nevertheless, no one, Wallich included, would ever wish to repeat the experience of disinflation in the future.

Lessons of 1979–83

The likelihood of such a replay would seem to depend crucially on what kind of enduring lessons have been learned during the last several years.

A monetarist experiment?   Probably nothing irritates a monetarist so much as hearing Paul Volcker called one, and all indications are that the chairman's reaction would be similar. There is no question that the Fed's policy initiatives during the 1979–82 period were far from the monetarist prescription of tight control of monetary growth, implemented through total reserves targeting. Thus, if monetarists reasonably should be allowed to have the final say as to what monetarism is, then the Fed's policy simply was not monetarism—period.

Nevertheless, that policy obviously was far closer to monetarist prescriptions than anything that had gone before, or, for that matter, than the policy adopted in the fall of 1982 and adhered to through the time of this writing (spring 1984). For three years, the significance the Fed attached to short-run control of the money supply was vastly greater than it was before October 6, 1979, and tolerance of interest-rate volatility was also much greater. Moreover, implementation of policy was guided by a reserves-based procedure which, though clearly not the monetarist prescription, was nevertheless cut from something of the same cloth.

In the author's view, the results of that experience suggest rather forcefully that the relationships between reserves aggregates and money (however defined), and more importantly between money and spending, are sufficiently variable that a highly rigid, "automatic" system of monetary control is not desirable. The success of monetary policy in reducing inflation was mainly due to its persistent restrictiveness, not to the detailwork of the operating procedures.[2]

The bulk of available evidence suggests that the greater volatility of monetary growth following 1979 reflects primarily disturbances of various kinds to the relationship between money and spending. Some of those disturbances could have been avoided, notably those associated with the 1980 credit controls program. Others, such as the sharp, prolonged decline in M1 velocity that followed the decline in inflation and interest rates during 1982, probably should have been expected, given the results of a number of sophisticated models of money demand. At least it appears so in retrospect; unfortunately, few of those results were available prior to 1982. Other short-run disturbances merely reflected inadequate seasonal adjustment of the raw money data, and they will vanish as revised seasonal adjustments become available.

Some economists interpret the large swings of monetary growth in recent years as indicating that the public's demand for money is unstable. Others point to highly complex econometric models of money demand that do reasonably well in explaining the plunge of M1 velocity. They suggest that money demand itself is stable, though the functional relationship is highly complex. The problem, on this view, lies with the conventional representation of the link between money and spending as velocity, which is merely a simple ratio.

The issue of the proper specification of money demand is not yet resolved—and indeed, it may never be—but one thing is clear. The Fed's annual targets implicitly assume a fairly steady growth of velocity over the year. If the new, sophisticated models of money demand are correct, then part of the problem with aggregates targeting is that the targets themselves are too simple. To a large extent, the Fed copes by specifying a range of acceptable target growth rates, but even so, such simple, numerical targets appear inherently prone to require interim adjustments. It is not clear what kind of target might replace them, but it assuredly would not be simple, and it probably would be subject to revision over periods shorter than a year.

On purely economic grounds, such an approach might have some appeal. But it would seriously diminish what many have regarded as one of the key attractions of targets in the first place—the ability to set a simple rule for policy and to use it to enforce accountability.

In view of the enormous amount of debate and research effort that economists have devoted to the fine points of monetary aggregates targeting and similar matters, it is somewhat ironic that the great policy lessons of the first four years of the Volcker Fed probably concern primarily expectations, real interest rates, and the robustness of financial markets and the economy in the face of volatile interest rates.

Expectations. If there is value in understanding that one does not understand, then perhaps economists and policy makers gained valuable experience concerning the formation—and change over time—of expectations, especially expectations of future inflation. The "ultra rationality" thesis popular in some economic circles implied that as soon as a credible and consistent long-run anti-inflation policy was announced, expectations would immediately adjust. Some economists conclude that this thesis was routed by the facts. Others note that the actual policy, replete with diversionary excursions into credit controls, stepped-up monetary volatility, and a swelling budget deficit, clearly fell short of such theoreticians' notions of consistency. On this view, the theory never had a fair test.

Probably the most visible shortfall was in the hoped for stability of monetary growth. But, in fact, it is not obvious that erratic growth really was a major problem. The survey of financial decision makers cited in Chapter 4 suggested quite strongly that most financial market participants had some understanding of the technical sources of M1 volatility and were not terribly disturbed by it. (In part, one suspects, that was because they perceived that the Fed itself was not disturbed, so that there would not be any consequences for interest rates.) Instead, they overwhelmingly viewed the chronically expansive direction of fiscal policy as the chief threat to a sustained policy of disinflation. Perhaps a more stable pattern of monetary growth would have contributed to a greater reduction of inflation expectations than in fact occurred. But, at the very least, it is not obvious that the improvement would have been very great. Almost certainly, a more restrictive fiscal policy would have had a much more significant impact.

In any event, real people do not appear to adjust their expectations rapidly most of the time, even if some austere economic models assume they do. In fact, one of the truly shocking aspects of the last several years was the long period of time required for many people to realize that anything fundamental had changed at all.

For example, in January 1983, the prestigious University of Michigan Survey Research Center asked a sample of respondents what the *actual* rate of increase of the consumer price index during the previous 12 months had been. The survey average was 7.6 percent, about double the actual rate! Fifteen months later, in April 1984, a similar survey turned up a 6.5 percent estimate—lower, to be sure, but still quite a bit higher than the 4.7 percent increase actually recorded in the consumer price index during the previous 12 months. At a minimum, one would have to conclude that most individuals simply do not have the quality of information necessary to support a rapid revision of expectations.

Naturally one would expect financial market professionals to be considerably more attuned to developing inflation trends than the average consumer, and there is some evidence that this is the case. But the differences appear to be less than one might suppose. The survey of financial market participants cited several times in earlier chapters found that 10-year inflation expectations in April 1982, at 6.76 percent, were a bit more than 2 percent lower than the peak reading of 8.82 percent in October 1980 (the earliest survey date). But between April 1982 and March 1984 (the most recent survey as this book was going to press), 10-year inflation expectations were almost unchanged.[3] The OPEC oil cartel was forced to lower its prices during this period, trends in the growth of wages were more favorable than they had been in decades, and actual inflation was substantially lower than the long-range expectation, but insofar as one can judge from the survey results, inflation expectations showed little response.

However, if ultrarationality appears not to describe observed behavior very well, the "adaptive expectations" hypothesis—which, reduced to essentials, implies that expectations of the future course of some variable such as the rate of inflation can be easily and accurately related to its past behavior—also had a distinctly spotty record. For example, the author is aware of no econometric model of long-term bond rates incorporating such an effect that is capable of explaining convincingly the convulsion that occurred in the long-term debt markets during the early 1980s. Similarly it is hard to imagine an adaptive process that would have kept the 10-year expectations of financial market participants essentially unchanged while actual inflation rates hit new cyclical low readings during 1982–84.

On balance, it is hard to avoid concluding that economists just do not understand much about the process by which expectations are formed. Nevertheless, most go about their business very much as if they *do* have such understanding or, in any event, they spend little time brooding over the lack of it. Their policy analyses tend to address other matters while leaving expectations to take care of themselves.

Volcker's approach was a clear break with that tendency. As we have seen, policy was formulated, whether rightly or wrongly, with its presumed psychological impact very much in the first rank of objectives. The Saturday Night Special, the credit controls program, and the abrupt tightening of reserve availability in late 1980, followed by continuing restraint during 1981 and early 1982—in all of these instances, the psychological impact of policy was thought to be of major significance in its own right.

Did it work that way in practice? The author is skeptical. It is inherently difficult to isolate any identifiable contribution of changing psychology to the dramatic slowdown of inflation. More likely, such change in expectations as has occurred has been the result of economic slack and the observed inflation slowdown rather than a product of any dramatic policy announcements. Nevertheless, the role of psychological factors in policy formulation remains an open issue. At the very least, Volcker's approach displayed a willingness to innovate, to cast aside conventional policy canons to master the inflation spiral. And if we do not know exactly *why* it worked, we do know that it *did work.*

Real interest rates. Chapter 5 enumerated several solid, economic-theoretical reasons why real interest rates are unlikely to be a satisfactory instrument for implementing monetary policy, and the experience of the Volcker Fed does not qualify that assessment. But the record does suggest one worthwhile lesson: whatever else a policymaker seeking to slow inflation in face of fiscal stimulus may do, he or she would be well advised to take care that real interest rates (calculated in some plausible fashion) remain distinctly positive.

No perturbation of measured monetary growth rates (and only the most extraordinary evidence of weakness in the nonfinancial economy) should be allowed to justify zero or negative real rates. To hold rates at such levels, as was done for most of the 1976–77 period, is to invite a replay of the inflationary consequences of that policy. Real rates, then, probably constitute not so much a fine policy indicator as a test of consistency between monetary policy and price stability.

Interest-rate volatility. Prior to October 6, 1979, it was conventional wisdom in some quarters that interest-rate volatility on anything like the scale witnessed during the last few years would destroy liquidity in the Treasury securities market and other financial markets. Dire effects would ensue for the economy generally and for the Fed's ability to execute open market operations in particular. Some also argued that volatile rates would destabilize certain sectors of the economy peculiarly sensitive to credit conditions. The experience of recent years suggests that these concerns, while not wholly groundless, tended to be exaggerated.

They were exaggerated primarily because of an underestimation of the economy's ability to invent new techniques for spreading the risk inherent in volatile rates. Such adjustments took time to achieve, of course. Indeed, in the days immediately following October 6, 1979, liquidity in the Treasury market almost vanished. Soon afterwards, as market participants became more familiar with the Fed's new operating procedures, liquidity returned.

The major difference was that bid/asked spreads were wider. For example, the best bid in the Treasury bill market previously might have been only a basis point or so different from the best offer. Because of greater rate volatility, such spreads widened to five basis points or more, sometimes considerably more. Spreads in other markets reacted similarly.

The widening of spreads definitely made active trading more

costly, but it hardly wrecked the markets' liquidity. Part of the reason why the reaction was not more severe lies in the nature of rate volatility. Large changes in interest rates may spell losses in some cases, but they also represent significant opportunities for anyone capable of anticipating them. Volatility deters risk-averse investors, but it also attracts risk-takers.

As merely one among many possible examples, increased volatility was a prime impetus to the burgeoning financial futures and options markets, which allowed participants to increase or decrease their risk exposure much more quickly and efficiently than they could do in the "cash" markets.

Unresolved issues

The years ahead will challenge monetary policy in a variety of ways. The most critical will be the maintenance of disinflationary momentum in the late stages of the recovery, when fiscal policy in all likelihood will continue stimulative. In fundamental respects, however, that challenge, though it will require an abundance of policy skills and determination, does not in itself raise any major analytical issues bearing on the role of the Federal Reserve and monetary policy. However, four issues promise to have major significance well beyond the present business cycle.

Financial restructuring and the lender of last resort. The most fundamental restructuring of the U.S. financial system since the 1930s is currently under way, and although its ultimate course is still unclear, several features stand out. One is that deregulation of banking and related activities is clearly having the same impact on the financial services industry that the earlier deregulation of stock brokerage commissions (1975), airlines (1978), and trucking (1980) had on those industries.

As banks and nonbanks increasingly compete on price—e.g., through the rates they pay on deposits—inefficient firms that previously had been shielded by the umbrella of regulation will either reform, sell out, or close down.

If the experience of the brokerage industry is any guide, the number of firms remaining in the financial services industry several years from now will be substantially smaller than it is currently. Indeed, some well-informed estimates suggest that through mergers and failures, something like one in three independent banks and thrift institutions may disappear by 1990. The resulting industry structure will probably consist of several dozen large organizations of essentially national scope, with a (diminishing) myriad of smaller firms ensconced in various market "niches." The end result should be a set of leaner, more competitive firms.

What is emerging is a new, increasingly electronic-based, system of banking services of extraordinary efficiency—or in any event, it will be, when it works. The real test of the system, of course, comes when everything goes wrong. One thinks immediately of the old saw, "to err is human; to really foul things up requires a computer."

New electronic payments systems will permit colossal errors (to say nothing of crimes) to be committed briskly and efficiently, and the urgency of their prompt detection and correction becomes correspondingly greater. But safeguarding accounts is nothing intrinsically new for banks, even if the means employed must be.

However, the increasingly electronic character of the payments system seems likely to make more difficult the Fed's role as underwriter of the liquidity of financial markets. The reason is time. With staggering volumes of transactions settling by the end of each business day, there may be very few hours in which to detect a problem, identify its implications, and take whatever measures are called for.

On a more fundamental level, the changing nature of the financial services industry is blurring the concept of banking. Securities firms offer a variety of accounts which, among other advantages, can be used to make payments in various ways. Credit cards are offered by a large number of firms. Banks, in turn, are rapidly entering fields previously considered off limits, such as insurance, securities brokerage, and securities underwriting.

This state of affairs has a number of implications for the Fed as lender of last resort. The most obvious is: should the Fed ever undertake to assist a nonbank participant in the payments system if a crisis threatened? Most would probably answer in the affirmative—in which case the question becomes: should such participants be subject to the Fed's regulatory oversight? The jury is still out on that one.

A senior Fed official expressed to the author another concern. In the past, the Fed has always felt that it could rely on banks for information about any difficulties that a nonbank firm might be experiencing. Now that banks are expanding into new activities, will they prove to be so reliable when their own nonbank affiliates are in trouble? The official plainly thought that to expect an equal standard of reliability under such circumstances would be asking a good deal of human nature.

Measurability of money.   As Chapter 5 made clear, the issue of the proper definition and interpretation of the money stock has been around for some time. But as overdraft facilities continue to proliferate, while various electronic devices allow more efficient monitoring and investing of available balances, the notion of spending decisions being related in some stable way to a measurable concept of money balances becomes increasingly tenuous. New measures such as Spindt's MQ may yet save the day, but that remains to be seen.

At the same time, it is clear that recent years have seen an extraordinarily large number of changes in deposit types serving a transactional role, at least to some degree. Some of these changes, such as money market mutual funds, were spurred by individuals' efforts to escape from burdensome interest rate ceilings on consumer-type deposit accounts. Others, such as NOWs and super NOWs, arose as those regulations were relaxed.

In the next several years, as complete deregulation of deposit interest rates becomes a reality, still further changes will probably occur. However, there are solid grounds to expect that the pace of such changes will taper off as the financial system adjusts to the new environment.

While some econometric models of money demand appear to have coped reasonably well with the impact of these changes, most analysts feel that explaining money demand would be easier in a stable regulatory environment. Hence the prospect of a distinctly slower pace of financial innovation holds out some hope that the ability to measure money and to analyze money demand may improve somewhat in the future.

Foreign dimension of domestic monetary policy. As the discussion in Chapter 11 suggested, there are a number of reasons for thinking that policy targets defined exclusively in terms of the domestic money supply may not give adequate consideration to the international aspects of policy. Unfortunately, there are no easy answers to the issue, and the incidence of domestic policy abroad is certain to be a continuing problem.

Attempts to manipulate foreign exchange rates seem likely to be even less effective in the future than they were in the past. The foreign currency reserves of the world's central banks simply do not appear adequate to the task. Rather, any exchange rate "policy" will probably be a reflection of the mix of domestic monetary and fiscal policy. That lends a major international dimension to the typically domestic debate over crowding out.

As noted in Chapter 11, Volcker has raised the possibility that as disinflation proceeds, monetary policy may gain more freedom to focus on currency misalignments. However, about all one can say at this juncture is that the time when that might be true has not yet arrived. And the historical ineffectiveness of central bank intervention in currency markets suggests that it may never be a realistic policy goal.

Communication and accountability. Monetary policy cannot be formulated and implemented for long in isolation from the political give-and-take of a democracy, and informed discussion of that policy requires efficient communication of its objectives. For the foreseeable future, monetary targets seem destined to continue to perform a critical role in communicating the Federal Reserve's objectives to the public and in providing the means by which the Congress can enforce accountability.

Yet one must wonder whether it could not be done more efficiently than it is now. Numerous redefinitions of the monetary aggregates, repeated modifications to growth targets, and the gradual, and sometimes not so gradual, smoothing of erratic growth rates through seasonal factor revisions—all these are the Fedwatcher's bread and butter. But is there no better way to communicate directly to a larger public?

And is there no better way to achieve accountability without depriving monetary policy of its essential flexibility?

These issues will be around for a long time to come.

A conclusion

This discussion appears to have led to one surpassingly basic yet often neglected conclusion. In framing monetary policy—or, for that matter, in ferreting out that policy through Fedwatching—judgment is central. There are no easy answers and no simple rules in monetary policy.

Notes

1. Henry C. Wallich, "Impact of Monetary Policy on Business," speech delivered at the Yale School of Organization and Management, March 30, 1983.

2. A similar conclusion is reached in Benjamin M. Friedman, "Lessons from the 1979–82 Monetarist Experiment," *American Economic Review*, May 1984, pp. 382–387. For a vigorous dissent, see Milton Friedman, "Lessons from the 1979–82 Monetary Policy Experiment," pp. 397–400 in the same issue.

3. Richard B. Hoey and Helen Hotchkiss, "Decision Makers Poll," A. G. Becker Paribas, Inc., April 17, 1984.

APPENDIX

A GUIDE TO FEDERAL RESERVE OPEN MARKET OPERATIONS*

Since many persons find the terminology used to describe the operational aspects of monetary policy complex and confusing, this appendix summarizes the major features of the instruments and strategy of open market operations. Readers desiring further insight into the daily routine of the Open Market Desk are referred to Paul Meek's excellent *U.S. Monetary Policy and Financial Markets,* available on request from the Federal Reserve Bank of New York.

Supplying reserves

In supplying nonborrowed reserves during the reserves maintenance period, the Fed typically tries to hit its target. The nonborrowed reserves target may be calculated by the staff on the basis of the FOMC's short-run growth objectives for primarily M1 as was the case during 1979–82, or it may be computed so as to maintain a desired level of "reserves pressure," i.e., discount-window borrowings.

In either case, the task is complicated by the at times highly erratic movements of the so-called operating factors. One of the most variable such factors is Federal Reserve float, the weekly average of which can swing by $1 billion or more in response to seasonal interruptions in the payments system or acute operational problems.[1] In contrast, the average weekly reserves provision called for by the Fed's monetary aggregates targets is only on the order of about $50 million. The upshot is that for the most part the Fed's open market operations are "defensive" in nature; that is, they are intended to offset a swing in reserves availability produced by float or some other operating factor, rather than to provide the small increment of reserves called for by the target.

In addition, given the overall need to add to or drain from the average level of reserves, the Fed still must decide the timing of open market operations during the reserves maintenance period.[2] Several factors influence the timing decision. First, the Open Market Desk's information about reserves availability generally becomes more complete and reliable as the period progresses. All other things being equal, then, the Desk would probably prefer to delay arranging any open market operations, unless the size of the projected imbalance of reserves supplies makes that course infeasible.

Also, the Open Market Desk on occasion may attempt to smooth out swings in the availability of reserves during the period so as to avoid unnecessary volatility in the funds market. Since banks must meet reserve requirements on an average basis for the period as a whole, intraperiod swings in reserves availability in principle need have no impact on the funds rate. Indeed, if banks were able to anticipate the movement in availability with confidence, they could passively allow their reserves positions to mirror the swing, and there would be no impact on the funds rate.

In practice, though, banks are highly uncertain about their reserves positions, and the funds rate is likely to respond to major daily imbalances between banks' "normal" reserves positions and actual availability.

Though such funds-rate movements may mislead some market participants, the Fed in recent years has been much less inclined than it was previously to smooth out swings in availability. Nevertheless, if projections suggest, for example, a very large excess of reserves emerging prior to the weekend, the Desk probably would want to offset the glut on Thursday or Friday, rather than see the funds rate temporarily depressed.

Similarly, if the reserves market appears generally in balance prior to the weekend, with a major excess supply expected to emerge later, then the Desk's natural inclination would be to delay the reserves-draining operation until after the weekend. On the other hand, moderate intraperiod swings in reserves availability probably would be ignored.

Smoothing adjustments may also be necessitated by variations in the distribution of discount-window borrowing during the period. The problem is rooted in the institutional phenomenon that virtually all discount-window borrowing by large banks (abstracting from long-term credit) is done on only the two Fridays and the final Wednesday.[3] If, as is usually the case, the discount rate is below the funds rate,

Friday is the day banks prefer to borrow. This is because borrowing on that day counts for three days, thus magnifying the favorable impact of the below-market discount rate on a bank's average funds costs for the week. (Primarily regional banks can succeed with such a tactic; discount window administration at the New York Federal Reserve Bank is generally acknowledged to be more stringent than in other Federal Reserve districts.)

Indeed, as Table A–1 illustrates, the Wednesday percentage of total borrowing is negatively related to the difference, or spread, between the funds rate and the discount rate, which is positively related to the overall level of borrowing. In 1976, when banks actually averaged net free reserves and the funds rate was low relative to the discount rate, Wednesday borrowing averaged about 40 percent of the total. During 1978–79, when borrowing traffic was much greater and the funds rate was correspondingly higher than the discount rate, the Wednesday percentage was about half as large, reflecting the greater attractiveness of Friday borrowing. However, during 1980–83 the Wednesday percentage on average was substantially higher than in 1978–79 and more erratic, despite the fact that average borrowing was about the same in both periods. Though the reasons for that phenomenon are not clear, it is probably related to the advent of the reserves-oriented operating procedures in late 1979 and perhaps to the effect of the discount rate surcharge on banks' borrowing behavior.

The substantial variability of the distribution of borrowing traffic during the reserves maintenance period can create problems for the Desk. For example, if for some reason borrowing is unexpectedly high early in the period, then the period's borrowing target may have been fulfilled, or even overfulfilled, leaving nothing to be done on the final Wednesday.

The result would be downward pressure on the funds rate unless the Desk entered the market to drain out some of the excess.[4] Such an operation would involve a deliberate, though probably temporary, departure from the intended relative supplies of nonborrowed and borrowed reserves, rather than merely a decision with regard to the timing of reserves availability during the maintenance period.[5]

Once the Desk has formed a view with regard to the desirable timing of any operations affecting reserves availability, it must choose an instrument to accomplish the objective. Basically, the decision involves a choice between (1) permanent reserves operations versus temporary ones and (2) various alternative kinds of temporary operations.

In order to avoid interfering with the market's determination of interest rates, the Desk tries to minimize its presence in the market. Thus, if there is a need to add reserves over a substantial period of time (e.g., during the late-year holiday season), the natural course is to make one or more outright purchases of securities. One way that

TABLE A-1

Behavior of Federal Reserve Adjustment Borrowing

	Average Federal Funds Rate Less Discount Rate (percent)	Average Borrowed Reserves ($ millions)	Average Net Borrowed Reserves ($ millions)	Wednesday Borrowing as a Percentage of Week Total			
				Mean	Standard Deviation	Minimum	Maximum
1976	−0.44%	$ 85	$−134	40.6%	24.4%	7.8%	82.1%
1977	0.06	464	250	29.4	22.4	7.6	92.8
1978	0.40	868	671	20.5	9.9	7.5	56.3
1979	0.88	1,338	1,116	19.6	9.0	7.0	47.7
1980	0.79	1,232	934	28.1	24.0	4.1	97.2
1981	0.11	1,266	964	27.2	15.6	7.5	89.2
1982	1.21	876	516	32.0	20.0	6.2	88.3
1983	0.59	664	167	33.5	21.7	3.7	86.3

Note: Borrowing data have been adjusted to remove extended credit advanced to certain institutions. The discount rate includes the discount-rate surcharges applied at various times during 1980–81. Since the surcharge was not binding for several months in 1981, the difference between the funds rate and the fully surcharged discount rate is deceptively small for that year.

can be done is to buy them from the foreign central banks for whom the New York Fed acts as agent and securities custodian. Such a transaction would be arranged internally and would involve no operations in the market. It thus serves as a convenient device to reduce the Fed's presence in the market. The major limitation of that kind of transaction is that the decision to buy or sell securities is made by the foreign customers, so that the Fed can take advantage of a timely opportunity to carry out its reserves-adding task this way, but it cannot create the opportunity itself.

In the event that no such opportunity appears, the Fed must instead purchase the securities in the market by asking dealers for their offers.[6] Regardless of how the outright purchase (sale) of securities is arranged, its purpose is to relieve the Fed of the necessity of repeatedly carrying out temporary additions (drains) of reserves for a protracted period of time.

In the event of a need to drain reserves over a substantial time period, a sale of securities to foreign accounts, if possible, would be convenient. But in this case, there is another nonmarket option as well: The Fed can bid to redeem some of its maturing bills at the regular weekly auction of Treasury bills.[7] To do so, the Fed simply submits its tender for a dollar amount smaller than its holding of the maturing issues. The major limitation of this approach is that the Fed obviously can redeem only as much as it holds of the maturing issues and in practice would not want to disrupt the auction process by concentrating a large redemption in a single auction. Consequently, only reserves drains in amounts of $500 million or so are likely to be implemented in this fashion. Larger operations will involve outright sales of securities in the market.[8]

When a reserves need is perceived to be temporary, affecting only one or a few reserves maintenance periods, the Fed's preferred action is to arrange repurchase agreements (RPs) with the dealers.[9] That injects reserves for the duration of the RPs and is operationally simpler and less obtrusive than would be an outright purchase of securities followed by an outright sale.

RPs arranged by the Fed for its own account are called System RPs. Those arranged by the Fed as agent for foreign central bank customers are termed customer RPs.

As mentioned briefly in Chapter 7, the Federal Reserve Bank of New York performs a number of banking services for foreign central banks and several international organizations. Typically, the Fed handles their very short-term investments by in effect doing RPs with them, using securities in the Fed's portfolio as collateral. The total of such short-term investment balances is sometimes informally referred to as the "internal RP pool," reflecting the fact that the investments are processed internally at the Fed for the most part, with no private market participants involved.

When the Desk wishes to inject reserves by reducing the portion of the pool invested with the Fed, it does so by executing some of the investment orders with the dealers as customer RPs. What remains of the pool is invested with the Fed and is described in a footnote to the Fed's balance sheet as "matched sale-purchase transactions with foreign official and international accounts." Fedwatchers call them simply "internal matched sales" (more on matched sales below).

When the Desk figures the reserves need, the internal RP pool is simply lumped together with other market factors. Accordingly, *both* System RPs and customer RPs inject reserves, though that fact is not always recognized by market participants. If they are functionally identical, then what explains the Fed's choice between them? As a rule, the Fed employs customer RPs when it estimates a reserves need to be small.[10] The largest customer RP ever arranged totaled only $3 billion, and the average size is about $1–2 billion.

In contrast, System RPs have been executed for amounts as great as $6–7 billion. Customer RPs are fundamentally limited by the available volume of foreign investment orders, which generally average $2–3 billion. Furthermore, since the foreign orders primarily constitute working cash balances of central banks, it is rather unusual for the Desk to arrange multiday customer RPs, though some have occurred. Thus, if a multiday RP is needed, a System transaction is the most likely alternative.

Moreover, in the past, more restrictive conditions on the securities eligible to serve as collateral for customer RPs meant that when the "floating supply" of collateral was scarce, customer RPs could be more difficult for the Fed to arrange than System RPs.[11] Under such circumstances, the Fed naturally preferred to rely on System RPs. However, collateral standards are now uniform for both types of RPs.[12]

In the event of a severe collateral shortage, the Desk may experience difficulty in executing the desired amount of System RPs. When faced with such a situation in the past, the Desk frequently has preannounced its RPs (e.g., notified dealers on Wednesday afternoon of its intention to do RPs on the following Thursday) in order to encourage dealers and their customers to keep collateral available for use with the System RPs.

A temporary reserves-draining operation is simpler in that matched sale-purchase transactions (MSPs), which are functionally equivalent to reverse repurchase agreements, can be used to remove the temporary reserves glut.[13] Here again, however, there may be a delicate problem of choice of technique. Frequently, market participants show relatively poor proposals to the Fed for multiday MSPs for an abundantly clear reason: They are being asked to extend the Fed a fixed-rate loan when they have at least some grounds for suspecting that the rationale for the MSPs might be to reduce the availability of reserves. All other things being equal, such an operation would raise short-term interest rates and thus would increase their costs of funding the loan.[14]

Proposals are more competitive for overnight MSPs or for multiday MSPs that market participants recognize as necessary to drain reserves. As a result, the Fed may well encounter a situation in which it is simply unable to drain a sufficient amount of reserves via multiday MSPs arranged, for example, on Thursday (without, that is, accepting rates well above the going market rate) and thus must return for more on Friday. This problem can be alleviated somewhat by offering simultaneously overnight and multiday MSPs.

Finally, if inadequate proposals prevent the Desk from achieving the desired reserves add (drain), the Treasury may be asked to alter the balances in its account at the Fed. Such an operation would take care of the problem if an additional drain is called for, but there can be difficulties when Treasury balances are used to inject reserves. The reason is that Treasury deposits must be collateralized, and if banks have insufficient collateral available, they will remit the balances back to the Treasury's Fed account, thus frustrating the reserve injection. In any event, manipulation of Treasury balances to adjust reserve positions is done relatively infrequently. In general, balances in the Treasury's Fed account are maintained close to a weekly average of $3 billion.[15]

Strategy of open market operations

During the year, reserves needs display a pronounced seasonal movement. Currency and demand deposits follow distinct multiweek swings and also fluctuate around certain dates, for example, holidays and tax-payment dates. Float behavior is also strongly influenced by holidays. In principle, even the large swings of reserves needs could be met through execution of large amounts of RPs, but a number of considerations argue against such a tactic.

First, the amount of collateral required easily approaches $10 billion or so and could well exceed the floating supply of "free" collateral in the hands of dealers and other financial institutions (mainly commercial banks). The result would be that the Desk would be unable to maintain borrowed and nonborrowed reserves at their intended levels. Moreover, even if the amount of collateral were adequate, the fact that banks would repeatedly begin the reserves maintenance period with a severe reserves deficiency (until the need was met through RPs) would probably create considerable upward pressure on the funds rate.

For these reasons, provision of at least some portion of the reserves need through outright purchases of securities is desirable, and accordingly the timing of outright transactions is closely related to swings in seasonal needs as well as changes in reserve requirements.

There are, of course, various ways to do outright transactions. First, as noted earlier, a suitable foreign customer order may present an opportunity for the Fed to effect the permanent addition (drain) of reserves without recourse to transactions with dealers. Such an approach is consistent with the Fed's desire to minimize its presence in the market, but it presents problems to Fedwatchers, who do not learn of the existence of the transaction until the Fed's release of reserves data following the week in which it was executed.

Another means by which the Fed can achieve a permanent reserves drain is to bid to reduce its holdings of maturing bills in a Treasury auction—for example, the regular Monday auction of three- and six-month bills. In such a case, Fedwatchers will learn of the redemption when the results are announced in the evening of the day of the auction. Since settlement for the auctioned bills is the following Thursday, Fedwatchers in this case will know the size of the reserves impact a couple of days before it actually occurs.

In many cases, the Fed will have no choice but to execute an outright transaction in the market. Such transactions are often arranged on Wednesday for settlement the following day, though they do occur on other days as well, sometimes for skip-day settlement. (That might happen if Wednesday were a holiday, or if the Treasury were having an auction that day.) Fedwatchers can only guess at the size of the transaction, since the Fed does not announce it. Typically, more than a week elapses before the size of the outright transaction becomes known to the market through the Fed's release of reserves data.

Given the decision to effect a permanent addition (drain) of reserves, the Fed must decide how many securities of what type to purchase (sell). The alternatives are Treasury bills, Treasury coupon securities, and federal agency securities.

In general, bills are the preferred instrument. The bill market is more liquid than the market for any other money market instrument, so that the large transactions arranged by the Fed (frequently on the order of $1–2 billion) will not have much impact on rates in the market. Since the Fed prefers not to exercise undue influence on market rates, that is an important consideration.

However, there is some incentive for the Fed to allocate at least some of its holdings to coupon securities, so as to provide a core of permanent reserves without the need repeatedly to roll over large amounts of maturing issues. Operationally, the problem with coupon purchases is that the amounts in dealer hands are frequently rather modest relative to the size the Fed requires, so that the Fed generally must solicit offers for a wide variety of issues in order to have the flexibility to obtain competitive rates and to maintain the desired maturity balance.[16] That involves a sizable job of computing yields for a large number of issues and extends the time required for the transaction to be processed. In other words, a coupon "pass" (i.e., an outright purchase) is an ordeal for the Desk.

Even worse is an agency pass. Since supplies of agency issues in dealer hands are typically light, even for short-term issues, offers must be solicited for many maturities of each agency's issues, necessitating an arduous computation of yields, followed by comparison of spreads between the rates on issues of different agencies. Thus, it comes as no surprise that agency passes are highly infrequent.

In the final analysis, the desired mix of permanent and temporary reserves injections must inevitably hinge on subjective judgments by the Desk manager. Nevertheless, there are certain situations for which temporary reserve injections or drains are particularly appropriate. A good example would be a pair of maintenance periods in which the first requires, say, a $1-billion average addition to reserves, followed by a $1-billion drain in the following period. This could be accomplished easily by executing $4.6 billion three-day RPs on a Friday ($4.6 billion × 3 days ÷ 14 days = $1 billion) in the first period and doing no RPs in the subsequent period, producing a $1 billion average reserve drain. That approach obviously has the merit that it minimizes the need for the Fed to enter the market.

In practice, of course, matters are rarely that straightforward. In the first place, estimates of reserves needs are only that—estimates. Second, at times, repeated execution of temporary reserves injection (drain) operations may serve an ancillary purpose by affecting the psychological attitude of funds traders.

For example, in an environment in which the funds rate has declined substantially in past weeks, funds traders may be apt to anticipate still further declines in the current maintenance period. One way in which the Fed may temper such expectations without departing from its objectives for borrowed and nonborrowed reserves (i.e., without temporarily forcing higher borrowing) would be to arrange open-market operations so that for several weeks RPs are necessary. Then banks would start each period short of reserves, and would therefore probably bid more aggressively for funds.[17]

To monetary policy purists, such behavior smacks of the old procedure of funds-rate targeting, and some critics have suggested that the Fed should reduce the frequency with which it arranges RPs.[18] Of course, the vast majority of temporary reserve injections (drains) are not related to the kind of expectations alteration described above, but are required by very short-term movements in the market factors. Even so, since late 1982 the Desk has executed some form of RP in the last three days of practically every reserves maintenance period, contributing to a level of RP activity substantially greater than that which earlier drew the critics' ire.

The object apparently is to guard against the possibility of the funds rate plunging due to an unintended, temporary excess of reserves. Whether one thinks the tactic justified or not thus has a great deal to do with whether or not one believes the Fed should do anything at all to damp interest-rate volatility.[19] Professional economists have sharply divided opinions on that issue.

Nevertheless, there is one respect in which the frequency of execution of RPs could be reduced with only a trivial change in techniques. It is not widely appreciated among market participants that multi-day system RPs are typically, but not always, "withdrawable"; that is, the dealer participating in the transaction may give notice to the Fed by 1:30 P.M. on the day the dealer wishes to terminate the agreement.[20] (The Fed also has the right to withdraw from the RP, but in practice that right is never exercised.)

As a result, if the Fed arranges, say, a seven-day RP on Thursday with a stop rate (the lowest accepted rate) of 10 percent, but the market RP rate declines to 9½ percent by Friday, then a substantial and essentially unpredictable portion of the dealers who entered into the RPs with the Fed on Thursday now have a palpable economic incentive to withdraw, leaving the Fed with the job of coming back into the market to arrange more RPs so as to prevent a reserves shortage from emerging. Not only that, but if rates rise after Thursday, and dealers respond by lightening their positions, then their reduced financing needs may also cause them to withdraw from the RPs, putting still further pressure on the funds market.

At this point, the reader may well be wondering why the Fed would allow its RPs to be withdrawable in the first place, especially since nonwithdrawable RPs are standard among other market participants. The best explanation appears to be that the withdrawable RP is an institution that has survived the circumstances that originally made it useful.

Before 1966, when the first MSPs were executed, any draining of reserves was accomplished through outright sales of securities. Thus, if the Fed had done RPs early in the week in response to a perceived reserves need, but had later found itself faced with a need to drain reserves, then to the extent that the soft funds rate caused RPs to be withdrawn, the reserves drain would be accomplished automatically and, in particular, without requiring an outright sale of securities.[21]

Obviously, however, MSPs make this particular feature of RPs redundant. Moreover, if an individual dealer firm withdraws from a large block of RPs, it has access to information not available to other market participants, who may not understand why the Fed entered the market to replace the RPs.

Presumably because of the interest-rate risk involved, dealers generally have participated in a smaller portion of the Fed's multiday MSPs and (very rare) multiday nonwithdrawable RPs than have their customers (primarily banks). Consequently, if multiday RPs were made uniformly nonwithdrawable, a smaller volume of less attractively priced proposals generally would be submitted, and that might impair the Fed's ability to execute as many transactions as desired.[22] One way to cope with that problem would be to offer one-day and multiday RPs simultaneously, as is frequently done with MSPs. Another would be to execute outright transactions more often.

With the exception of customer RPs, the Fed does not disclose the size of a temporary addition (drain) of reserves, and that presents problems for Fedwatchers and other market participants. Some participants attempt to cope by monitoring the stop rate on the transaction.

CHART A–1

Hypothetical Distributions of Proposals for Repurchase Agreements and Matched Sale-Purchase Agreements

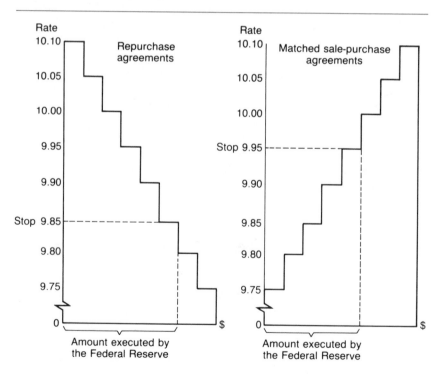

The conventional wisdom is that a low (high) stop on an RP (MSP) relative to the market rate indicates an "aggressive" operation. But, in fact, monitoring the stop is a very poor substitute for knowing the size of the transaction relative to the size of the reserve need. The reason is that the stop rate in general depends on the size of the transaction and the distribution of proposals submitted to the Fed.

As Chart A–1 illustrates, the flatter the "tail" of the proposals (i.e., the narrower the range from the highest to the lowest rates shown to the Fed), the less responsive is the stop rate to variations in the size of the transaction. Consequently, there is no unique relation between the stop relative to the market and the aggressiveness of the operation. Furthermore, in some circumstances, dealers and perhaps also their customers are likely to be loath to submit very competitive proposals to the Fed—for example, multiday MSPs in general, and RPs when dealers are holding negligible or short positions.

Notes

* Adapted from William C. Melton, "Fedwatching and the Federal Funds Market," Chapter 20 in *The Handbook of Economic and Financial Measures,* ed. Frank J. Fabozzi and Harry I. Greenfield (Homewood, Ill.: Dow Jones-Irwin, 1984). An earlier version appeared as Chapter 45 in *The Handbook of Fixed Income Securities,* ed. Frank J. Fabozzi and Irving M. Pollack (Homewood, Ill.: Dow Jones-Irwin, 1983).

1. Float occurs when the scheduled availability of credit to banks receiving checks and other payments processed by the Fed is out of synchronization with the charging of banks making such payments.

2. Prior to February 2, 1984, the reserves maintenance period was *one* week from Thursday to the following Wednesday. Since then, the maintenance period has been *two* weeks, starting on Thursday and ending on the second Wednesday following.

3. When small banks borrow from the discount window, they frequently do so for every day of the statement week. The reason is that such banks almost always are sellers of federal funds, so that if they have sustained a reserve drain so large that it cannot be covered by reducing their funds sales, there may be little alternative to seeking accommodation for a number of days.

4. In a sense, borrowing before the last day of the maintenance period is "demand-determined," largely reflecting banks' efforts to take advantage of a (possibly) below-market discount rate. By the final Wednesday afternoon, however, the total amount of borrowing remaining to be done is almost completely determined by reserves supplied earlier in the period. That means that on the final Wednesday (and perhaps somewhat earlier), the funds rate responds to the scale of borrowing and not the other way around.

5. On not a few occasions, the Desk has made precisely such a departure in nonborrowed reserves provision in order to offset swings of borrowing. For details, see Paul Meek and Fred J. Levin, "Implementing the New Operating Procedures: The View from the Trading Desk," in *New Monetary Control Procedures* (Washington, D.C.: Board of Governors of the Federal Reserve System, 1981).

6. By law, the Federal Reserve may not bid to increase its holdings of maturing Treasury bills or coupons in an auction. The original purpose of this restriction apparently

was to prevent the Treasury from selling unlimited amounts of securities directly to the Fed. Instead, the Treasury was to be subject to the discipline of the market. At present, the main practical justification for the restriction is that any attempt by the Fed to enlarge its holdings in an auction would in effect reduce the size of the offering to the public below the size announced, thus tending to produce an unexpectedly high price (low yield) on the issue. That could be disadvantageous to securities dealers and others submitting competitive bids for the issue.

7. Specifically, the Fed bids for the amount of maturing bills it wants to redeem by submitting a tender at a price certain to be rejected. The rest of its maturing bills are bid for on a "noncompetitive" basis, which assures an award of the amount bid for at the average price of accepted "competitive" tenders. For more details of Treasury auction procedures, see Marcia L. Stigum, *The Money Market* (Homewood, Ill.: Dow Jones-Irwin, 1983); and Kenneth D. Garbade, *Securities Markets* (New York: McGraw-Hill, 1982).

8. In practice, outright sales of securities are rather rare. They sometimes occur early in the year to implement a seasonal drain of reserves. In addition, outright sales tend to be associated with reductions of reserve requirements, which otherwise might produce a substantial excess of reserves.

9. In effect, an RP is a collateralized loan. When a dealer arranges an RP, he or she transfers title to a security to the lender in exchange for cash. At maturity, the transaction reverses. The security is returned to the dealer, and the lender receives the original principal plus interest due. A "reverse RP" operates in exactly the same way, except the dealer temporarily lends out cash in exchange for a security. For more details on RPs, see Stigum, *The Money Market*.

10. When the Fed was targeting the funds rate, customer RPs frequently were employed to signal that the Fed had no objection to the current funds rate but wanted to add reserves to meet a modest estimated reserve need. The nonborrowed reserves targeting procedures have obviated that practice.

11. A collateral shortage may exist when the floating supply of eligible securities in the hands of dealers and their customers is relatively small, as when widespread expectations of rising interest rates cause dealers and banks to trim their holdings of securities.

12. Until a few years ago, collateral for customer RPs was priced at market value, while collateral for System RPs was priced at par value. That meant that dealers required more collateral per dollar of customer RPs than of System RPs. Currently, collateral for both forms of RPs is priced at market value, including any accrued interest.

Until very recently, there was also an important difference in the types of securities that were eligible collateral for customer and System RPs. Only Treasury and agency securities are eligible collateral for customer RPs, while those securities as well as certain bankers' acceptances were eligible for System RPs. As of July 1984, however, acceptances ceased to be eligible collateral for System RPs, so that there now are no remaining differences in collateral eligibility.

13. Since the Federal Reserve Act prohibits the Federal Reserve Banks from borrowing from the public, reverse RPs were and are viewed as an illegal transaction for the Fed. However, in 1966, a sudden, temporary increase in float resulting from a disruption of airline service prompted the innovation of the matched (cash) sale (forward) purchase agreement. The agreement is structured as two separate transactions, and is therefore legal under the act's authorization to buy and sell securities. Moral: There's more than one way to skin a cat! Operationally, MSPs are less time consuming for the Desk than are RPs, since the Fed controls the collateral. That is, the Fed can specify the one or two bill issues in its portfolio that are to be used in the MSPs and set the

prices easily. For RPs, however,the Fed must accept whatever eligible collateral the dealers wish to offer, and the pricing task is commensurately greater.

14. On the other hand, if the MSPs are widely perceived to be required to offset a reserves excess due to movements of the operating factors, then dealers will be more confident of their financing costs, and proposals likely will be more competitive.

15. This procedure was reintroduced in November 1978, when new regulations were adopted governing Treasury tax and loan accounts. For details, see Joan E. Lovett, "Treasury Tax and Loan Accounts and Federal Reserve Open Market Operations," *Quarterly Review*, Federal Reserve Bank of New York, Summer 1978, pp. 41–46.

16. This problem is obviously less severe in the period immediately following the settlement of an auction of Treasury coupon securities when dealer holdings typically are rather ample. Not coincidentally, most of the Fed's purchases of coupon securities are made at such times.

17. A simpler way to achieve the same objective would be to undersupply nonborrowed reserves, but that approach obviously would involve a departure from the nonborrowed reserves path.

18. For example, Milton Friedman has criticized the Fed for an excessive amount of RP activity. See Milton Friedman, "Monetary Policy: Theory and Practice," *Journal of Money, Credit and Banking*, February 1982, pp. 98–118. For a critique and correction of Friedman's charges by two officers of the Open Market Desk, see Fred J. Levin and Anne-Marie Meulendyke, "A Comment," *Journal of Money, Credit and Banking*, August 1982, pp. 399–403, as well as Friedman's reply in the same issue, pp. 404–6.

19. In terms of the graphical exposition employed in Chapter 5, the object is to maintain banks' reserves demand schedule on the sloped portion of the reserves supply schedule *at all times* during the reserves maintenance period so that an unintended increase in nonborrowed reserves does not prompt a plunge in the funds rate.

20. Nonwithdrawable RPs are principally used during periods when a prolonged shortage of free collateral is expected.

21. Sometimes, however, the withdrawal of RPs in those days was not altogether automatic. The story is told of a Desk manager who was confronted with a need to drain reserves after multiday RPs had been executed earlier in the week. Though the funds rate was softening, no withdrawals were forthcoming. Upon investigation, it turned out that a large block of the RPs was held at a major dealer firm. Accordingly, the manager called the firm's head trader and asked whether he would like to withdraw his RPs. The head trader replied that he was not interested. Then the manager said that he would appreciate it if the RPs were withdrawn. Again the offer was declined. Before hanging up, the Desk manager observed that he was certain to remember this event the next time the head trader was in a jam and needed a favor. About 10 minutes later, a phone call to the Desk announced the withdrawal of the RPs.

22. Dealers desire to do RPs primarily to finance their inventory of securities, though many also run a "matched book" quite independently of their securities position. Suppose that a dealer's inventory were suddenly reduced. If that position had been financed in large part through a multiday nonwithdrawable RP, the dealer would be left holding uninvested cash that could not be eliminated by the simple device of withdrawing from the RP. Thus, because of their greater flexibility in matching financing sources to securities positions, withdrawable RPs are usually strongly preferred by dealers. Banks normally have much less of a need for flexibility in financing their investment portfolios. For that reason, dealers' customers do a much larger portion of nonwithdrawable RPs than of withdrawable RPs. Similarly, customers account for a larger than normal portion of multiday MSPs as well as RPs when dealers have very light or net short positions.

GLOSSARY

Adjustment credit   Loans extended by the Federal Reserve to banks and other depository institutions to meet reserves needs lasting only a few days.

Annual target   A target growth range for a monetary or credit aggregate, generally defined from the average level of the aggregate in the fourth quarter of the previous year to the fourth quarter of the target year. Sometimes also referred to as a long-run target.

Borrowed reserves   Equal to adjustment borrowings plus seasonal borrowings from the Federal Reserve.

Contemporaneous reserve requirements (CRR)   A system in which banks and other financial institutions maintain reserves required to support their transactions deposits during a time period approximately simultaneous with the time period during which deposits are calculated.

Demand deposits   Deposits at a bank that are legally payable on demand.

Desk   Familiar term for the Open Market Desk.

Discount window   Familiar term for the division of a Federal Reserve Bank that extends loans to banks and certain other financial institutions.

Directive   Written instructions from the FOMC to the Federal Reserve Bank of New York indicating how open market operations are to be conducted between FOMC meetings. Adopted at each FOMC meeting.

Discount rate   The interest rate charged on short-term adjustment credit extended by the Federal Reserve Banks to banks and certain other financial institutions.

Excess reserves   Reserves held by banks and certain other financial institutions in excess of their required reserves.

Extended credit   Loans extended by the Federal Reserve to banks and certain other financial institutions to meet protracted reserves needs.

Eurodollar deposit   A dollar-denominated deposit held at a bank or bank branch located outside the United States.

Fed funds   Familiar term for federal funds.

Federal funds   Immediately available funds borrowed by banks from certain other financial institutions and government agencies; exempt from reserve requirements.

Federal funds rate band   A range in which the FOMC anticipates that the interest rate on federal funds will trade. The band is specified in the directive, and if the funds rate appears likely to trade outside of it, an FOMC telephone consultation may be called.

Federal Open Market Committee   Committee of the Federal Reserve System responsible for monetary policy.

Float   Occurs when the Fed, in the process of clearing checks or other payments, posts credits to the reserve accounts of receiving banks asynchronously with the posting of debits to the reserve accounts of paying banks; may add or drain reserves depending on the timing of credits and debits.

FOMC   Federal Open Market Committee.

FOMC minutes   A highly condensed record of discussion and policy actions taken at an FOMC meeting, including the text of the directive. Released to the public a few days after the following regularly scheduled FOMC meeting.

Free reserves   Equal to excess reserves less borrowed reserves; also equals the negative of net borrowed reserves.

Lagged reserve requirements (LRR)   A system in which banks and other depository institutions maintain reserves required to support their deposits during a time period later than the time period during which deposits are calculated.

Match   Familiar term for matched sale-purchase agreement.

Matched sale-purchase agreement   A sale of securities by the Federal Reserve to a primary dealer for immediate delivery and payment, executed simultaneously with a purchase of the same securities to be delivered and paid for on a future date; functionally identical to a reverse repurchase agreement. Drains reserves temporarily from the banking system.

Monetary base   Equal to total reserves plus currency in the hands of the public.

Money demand   The functional relationship between some measure of money and other variables such as wealth, income, and interest rates.

M1   Consists of currency in the hands of the public, travelers checks of nonbank issuers, net demand deposits, and other checkable deposits (primarily NOW accounts). Excludes deposits due to domestic banks, the U.S. government, and foreign banks and official institutions.

M2   Consists of M1 plus overnight (and continuing contract) RPs issued by banks, overnight Eurodollar deposits issued to U.S. residents by foreign branches of U.S. banks worldwide, money market deposit accounts, savings and time deposits in amounts less than $100,000, and balances in both taxable and tax-exempt noninstitutional money market mutual funds. Excludes IRA and Keogh balances at depository institutions and noninstitutional money market funds, balances held by U.S. commercial banks noninstitutional money market funds, foreign governments and banks, and the U.S. government, as well as other miscellaneous items.

M3   Consists of M2 plus large denomination time deposits and term RP liabilities (in amounts of $100,000 or more) issued by commercial banks and thrift institutions, term Eurodollar deposits held by U.S. residents at foreign branches of U.S. banks worldwide and at all banking offices in the United Kingdom and Canada, and balances in both taxable and tax-exempt institutional money market mutual funds. Excludes balances held by depository institutions, the U.S. government, money market mutual funds, and foreign banks and official institutions, as well as other miscellaneous items.

Negotiable order of withdrawal (NOW) accounts   Interest-bearing deposits that are effectively payable on demand.

Net borrowed reserves   Equal to borrowed reserves less excess reserves; also equals the negative of free reserves.

Nonborrowed reserves   Equal to total reserves less borrowed reserves; also equals reserves supplied by the Federal Reserve through open market operations and extended credit.

Open Market Desk   Personnel at the Federal Reserve Bank of New York who carry out open market operations for the Federal Reserve System and perform a number of other functions.

Open market operations   Transactions between the Federal Reserve and primary government securities dealers arranged by the Open Market Desk in order to alter the amount of reserves available to the banking system.

Operating target   A target for some variable—such as the federal funds rate, nonborrowed reserves, or total reserves—that the Open Market Desk can use to guide its open market operations.

Outright purchase (sale)   A transaction in which the Federal Reserve buys (sells) Treasury or government agency securities for its portfolio and creates a permanent injection (drain) of reserves.

Primary dealers   Government securities dealer firms maintaining a trading relationship with the Open Market Desk; identical to reporting dealers.

Reporting dealers   The official Federal Reserve designation for primary dealers.

Repo   Familiar term for repurchase agreement.

Repurchase agreement   Transaction in which a securities dealer borrows cash and transfers to the lender a security that is to be returned by the lender at the end of the term of the loan. When executed by the Federal

Reserve, injects reserves into the banking system temporarily. So-called customer repurchase agreements have mechanics slightly different from System repurchase agreements but have the same effect on availability of reserves.

Required reserves   The total of reserves that banks and other depository institutions must hold to satisfy the reserve requirements on their deposits.

Reserve requirement   Fractional amount of a deposit or other liability that a bank or other depository institution is required to hold in eligible reserves.

Reserves   Collected deposits held at a Federal Reserve Bank plus vault cash held by an institution subject to Federal Reserve reserve requirements.

Reserves maintenance period   Period of time during which a bank or other financial institution must hold average reserves at least equal to its average required reserves. Currently the reserves maintenance period is 14 days long, beginning on Thursday and ending on the second Wednesday following.

Reverse   Familiar term for a reverse repurchase agreement or a matched sale-purchase agreement.

Reverse repurchase agreement   Transaction in which a dealer borrows a security in exchange for cash; functionally the opposite of a repurchase agreement.

Reverse RP   Familiar term for reverse repurchase agreement or matched sale-purchase agreement.

RP   Familiar term for repurchase agreement.

Short-run target   A target indicating a desired growth rate for a monetary aggregate over a period of a few months. Specified in the FOMC directive.

Street   Familiar term for Wall Street, often used to refer to all securities broker-dealer firms as a group.

Total reserves   The total of all reserves held by banks and other financial institutions subject to Federal Reserve reserve requirements.

Velocity   Gross national product divided by a monetary aggregate; indicates how many times per year, on average, the aggregate is used in income-generating transactions.

INDEX

A